PIONEERS
IN
PARADISE

D1601308

Sophie Britten

PIONEERS
IN
PARADISE

A Historical and Biographical Record
of Early Days in Three Rivers, California
1850s to **1950**s

Sophie Britten

gatekeeper press
Columbus, Ohio

This book is a work of nonfiction. The names, characters, and events in this book have been researched and verified to the best of the author's ability.

Pioneers in Paradise: a Historical and Biographical Record of Early Days in Three Rivers, California 1850s to 1950s

Published by Gatekeeper Press
2167 Stringtown Rd, Suite 109
Columbus, OH 43123-2989
www.GatekeeperPress.com

ISBN (paperback): 9781662908590
ISBN (eBook): 9781662908606

Revised Edition

Cover Photo: Nell Sivertson Britten (wife of Noel Britten and Ernest Britten), preparing their wagon for the "Days of 49" Wagon Train to Woodlake in 1926.

Dedication

This book is dedicated first of all, to the late Frankie Luella Welch. Without her news clippings and notes that she wrote over the years, this book would never have been written.

Next, to Ord Loverin, who instilled in this author the curiosity and love of local history and the wonder and lore of the mountains that surround and shelter us.

And lastly, to my beloved husband, the late John Britten, Sr.; you are still, and always will be, the "Wind Beneath My Wings."

Preface

Once upon a time, in a small community in the Sierra foothills, a new widow was trying to recover from the recent loss of her husband and she wondered what she could do with the rest of her life to give it some meaning. She saw the future stretching out endlessly before her and she felt lost, as if she had no more purpose in her life.

Then one day, while cleaning out her basement, she came upon two or three cardboard boxes, full to the brim of news clippings, some very old; as well as many handwritten notes in pencil on legal-sized newsprint and the backs of used envelopes. Upon investigation, she saw that they had been cut out of the Fresno and Visalia papers, dating back to 1924.

What a treasure trove she had discovered! These clippings and notes were articles that had been written over the years by Frankie Luella Welch. Obviously, Frankie had intended to use them for a history of Three Rivers that she meant to write someday.

Spanning the years 1924 to 1977, the year before her death, Frankie wrote news articles for the *Fresno Bee* and the *Visalia Times-Delta*. Since she was paid by the published "inch," she was very careful to save every article that she wrote.

From this discovery, this lonely widow found something meaningful to do with her life: to complete what Frankie had intended and record the history of Three Rivers.

It took at least two years to sort and categorize all of the information in the material. She sorted it two ways: by events, places and things and by families. Thus, this book is divided into two parts. The first part is events, places, and things; the second part is brief sketches of these early-day families and their histories.

Three Rivers has been settled for approximately one hundred and sixty years, yet in that time many people have come here and left, some to live other places, some to stay on their land, raise their families and eventually die here.

This history reflects only a small part of what the early pioneers endured to keep their homesteads intact and make a living for their families. Their desire was to come west in search of El Dorado, looking for opportunities in the Golden State, or just finding new freedoms and a place to start fresh for themselves and their families.

The reader will note that these pioneers endured two forces of nature; namely, fires and floods. Many homes and other buildings were destroyed by fire, probably because of the use of wood stoves and easily combustible building materials. In many cases, the settlers re-built as soon as possible and got on with their lives.

The other force of nature with which those early settlers had to contend was water, since settling near the rivers was a necessity for their water supply. However, the periodic floods that occur and wash down the canyons did considerable damage over the years and forced those families to build on higher ground, digging ditches to bring the water to irrigate their lands and homes.

Many changes have come about since Hale Tharp rode up the Middle Fork and encountered the friendly tribe of Yokuts; however, Three Rivers remains essentially the same today. This is evident when members of the community come together to care for one another, and their willingness to help in times of trouble.

These early day pioneers shared an important common goal: to make the best life possible for their families and to help each other in the community through good times and bad.

The author sincerely hopes she has been accurate in relating the stories and history she has presented here and apologizes in advance for any inaccuracy. The author does not intend that this book should be the final authority on the facts as they are presented. She has discovered the materials contained here only by conducting extensive research. All incidents recorded here are based on the documentation provided and are referenced in the book. There were more early settlers not included in this work. That was not by design; but because there was not enough information available.

Please enjoy the book; it is a joy to give the reader a glimpse of our local history.

Acknowledgments

A lthough this project has been in the "works" for at least ten years, it needed a catalyst or impetus to really give it validity. That came in the form of a grant from the <u>Tulare County Historical Society</u>. The author wishes to give sincere thanks to the Society and its liaison, Lari Ommen. The award of the grant has not only made this project possible, but it has confirmed the necessity of a recorded history of Three Rivers and its pioneers.

In addition, the author wishes to thank and acknowledge the following for their help and encouragement:

<u>Louise Jackson</u> - for proofreading and editing my drafts in spite of trying to finish her own book and who gave me the idea of applying for a grant in the first place. Did you ever think I would finish?? Thank you for having faith in my ability.

<u>Jana Botkin</u> - my other proofreader and editor who put up with my typos and apostrophes in the wrong places! Your willingness to help and your practical suggestions have kept me going.

<u>Anne Lang</u> - her gentle question, "How's the book coming?" asked very frequently kept me on track and our discussions of local history were an inspiration.

<u>Bruton Peterson</u> - who furnished the lovely photos of the East Fork of the Kaweah River as well as the pictures of Harry and Mary Trauger.

<u>Earl and Gaynor McKee</u> - who endured my many questions and graciously shared Norma Hardison's book, *Memories,* as well as photos of their parents and grandparents.

<u>Tom Logan</u> - who kept asking "Where's the book?"

<u>Norman Polly</u> - who gave me so much encouragement in his gentle, sweet way.

<u>Three Rivers Historical Society Museum</u> and Tom and Dody Marshall who gave of their time and shared photos in order to facilitate the completion of this book.

Gene, Catherine and Mike Whitney - who invited the author into their home to share news articles and information about their family. Special thanks to Mike who made the special trip to Big Oak Flat in order to take pictures that are included in this book.

To many other friends and people who have inquired and shown enthusiasm for this project - your faith and appreciation for the project has motivated this author and helped her to finish the work.

Contents

Part One

Events, Places, and Things

Chapter I

Chapter II

Chapter III

Chapter IV

Chapter V

Chapter VI

Chapter VII

Chapter VIII

Chapter IX

Part Two

Family Histories

1850–1860s

1910s

1920s

Special Section

PART ONE

Events, Places, and Things

CHAPTER I

Agriculture

Orchards of Three Rivers

For many years, October was the month of the apple harvest in Three Rivers. Summer sun and the waters of the Kaweah brought the fruit to full maturity and the trees were laden with their fragrant, juicy and flavorful apples. They ranged in color from the deepest red to a delicate yellow. The fruit was hauled to apple sheds, washed and graded; the best was loose boxed for eager buyers. The smaller apples were then made into cider.

Hundreds of valley residents would drive into the hills here each fall to buy apples, pears and cider. As they came into Three Rivers on Highway 198, they would see signs of the apple harvest directing them to the Sequoia Cider Mill. Originally started years ago by Dr. D. D. Nice, and expanded later by Paul Spotts, it was known as Spotts' Cider Mill. The Cider Mill was a roadside stand and a very pleasant stop for the motorist. The stand specialized in fresh cider the year round. At one point, it was operated by Gus Wohler, who gave it the name of "Sequoia" and later owned by Mervin McCoy, then it was turned into a restaurant which unfortunately burned to the ground in 2012. It was re-built and is currently known as the Sequoia Cider Mill.

Turning left across the main river and driving up the North Fork Road into historic Kaweah, the driver would discover a large and flourishing apple district. Members of the old Kaweah Commonwealth Colony put out many orchards after the Colony disbanded, adding to those already planted by the pioneers. Most of these plantings have died out or have been taken over by homesites.

It was in this area in 1896 that Fred Savage started an orchard of Ben Davis and Winesap variety apples. It was enlarged to a twenty-acre planting in 1897-98. His sons, Kenneth and Alan, continued the operation then known as the Savage Brothers Apple Ranch. The making of cider originally used a hand-cranked mill and the apples were ground by hand and then dropped into a slatted press. When this was full, a "follower" was screwed down, and the juice began to flow. This mill was later replaced by a bigger, commercial cider mill.

In the past, it was common practice to feed the "pummy" left from making cider to the family drove of pigs that was common to most farms and ranches at the time. One of the ranchers did not feed the pulp to his hogs for a few days after the apples had been ground; later that day, his little girl came running to the house, crying, "Mama!, Mama! The pigs are all dead!" The wife hurried to the pig pen and found the motionless pigs sprawled about, seemingly expired. When she picked up a stick and prodded one of the prone sows, the animal pulled herself up on wobbly legs, staggered and pitched forward, ramming her snout into the earth. The pigs had not gone to pig heaven after all; they were just very inebriated from eating the fermented leavings of the apples!

Regarding more history of orchard planting, the Mehrten family came to the Three Rivers country in 1906 and bought the old Purdy place on the North Fork, which already had its own orchard. Nearby at that time was one of the finest and best-kept orchards in the country. It was owned by Edmund Taylor. After his death, the new owners, having no sentiment about the cultivation of apples, let it go back to its original state, even though it was good for more years of productivity. It was given over to more homesites and horse pastures.

In the early days, poor road conditions into Three Rivers discouraged the public from driving up to the orchards for their apples and it became necessary for some of the apple growers to take their own fruit into town to sell. One of these was Marion Griffes; he had a large orchard on what eventually was to become the Thorn Ranch. He would put hay in the bottom of his wagon, pour the sweetly scented apples onto it and head his team for the valley. From door to door in towns and countryside, he sold apples by the buckets full. Sometimes he would go as far as Hanford and be away from home a week at a time.

He was very smart at his business of selling apples. In the fall, he sorted them, selling the large ones for a good price. After the holidays when the supply of apples became more scarce, he would bring out the small ones and get almost as much for them as he had earlier for the larger ones.

When the Thorn family bought the ranch in 1917, it was no longer necessary to take apples to the valley to sell; instead, the public came to Three Rivers to buy them. By that time, the roads were better and the family trade was good. Mrs. Bernice Thorn remembered that, in one year, eighty tons of apples were sold at the ranch.

Winesaps, Stamen Winesaps, Ben Davis, Black Twig, Arkansas Black, Delicious and White Winter Permains were some of the many varieties of apples grown. Kenneth Savage, who always enjoyed a good joke, told about his favorite apple, the Ben Davis, which is a large, well-flavored apple, especially good for baking purposes. Once, when Savage was peddling apples, he met another apple peddler and stopped to pass the time of day.

"What kind of apples you selling?" the peddler asked. "Mostly Ben Davis," replied Savage. "Why, them apples ain't no good," the peddler laughed. With a twinkle in his eye, he told about a man who boasted that he could tell any apple by the flavor. They blindfolded him and gave him a slice of Jonathan and he named it correctly; then they gave him a piece of Delicious, of Winesap then Black Twig and each time he came up with the right answer. Then they gave him a piece of cork. After chewing on it for a while, he said, "Might be a Ben Davis, but it is juicer than any I [have] ever tasted."[1]

When apple production was at its height, the community held apple festivals in a big dance pavilion built by H. P. Moffitt in Kaweah Park. Elbert Wing and Josiah Belden were prominent apple growers at this time and along with other producers, displayed quantities of bright-hued apples, pears and other produce. There was dancing in the center of the big floor, and a dinner was served with, of course, apple pie.

Mrs. Frank Finch, dinner chairman one year, staged a pie-eating contest between two teams of boys. One of the boys was the then-young Ernest "John" Britten. "We were eating pie as fast as we could," he recalled, "but we saw that we were getting behind and had to do something, so we smeared our faces as well as our mouths. It stuck and we emerged from the contest, smeared and triumphant!"[2]

Horace Taylor, who owned the Taylor Ranch, dug a big cellar to store apples and then built a dance hall over it. He thoughtfully provided shelves where the babies could be laid while the mothers danced. If a child cried as the caller sang, "All join hands," the mother would break away and rush to see if her baby had fallen to the floor. The late Mrs. Bessie Akers of Exeter went to the dances with her father Frank Britten, who played his fiddle for the dancers. She remembered how the community would dance the night away with the fragrance of the apples coming up from the cellar.

Traces of old apple orchards can still be seen up and down all branches of the Kaweah River, reminding us of the hopes and ambitions of the early-day settlers. Since the earliest time, orchards have been closely associated with the idea of "home." As soon as a settler could get a little stream of water to his clearing from a spring or the river, his first development would be to put out some fruit trees.

One of these was Ira Blossom, an early-day pioneer. He settled on the South Fork and took out a ditch in 1886 for his young orchard. To this end, he carried young fruit trees on his back up to Big Oak Flat from Lemon

---

1   *No Apples for the Teacher*, manuscript by Frankie Luella Welch
2   Ibid.

Cove, and then down the trail to his place before there was a road into Three Rivers.

L to R: Lizzie Alles, Charles Blossom, Wes Warren, Max Dungan (in tree), little Frank Devoe, Mrs. Curtis (on horse), and Joe Palmer. *Photo from Author's Collection.*

The Enoch Work family was credited with putting out the first orchard. They settled on the lower South Fork, a short distance above where it meets the Middle Fork. Mr. Work dug a ditch and planted fruit trees in 1865. This orchard had a short and tragic life, however; the big flood of 1867 wiped it out.

A small orchard on the Mineral King Road was probably planted in the mid-1870s by Harry and Mary Trauger. Sam Halstead planted his orchard on the North Fork in 1879 where Trailer Isle is now located.

In 1882, Orlando Barton brought water to his orchard by extending the ditch from the South Fork through to the Britten Ranch, allowing him to provide water to his orchard. Jason Barton, sometimes called the mayor of Three Rivers, lived on the Barton Ranch on the North Fork. One day, a passing neighbor saw him cutting down an apple tree. "What are you doing, Jason?" he called from the road.

Big, jovial Jason rested his axe on the ground and answered, "Grubbing out this old mothy apple orchard." He drew a red bandana from his overall pocket and mopped his brow. "When there is a worm in every apple, you can eat around 'em. But when there are five worms in every apple, it's time to go into something else. I'm going to oranges; they don't have worms." Then he poked the red bandana in his pocket and resumed swinging his axe into the shuddering apple tree.[3]

The Glenn family started an orchard on the South Fork in the 1880s on a place first irrigated by the Gilstraps in 1879. This place was later developed by Barney Mehrten and his son David into one of the best mountain apple orchards. Other orchards started along the South Fork about the same time were the Boltons, the Busbys, and the Alleses, who came here in the late 1880s to file for a homestead on their place.

A peculiar fate befell a young orchard on the old Putman place, known today as the Wells Ranch. In the early 1890s, the country was overrun with hogs, which roamed the hills as cattle do. There were very few fences and one day in the summer, hogs hungry for something green invaded the orchard and tore it to pieces, limb by limb, even climbing up into the trees to reach the upper branches.

Joe Lovelace, nephew of the North Fork pioneer of the 1860s, put out an orchard in 1889 on the Middle Fork across the river from Kaweah Power Plant No 2.

Another location used for planting was again on the North Fork by the Kaweah Colonists; they also planted fruit trees along their road into the Sequoias. There were a few trees planted at Hospital Rock, supposedly by James Wolverton, who was stationed there in the early 1890s to keep Hale Tharp's stock from drifting out of the mountains. Then there was Bill Case, who used to haul cedar [building] shakes out of the Salt Creek Pinery with a horse, a mule, a donkey and an ox, all harnessed together; he was credited

---

3   Ibid.

with planting apple trees which grew for many years among the pines on Case Mountain.

Abe Burdick also planted a large apple orchard near Yucca Creek on the North Fork, clearing the ground of brush, digging the holes and tending the trees entirely by hand.

The W. F. Dean hillside orchard was also started at an early date. Professor Dean hired George Welch, a pioneer civil engineer, to survey the irrigation ditches; the ditches had to turn and twist considerably to maintain grade on the irregular ground. It was a standing joke between the two friends that "Welch did some [really] crooked work there."[4]

The Clarence Dinely orchard on the Middle Fork, which produced exceptionally fine big red apples, is now entirely taken over by homesites. The name, Dinely Road, is all that remains. Apples planted by Walter Braddock, a North Fork pioneer, won many prizes at county fairs. In the early 1890s, J. W. Griffes, father of Marion Griffes, moved to a mountain ranch to the north of the Mineral King Road. This ranch had originally been started by a man with the last name of Arnold. By the late 1890s, Griffes had nine acres of apples and berries; this orchard was at an elevation of 5,000 feet, and was the highest orchard in the area. The quality of the fruit was excellent, [Even in the 1950-60s, this author can remember the wonderful old apple trees in the orchard at the Griffes' Milk Ranch; particularly the flat green apples that my dad—Ord Loverin—said were called "Grindstones"; they were the best tasting and made the most wonderful pies and applesauce!][5] but marketing was always difficult because of the precipitous mountain roads. Tom Dungan of Exeter, hauling out a load of apples one time, went over the grade when his horses became frightened and rolled almost 1,000 feet to the river's edge. Miraculously, neither he nor the boy with him, nor the horses were seriously injured; even the wagon was not badly damaged, but the apples never made it to town.

The Grunigen family put out a small family orchard at Lake Canyon on the Mineral King Road in 1896.

---

4   Ibid.
5   Memories by the author.

Grünigen Homestead and Inn at Lake Canyon.
August 2, 1918

Orchards at Lake Canyon. *Photo from Author's Collection.*

Farther down at Oak Grove, on a place first owned by a man named Eldridge, A. O. Griffes had a small orchard. A very early orchard was planted by Almer Lovelace, a grand-uncle of the one-time county surveyor named Byron Lovelace. He came here in the mid-1860s and settled near the junction of the North Fork and the Middle Fork. This place was later purchased by Montgomery Barton in 1880, and subsequently by the Pierce family. It was developed by James H. Pierce into a profitable commercial orchard.

These and many other old orchards along every branch of the Kaweah are now only memories. Although traces of some of them are still to be found, the ones that are left stand in lonely testimony to the hopes and ambitions of those early-day settlers. They are reminders that at one time apples played a very important part in the development of the Kaweah Canyon and the Three Rivers country.

CHAPTER II

Churches and Cemeteries

Some Early Three Rivers Churches

"That Old-Time Religion"

Most pioneers, and probably Three Rivers settlers as well, had a deep religious faith and some came west for the same reasons that groups such as the Puritans left Europe: to find a place where they could practice their faith without being persecuted or thought eccentric. Many saw the West as a place for freedoms that appealed to them. Strong religious faith added to the strength a pioneer needed for the times in which they lived; hardship, illness and death were their constant companions. Couples often had several children with the awareness that probably half would not survive to become adults. Diphtheria, smallpox, typhoid, scarlet fever and pneumonia took a heavy toll on families. Even the rich and influential could not prevent the ravages and heartbreak which wiped out large groups of children during the diphtheria epidemic of 1878-1879. Believing that there was a "Better Land" beyond the grave was helpful to the grieving families.

Religion was taken seriously and "practiced" by the old-timers. They went to church and Sunday School wherever and whenever the opportunity was presented; not only on Sundays but often to mid-week prayer meetings. In addition, there were circuit-riding ministers and priests who took religion to isolated areas. It was not illegal in those days to hold church or Sunday school in the local schoolhouse.

Camp and tent revival meetings were very popular, not only to refresh the soul, but were also fun and great opportunities for socializing. They were held usually in the late spring or early summer, in the many beautiful spots along streams in the foothills, such as the Venice Hill area. Families loaded bedding and food into their wagons or buggies and spent as much time as a week listening to several preachers who spoke with different styles for sinners to be saved; many a backsliding old reprobate was "born again" during the fervor of the moment and many lives were changed as a result.

Camp meetings were a good place for young people to meet, hold hands, walk through the meadows, and get to know each other. No singles bars in those days!

Locally, the first Christian church began very humbly. In the 1890s, "Grandma" Christina Alles began a Sunday School in her home. In the 1920s, following the reorganization of the Sunday School, services were held regularly at the Three Rivers schoolhouse, at the corner of Blossom Drive and Old Three Rivers Drive. With the election of Mrs. Jessie Finch to Sunday School superintendent, it was hoped that interest in Sunday School would receive a renewed attendance.

COMMUNITY PRESBYTERIAN CHURCH HISTORY

On November 5, 1939, one hundred people met in the Three Rivers schoolhouse and the first church was organized by the Presbytery of San Joaquin, with 45 communicant members. Immediate plans were made for a building; Dan Alles, his wife Margaret and her daughter Beulah Beam, bought the knoll from Armin Grunigen and gave it for the establishment of the new church. Mr. Walter T. Wells, Sr. and his wife Mary hired an architect at their own expense. They then proceeded to cut and donate lumber, milled on his land at Silver City, and he paid for all the hardware. Using sand from the river, men of the community built the church, and because of the amount of labor and materials donated, the cash cost was only $5,000; half of that was covered by an interest-free loan from the Board of National Missions.

On November 2, 1941, the new building was dedicated and the first pastor, the Rev. John Buchholz, was installed, having already been serving in this capacity for a year. The manse (minister's residence) was built and dedicated April 11, 1948; it was considerably renovated in 1970. Another milestone was passed in 1953, when after twelve years of financial aid from the Presbyterian Board of National Missions, the church became self-supporting; at the same time, the loans on both church and manse were paid off and the mortgage burned. Although the manse has been replaced with Harrison Hall, the church still stands today on its knoll and is known as the Community Presbyterian Church.

SAINT CLAIR'S CATHOLIC CHURCH HISTORY

Yearning and dedication in large amounts were the driving forces behind the creation and establishment of the Three Rivers Catholic Church. In 1947, Rev. James Kelly came to the Sacred Heart Church in Exeter from County Clare, Ireland. This was at the time that the Exeter Church became an official parish. Father Kelly served the faithful attendees of Exeter, Woodlake, Lemon Cove, Three Rivers, Sequoia National Park and Wilsonia. Eventually, the St. Francis Cabrini Church in Woodlake became a mission of the Exeter Church and remained so until 1963, when it became its own parish. It was at this time that St. Clair's of Three Rivers became the mission church of the Woodlake parish.

George St. Clair, an acquaintance of Father Kelly and a local developer, offered a gift of three acres of land in Alta Acres. The church was subsequently named in honor of this benefactor. As an interesting note, after Mr. St. Clair left the area, he subsequently became a Catholic. However, when the property was first offered to the church, it was refused by the Bishop due to a potential problem with water rights. The issue was resolved and the donation of land was gratefully accepted.

Plans were drawn by architect Frank Robert, who donated his time. He paid for a structural engineer to assist with the drawings. Mr. Robert had arrived in Three Rivers just after WWII, where he had been a pilot in the Army Air Corps. He had studied under Frank Lloyd Wright and later became very successful designing hotels in the Hawaiian Islands, and he built a number of homes in Three Rivers as well.

Financing of the building of the church was accomplished on the "pay-as-you-go" theory. No monthly pledges were solicited, but monthly fundraising activities were organized. This was the start of the annual turkey dinners, held at the original Three Rivers Woman's Club House on North Fork Drive. Don Reimers and John Wollenman donated the turkeys, with their wives cooking them at home.

Trembley's Drive-In [We Three Bakery] was the scene of many card parties where local folks played bridge, pedro and canasta. Other fundraisers were rummage and white elephant sales, Valentine's Day bake sales and raffles.

As the construction of the building progressed, enthused visitors and generous members of the congregation contributed to the weekly second collection for the building fund. Because of assistance provided by local Catholics, receipts from the Masses said in Sequoia National Park were given to the building fund as well. Tom Crowe, a Visalia attorney and cabin owner in the Mineral King area, was very friendly toward the church, and when his mother died, he donated a great deal of antique furniture to be sold for the benefit of the building fund. The hustle and humor of John Wollenman as the auctioneer helped to make the sale a great success.

Construction began with Floyd Hill in charge of the project. Volunteers gave their time and efforts. Mr. Hill also obtained help from the boys' camp located at Hammond Fire Station, at that time a juvenile correctional facility. The boys came down on weekends to assist with mixing cement and other jobs. By the time of the ground-breaking ceremony, considerable work had already been done at the site.

The steel for the building was donated by a person who was erecting a structure on Kaweah River Drive. His plans changed and he gave the steel to the church. It was moved, two pieces at a time, to the building site by John Wollenman and Jim Ady. This was accomplished by strapping the beams underneath John's 1949 Studebaker. All went well until the car reached the highway where the steel began to hit the high center of the road. When that happened, Jim would drive and John would position fence posts under the car wheels in order to move ahead. Earl Davis' father owned a well-drilling rig, which he used to raise the cross and steel beams.

As construction proceeded, additional money was needed; the Catholic *Extension* magazine was contacted, and they provided both a loan and a gift. At this point, the church could then afford to pay the carpenters, Hill and Jackson, so they could stay on the job all week and speed completion of the project. Later on, Bill Stroh and Loren Finch had to erect special scaffolding to finish the high interior redwood walls.

During the planning, Mass was said in a room adjoining Trembley's Restaurant or at the home of John and Bernie Wollenman. After the pouring of the concrete foundation slab, Mass was celebrated continually from then on. People attending St. Clair's at that time sat on makeshift pews of construction lumber.

As the church was being completed, a list was made of items that were necessary, such as interior furnishings, inside and outside lighting for the restrooms, parking lot paving, etc. Pews were built by the church members. Bill Stephenson did the plumbing for the restrooms. The altar was made of redwood plywood. Stations of the Cross were obtained by friends of the Ady family from a Catholic church in Lomita that was being demolished.

At that time, the Ted Ady family lived next door to the Redwood Shop (in 2012, the studio of Nadi Spencer), a business in the village owned by Virgil Chaboude, who had been stricken with polio in his younger years. One day, after a period of rain, the Ady's six-year-old son Tom was playing out by the shop. One of the logs came loose from the pile and rolled onto him, pushing the boy face down into the mud. Mr. Chaboude was somehow able to wrest the log away and used artificial respiration to revive the child. Young Tom was taken to the hospital and had surgery for liver damage but ultimately regained his health. It is said that the next day, five men couldn't move the log. This is one of the "small miracles" that are part of St. Clair's history. The altar rail, donated by the Adys, was made of that same redwood log.

Another amazing incident involved Clyde Bradshaw, a powder man and general handyman around town, who was blasting a boulder out of the church parking lot. He had laid a heavy wire mesh gravel screen nearby and when the charge was set off, the screen flew into the power lines overhead. Clyde was leaning against his pickup and when the electrical current came down, it went through his body, tore off part of his pants and burned his legs. He had to be hospitalized but, thankfully, he recovered.

The bell, previously mounted on the sacristy roof, arrived in a roundabout way from St. Mary's University. It was brought to St. Clair's by a visiting Jesuit priest and teacher at Loyola University, Father J. J. Markey. He spent several summers in the area and would say Mass while here. He brought the bell one Sunday in the trunk of his car.

Father Gregory Wooler, Order of the Franciscans, came to Three Rivers in 1955 to establish a Franciscan Retreat. During early construction of the Retreat Center, he had a house trailer on the church grounds. He lived there, serving as both celebrant and security guard. During Father Gregory's residence in Three Rivers, he did much to promote a warm and mutual friendship between the congregation at St. Clair's and the Franciscan Order.

During the past fifty years, there have been many priests and brothers who contributed to the spiritual welfare and guidance of the St. Clair's Catholic community. The congregation has changed through the years, but always with people who have enriched the church with their unique abilities to keep the Spirit of Christ alive in the community.

Three Rivers and Other Local Cemeteries

The Three Rivers Cemetery was established by a group of early settlers who realized the need for a concentrated location to bury their dead. A hillside spot overlooking Old Three Rivers and the Kaweah Middle Fork Canyon was selected. Sharply rising mountains behind the site gave it a feeling of shelter.

On March 19, 1909, a deed was executed and signed by Charles F. Bahwell granting the Three Rivers Cemetery Association of Three Rivers, Tulare County, California one acre of land for the sum of $10.00. This was witnessed by Pirey Johnson and Isham D. Mullenix. Thus, the Three Rivers Cemetery was established. When the need of additional land was foreseen, Noel Britten, who had acquired the Bahwell property, gave an additional half acre to the east; the same was done by Byron Allen to the west.

Digging a grave at that early time was laboriously done with pick and shovel and if the excavating was unusually hard, it was barely completed by the time the hearse arrived. In the early days, there was no caretaker for the cemetery. Instead, pioneer women walked across the hills each spring to rake and tidy up around their families' graves. They encircled each resting place of their loved ones with a line of stones since there was no curbing in place at that time.

In the beginning, the cemetery had no funds for upkeep; people took care of their own family plots and when there was a death, the neighbors dug the grave. In 1942, Tulare County took over and a special district was formed, called the "Three Rivers Public Cemetery District"; it is administered with tax monies and served by a Sexton and a Board of Directors.

The first officers were J. W. Griffes, C. W. Blossom and George Welch. Frank Finch, J. W. Carter, I. D. Mullenix and H. Y. Alles were Trustees of the Association.

The original plots sold for $10.00 each. J.E. Barton, M. M. Barton, Ira Blossom and C. W. Blossom donated land for a road into the property and each received a cemetery lot in return. At that time, the cemetery board also agreed that Conrad Alles could pasture his cattle on the unused portion of the cemetery grounds until it was needed or fenced. Montgomery Barton was the first resident buried in the new cemetery in 1910.

Although the cemetery represents a small community, it nevertheless has some memorable residents interred there. The most notable of these is Major Frederick Burnham, one of the world's great adventurers and scouts. He was very useful to the British Empire during the Boer War, and was invested by that country with the Distinguished Service Order.

Other Local Cemeteries

There have been a number of family plots and small cemeteries in the Three Rivers District where members of families and various communities have been buried before the establishment of the Three Rivers District Cemetery. Those known to this author and gleaned from various records are:

Back of the Kaweah Post Office: three or four people buried there. (Names unknown)

Old Bear Ranch - one man, Jim Wolverton

Kaweah Colony:
George Dillon
Professor Eahrler
...Elfritti
Andrew Larson
Davis Mac Key
Infant of P.J. Martin
Mrs. ...Pierce
Mrs. Louise Stewart
Mrs. Charles Tousley
Frank Wigginton

Mineral King - one man, Robert Duggan
Oak Grove - one man, Alpheus Fife

CHAPTER III

Community Events

Three Rivers "Days of 49"

(In 1926!)

The year 1926 saw a community event in Three Rivers like none other before or since. Two hundred and fifty members of the Three Rivers community took part in an exciting adventure; they turned back the pages of time to recreate the days of the forty-niners, and participated in an exciting pageant of history. They hooked their wagons to horse or mule teams and made a "trek" to Woodlake for the celebration. Where did all those wagons come from at that time and where have they gone in the past 86 years? Luckily, we have a detailed account of the activities that occurred then. The following is a record of the event from the *Fresno Morning Republican*:

> The residents of Three Rivers rode into Woodlake on horseback and in covered wagons, bringing with them all the

romance, color and characters of the days of 1849, traveling down Highway 198 and taking the road into Woodlake. In direct contrast to the wagon caravan, all other roads brought hundreds of autos, each carrying its full quota of passengers. Woodlake hosted over 5,000 people as guests of the community.

From the moment the first "Indian scout" was sighted, as he led the procession winding its way off the mountain highway to Woodlake, to the moment the last guest had departed late that night, the day was voted a great success.

The Days of '49 celebration was staged by residents of Three Rivers as its contribution toward raising a fund with which to later produce a pageant, the resulting funds of which would be given for the benefit of Woodlake High School.

At approximately 2 p.m., the caravan of 21 covered wagons from Three Rivers entered the city, being met on the highway by city officials, who welcomed them and offered a site for their camp, whereupon the caravan encircled the business district and formed the wagons in a circle on a vacant lot in the heart of the city, making camp for the night.

Leading the procession was Professor Wm. F. Dean, dressed as an Indian scout, who, with a long telescope, kept a watchful eye out for Indians. Professor Dean was one of the pioneer settlers of Three Rivers and the role he played then was not new to him.

Following Dean was Jason Barton, captain of the caravan; Jeff Davis, who was costumed in a garment of skins and gave an excellent interpretation of Buffalo Bill; Noel Britten, a scout and Phil Davis, lieutenant of the party. These all rode horseback and were dressed appropriately in the garb of that period.

The first of the covered wagons, of which there were 21 in all, was driven by Henry DeLong, age 78, who crossed the plains in a covered wagon during the early days of the West. With him as passengers were others who had also come to the West by covered wagon. Among these were Commodore P. Murray, J. H. Pritchard and Mrs. Betsy Purdy, all of Three Rivers. Commodore Murray had the distinction of being the first white child born in Tulare County, August 7, 1853 in the area later known as Visalia. His father and mother were members of a party who came overland from Missouri and were the first settlers in the Visalia district.

Just behind the first covered wagon was an interesting trio on horseback: Dr. D. D. Nice as the "parson," Mrs. Frank Finch and Mrs. J. H. Butts, who rode sidesaddle, garbed in the dress of 1849; Mrs. Finch sported a corncob pipe for extra drama. Accompanying them afoot was Ben Packard dressed as another Indian scout.

Scattered throughout the caravan were numerous characters of the days of '49, afoot and on horseback. Among these was Phil Davis, chairman of the committee staging the celebration, dressed as "Daniel Boone"; Phil Alles, dressed as a miner; Frank Finch, a fiddler who played "Susannah" as the caravan rode through the city. In addition, there was Hudson Barton, who drove a 4-horse team across the plains at the age of 21; Bill Swanson, purported to be the first white child born in Three Rivers; Mrs. Bob Barton of Three Rivers, wearing her grandmother's 100-year-old dress. Also Lon Colvin as an "Indian," Henry Alles as "Jim Burger" the groom, Barney Mehrten, Jason Barton, wagon train leader; Marcella and Viola Britten of Three Rivers, riding sidesaddle, wearing dresses 75 years old—they scored a decided hit. Ernest John Britten, 14, created a lot of amusement when he rode in the parade astride the family cow.

In addition to the 21 wagons, each carrying at least 10 people, everyone appropriately garbed and carrying all the needed articles for camp life, there was 57 head of loose horses and 22 head of cattle which brought up the rear of the train. These were under the charge of Byron Allen, Alf Hengst, Girard Davis and Bill Swanson. The horse train was herded by Bert Nice, Lon and

Albie Lane, Irving Maxon, Craig Thorn, Clarence Dinely and Frank Door.

What was declared to be the most complete and authentic covered wagon equipment was that driven by Harold "Shorty" Hengst, who entered the town driving his team while barefoot and in his impersonation gave an excellent display of a backwoodsman. Strapped to the rear of his wagon was a crate of geese, while all the needed equipment was loaded inside.

John Britten and His Bobcat. *Photo from Author's Collection.*

After the wagons had formed a circle and campfires had been started at each wagon, where the women and girls prepared their dinner, there centered about the caravan the atmosphere of the

West as experienced so many years ago. Striding into camp was an Indian who was found to be friendly; he was given a handout at the Finch wagon and sent on his way. Noel Britten, one of the hunters of the outfit, soon returned to camp with his father's Kentucky rifle, carrying a large deer, creating much interest from camp visitors and observers. The "deer" was actually a cleverly stuffed hide which looked very real. However, Ernest John Britten, 14, won a lot of attention when he walked into camp, proudly displaying a wildcat which he had killed that day a short time before nearing Woodlake. The deceased cat was viewed at close range by all visitors; this stunt was one not included on the program, but proved to be one of the biggest hits of the day.

J. F. Righter, a gold miner of Mariposa County, attracted much attention with his equipment for panning gold, made even more interesting when a small nugget of virgin gold, valued at 30 cents was discovered; his demonstration of how gold is washed out of crushed rock and sand was most educational and added another bit of color and atmosphere to the day's entertainment.

L to R: Maud Loverin, Noel Britten, Ord Loverin and Jason Barton. *Photo from Author's Collection.*

During the afternoon and evening, old-time dances were enjoyed, excellent music being furnished by the Poison Oak Orchestra of Three Rivers, with Frank Finch as director. The old dances were called by Jason Barton while Jeff Davis proved himself an artist at "shaking the bones."

George Welch, 95, a pioneer in engineering and road building in the Three Rivers and Sequoia Park district, was a distinguished guest of the caravan celebration and was the oldest person in attendance. He took a keen delight in the entertainment of the day and entered into the spirit of the day with much enthusiasm.

Motion pictures of the picturesque celebration were taken by representatives of Pathe, Fox, Universal, Lasky and International film companies and plans were made to release them for screening.

Words of praise were heard from all sides for Phil Davis of Three Rivers, who originated the covered wagon caravan idea and did much to make it the success that it was. According to him, 250 residents of Three Rivers participated in the celebration, marking it as the most successful entertainment of its kind ever staged in the Valley, and bringing to Three Rivers and Woodlake much valuable advertising.[6]

[Ed note: one reel of the Pageant was eventually located by Earl McKee and converted into VHS format. It is the possession of the Three Rivers Museum and is viewed occasionally.]

---

6   *Fresno Morning Republican*, February 7, 1926.

Pioneers Rolled Back The Years---

Three Rivers, California, February 8, 1926

——— ———

Photo from Author's Collection.

CHAPTER IV

Community Organizations

Sequoia Hall

[Three Rivers Community Hall]

While doing research into the history of the old Three Rivers Community Hall, also known as, "Sequoia Hall", the author found an article written a number of years ago by the late Thelma [Alles] Crain. This article was in the first newsletter published by the Three Rivers Historical Society. Since Thelma had experienced firsthand many of the activities that took place there, her story is included here with only slight editorial changes:

"Sequoia Hall"

by Thelma Crain

Since there was no church building in town at the time, each Sunday saw church-goers gathering there to worship and one can still imagine the strains of "When The Roll Is Called Up Yonder" wafting through the air; the ample voice of Professor Dean easily heard above the others.

Each year, the annual Christmas Party was held at the Hall with Santa, fun and games, and a gift from the tree for each child in the community, usually followed by the swapping of gifts, in the hope of acquiring something more to one's liking.

Perhaps the favorite and best remembered of the activities were the dances where singles and couples came to dance away the evening to the music of one of the local bands. The "Poison Oak Band" was a favorite of the 1920s; its members' names reading like something out of the Audubon Society. There was Frank Finch, Edna Finch, Zola Finch, Jesse Finch, Ben Hardin, Carrie Swanson and others. In 1934, the music was furnished by Calva Stuart, Carney Franks, Lother Lutrell, Wesley Smith and other musicians.

The dancing usually started at 8PM and continued until midnight when everyone gathered downstairs for homemade cake and coffee - no prepared cake mixes in those days! Also, this was the time before the invention of "baby-sitters" and unless one had a cooperative grandparent in the home to tend the children, they accompanied their parents. The children were bundled up and put down to sleep on the stage or on the floors in the cloak rooms.

Sequoia Hall was the meeting place for the Woman's Club, box socials, Red Cross sewing, school programs, PTA and all manner of community festivities and activities.

The Hall had an interesting history, being built in 1909 on a site donated by Charles Bahwell on the river near the junction of Highway 198 and North Fork Drive. Construction of the building was under the supervision of Robert Dillon, father-in-law of Armin Grunigen. Dillon was paid $2.00 per hour for his services and money was raised by the sale of shares which went for $5.00

each. Materials were hauled from Lemon Cove by Robert Dillon and Jason Barton, using teams pulled by six horses each. The building, when completed, measured 30 x 60 feet and was heated by a large wood stove. The inside walls around the dance floor were equipped with hinged sides which could be used as tables when needed.

The Sequoia Hall Association was incorporated in 1911 and in 1928 the building was raised up a level so that a kitchen and dining area could be provided downstairs. This project was directed by Jason Barton; the Three Rivers Woman's Club donated $600.00 for this purpose.

Eventually, when fire prevention laws became more stringent, it was found to be too expensive to bring the building up to code. The County Fire Department refused it as a gift for the same reason and in 1955, a crew from the Woodlake Prison Camp was engaged to tear down the two-story structure and the scrap lumber was hauled away to other county projects.[7]

Sequoia Hall Demolition. *Photo from Author's Collection.*

---

7   *Heritage*, from the Three Rivers Historical Society, Vol I, No. 1, February 1992, pg. 01.

The following clippings from early newspapers serve to illustrate some of the events held at the "Hall" and enjoyed by the community:

"Benefit Dance At Three Rivers for Injured Mailman"

The old-time party given at the Community Hall Saturday evening for E. J. Briggs, who was seriously injured in an auto wreck while carrying United States mail between Three Rivers and Hammond, was a successful affair.

Modern as well as old-time dances were enjoyed to music accommodatingly furnished by different musicians during the evening. At midnight a supper, prepared by the women of the community, was served in the banquet room.[8]

"A masked ball was held at the Community Hall Saturday Evening"

Tom Phipps and Miss Myrtle Barton were awarded the prize for the best costumed couple and Dixie Clarkson of Lemon Cove took the prize for the best single costume. Mmes. Frank Finch, Phillip Alles, John Alles and Tena Austin and the Misses Rena Alles and Zola Finch, all dressed as sunbonnet babies, won the group prize. Mr. & Mrs. John Washburn of Lemon Cove were given a prize for being the most graceful waltzing couple. [9]

A party was given at the community hall Saturday evening. Each person had been requested to bring a costume wrapped in a package. As the packages arrived, they were deposited with a custodian, the men's and women's separately, and each depositor tagged with a number. The numbers were matched later for partners in the grand march. When the time came for putting on the costumes, each person drew a package and donned its

---

8   *Visalia Times-Delta*, March 18, 1924
9   *Fresno Bee*, Dec. 16, 1924

contents, irrespective of size or fit. Gales of laughter swept the hall as dignified members of the community emerged from the dressing rooms wedged into garments half their size or garbed in outfits so large that they dragged on the floor.

The grand march was formed and elaborate figures executed up and down the hall by the grotesquely garbed dancers. A prize for the funniest couple was awarded to Clarence Britten and Miss Marjorie Finch. Much added merriment was afforded when the affair was turned into a leap year party with the women requesting the pleasure of dances from the opposite sex.[10]

"Four Hundred Attend Dinner at Three Rivers"

Four hundred people packed the Community Hall Friday evening when Three Rivers entertained friends from the valley towns with a free chicken dinner and an old-time dance. The crowd was so far in excess of the capacity of the banquet room that plate suppers had to be served upstairs to a large portion of the guests.

The banquet room was prettily decorated with flowers, holly and huge baskets of apples and oranges. A feast of baked chicken and all its attributes weighed down the tables. Dancing, though difficult on the crowded floor, continued until a late hour and a spirit of merriment and old-fashioned friendliness prevailed.

The affair was given under the auspices of the Hall Association to friends of the community who have been coming to dances here for many years past. Jason Barton, as chairman of arrangements, was ably assisted by men, women and young people of the neighborhood in this expression of old-time hospitality.[11]

---

10   *Fresno Bee*, Jan. 8, 1925
11   *Visalia Times-Delta*, December 6, 1926

Three Rivers Chapter of the Red Cross

Promptly after the United States entered World War I, Three Rivers joined the rest of the country in the organization of a Red Cross unit. A mass meeting was called and a large membership was promptly enrolled in what was named the Three Rivers Branch of the Visalia Chapter of the American Red Cross.

Mrs. Anna McMullin Hays was the first chairman and served until after the close of the war. Under her enthusiastic leadership, a very high standard of support and service was maintained. The whole community responded with zeal. Funds for supplies were raised by public subscription and by entertainments. One very successful occasion was the "Pie Sale" in Giant Forest. The Woman's Club suspended its own meetings and co-operated in every way. The Red Cross met every Wednesday at the Hall [old Sequoia Hall] for all-day work sessions.

A Junior Red Cross Chapter was also organized at the Three Rivers School, as well as the Sulphur Springs School; both did faithful work for the Red Cross as well.

After the war, the Three Rivers community kept its organization active and maintained a high membership, continuing to contribute liberally to any emergency call and was on the alert to care for local cases of need until theThree Rivers Womans Club took on this endeavor.[12]

---

12   Notes of Frankie Welch.

Photo from Author's Collection.

Three Rivers Woman's Club

The Three Rivers Woman's Club began in 1915 as a sewing circle which met only occasionally; it was soon organized into an active and purpose-filled woman's social club. The late Carrie Swanson told it this way:

[I]t all started back in the autumn of 1915 when one bright little woman asked the other women of the community to gather at her home for a social afternoon. A few other meetings were held at different homes during the winter. Memories of those pleasant gatherings freshened as the autumn of 1916 arrived and other meetings were arranged. An unwritten rule prevailed for a time that the first guest to arrive at the home where the meeting was being held would receive the group the next time.

Other activities than just the social hour began claiming the group's attention. An entertainment or two—some dances—were given to supply funds for various needs in welfare work. The necessary organization was discussed and in March 1917, the Three Rivers Woman's Club was officially organized and federated within the San Joaquin Valley District. Then came the war [World War I]. Regular meetings of the club were discontinued and the members turned all their time and efforts to Red Cross work. The Three Rivers chapter had as their president Mrs. Anna McMullin Hays and through her genial leadership a great amount of work was done—sewing, giving dances and other entertainments for raising relief funds. When the necessity of such work was over, regular meetings of the club were resumed. [13]

Hard Times Dance *Photo from Author's Collection.*

In May 1917, the Woman's Club reported a total of $600 for that year, which was used to benefit the community. The club gave seven entertainments and dances to realize this amount. They also worked for the Three Rivers exhibit at the Citrus Fair and were presented with a silver cup by J. E. Barton as a token of appreciation.[14]

---

13   Manuscript of Carrie Swanson, undated.
14   Notes from *Remember When*, by Pauline Grunigen in the *Sequoia Sentinel*, date unknown.

Before World War I, the group helped to remodel the old Community Hall and had their meetings there for a few years. In time, the large size of the building and the cold temperatures did not work out and so they searched for a new place to call home.

This opportunity came in 1924 when one of their staunchest members died and her son gave her home to the Three Rivers Woman's Club to use for as long as they needed it. This lady was the same Mrs. Hays who had been so instrumental in the club's formation and activities and played such a large part in the community. The house had originally been built by Dan and John Hunter; it had been designed for an invalid girl, Elizabeth Maxwell, whom the doctors had sent to the hills for her health, but she died before it was completed. Mrs. Hays bought it for $1200.00 and lived there until her death.[15] The building is now the home of the Three Rivers Arts Center, just across the Middle Fork Bridge.

This gift of the building was the opportunity for the Woman's Club to have their own home. The women happily tied on aprons and went to work giving dinners, dances, card parties and various entertainments which would bring in money for remodeling the Hays' home. Partitions were torn out, an oak floor laid and furnishings were purchased. Now the club members could gather cozily around a leaping blaze in the big fireplace for meetings or refreshments.

The club became a social and civic center; community activities, musicals and many other social gatherings were held there. They held art exhibits and even put on an Heirloom Tea, which drew undreamed-of treasures from the past that had been hidden in many Three Rivers homes. For nearly 30 years, the club entertained the oldsters of the community with a dinner and program each fall. This Pioneer Dinner became a tradition to which all the attendees looked forward to enjoying.

In 1921, the club was federated with state, district and county clubs. This brought state speakers and district meetings to Three Rivers. The clubhouse was remodeled and enlarged several times to make it more suitable for community and public gatherings.

---

15   *Heritage*, by Joe Doctor, July 22, 1987.

However, there were still some inconveniences at the clubhouse—the water system had a way of quitting when most needed—but the pioneer women always managed to carry on. Mrs. Grace Alles, four-time president of the club, recalled that on one occasion she carried water by the buckets full from the river for a big dinner.

Backed by tall trees suggesting a lovely landscape painting, the clubhouse had a view up the Kaweah River to the Sierras and the Giant Sequoia second to none. It logically followed that the club chose the sequoia tree as its official emblem.

One of the annual Pioneer Dinners was held October 30, 1926 and it was reported like this:

Honoring the old people of the community, the Woman's Club of this place gave a dinner and afternoon entertainment for them at the clubhouse Wednesday. But as one mingled with the guests and caught the spirit of the gathering, one was inclined to wonder where the "old people" were and to feel somehow that the term was a misnomer.

The oldest man there, A.B. Burdick (88), who manages an apple ranch all by himself 13 miles above here in the mountains, walked the greater part of that distance to the affair. And the oldest woman present, Mrs. Betsy Purdy, 86, slim and boyishly bobbed, read an entertaining paper before the assemblage - without glasses.

The guests, numbering 18, were seated at two prettily decorated long tables in the spacious and hospitable main room of the clubhouse and [were] served a repast which did credit to the committee in charge. Mrs. Frank Finch, president of the club, acted as hostess. Halloween favors and caps added to the gaiety of the affair.

The article continued on with more interesting facts:

After dinner, numerous pictures were taken and much interesting data gathered by persistent newspaper men. Then followed a program furnished in large part by the guests themselves. "Grandma" Alles, as she is affectionately called by the neighborhood, belying her 84 years, played and sang a number of German hymns. John Rice and "Doc" Mullenix, old-timers, played spirited jigs and swinging waltzes on the violin. Mrs. Betsy Purdy gave a reading and Mrs. Julia Topping sang "God Bless You," which she sang 53 years ago on her wedding day. Mrs. N. Sivertson, born in Norway, sang hymns in her native tongue; Enos Barton convulsed his hearers with a humorous recitation, "The Boat Captain Preacher" and J. A. Eggers sang "California Hills" among which he has lived for the past 49 years.

It was further recorded:

To A. B. Burdick went the honor of having attained the greatest number of years; Mrs. Betsy Purdy the honor of the oldest woman there. Others who had reached the required age of 70 or over were as follows: I.D. ["Doc"] Mullenix, born 1844 in Tennessee; Mrs. N. Sivertson, born Norway 1846; Ben Southward, born 1848 Ohio; Enos Barton, born 1849, Illinois; William Morrow, born 1849; Henry DeLong, born 1849; Mrs. Molly Griffes, born 1849; John Rice born 1850; Mrs. Julia Topping, born 1853; J. A. Eggers, born 1854; Mrs. Henry DeLong, born 1855; Mrs. Molly McKee, born 1855; Lowell van Allen, born 1854. Mrs. M.L. Thorn and Mrs. J.A. Eggers were among the guests, although they have not qualified as to age. The Woman's Club plans to make this affair a yearly event.[16]

Although the Hays' home continued to be used by the Woman's Club for many years, eventually the majority of the club members wished to be

16   *Visalia Times-Delta*, October 30, 1926.

relieved of the upkeep and responsibility of the clubhouse; they moved to their present place of meetings at the Memorial Building on Highway 198 where they continue to this day to hold community activities and generously donate to the various needs of the community.

Oct. 20, 1925 Pioneer Dinner

Front Row, L to R: Mrs. Christina Alles, Mrs. Henry Delong, Mrs. Nils Sivertson, George Welch, John Pritchard, Mrs. A. O. [Mollie] Griffes, Mrs. Fred Maxon, Mrs. B.C. Purdy.
Second Row: Nils Sivertson, Henry DeLong, Enos Barton, W. S. Morrow, George Grove, W. F. Dean, A.O. Griffes, Col. George Stewart.
Back Row: Mrs. Addie Stewart, Mrs. Laura Hopping, Mrs. C.A. Hyde, Mrs. Mollie McKee, Mrs. J.E. Eggers, J.E. Eggers, Judge W.B. Wallace, Fred Maxon, John Spenser.
Photo from Author's Collection.

[NOTE: Why is it called "Woman's" Club and not "Women's" Club? The author was given this information by a reliable source:

I received your question and all I can say it was a matter of choice when clubs picked their names. Clubs that chose Women's took the view that they were a group of women and that was their club. The ones that chose Woman's (which is the majority) picked that because they wanted the member to feel it was their club and club for a woman.][17]

---

17   Information from Toby Kahan, Vice-President, California Federation of Women's Clubs.

CHAPTER V

Early Business Ventures

Atwell Mill

Logging Industry

Some of the following information was taken from an article written by the late Grace Alles.[18]

Isham Dykes Mullenix (known as "Doc") and father of Grace, went to Mineral King to work at the mines in 1878 with Dan Overall and William Wallace. Evidently, they were put to work in the construction of the stamp mill; this type of work did not agree with them and they stayed only a few days. Mullenix left to go down to what is now the Atwell Mill area, where he started making pine shakes for the inhabitants of Silver City. In 1879, he filed for a homestead on 160 acres there at Atwell which was "proved up" in 1883 and became his property. Subsequently, he sold it to Judge A. J. Atwell in 1886, withholding the original house lot (the site of the present

---

ranger station) and either withheld then or bought later, 20 acres up on the hill above this site.

Atwell built his mill in 1887. He used mostly pine, fir and cedar trees for the endeavor. The judge died in 1890 and his heirs owned the mill until 1915. The Kaweah Colony operated the mill in 1891 when the Federal Government stopped their operation at the Colony Mill site on the North Fork drainage. The Colonists leased Atwell Mill from Mrs. Atwell, sawing and cutting their lumber there for one year.

In 1896, Henry Alles and Jeff Davenport leased the mill and then sub-leased it to the Mt. Whitney Power Company in 1898. The power company then cut enough *Sequoia Gigantea* there to build the flume from Oak Grove to Powerhouse No. 1 at Hammond. This was continued until 1901; Henry Alles took over in 1902, running the mill until 1918 when his brother Phil, took over the operation. Phillip Alles moved the mill to Silver City in 1937 and sold it to Walter Wells, until Wells had milled all the lumber he needed. Subsequently, the business was sold to someone from Springville.

The wheel in the meadow that can still be seen is the flywheel of the engine from the mill and has been there since 1886; Judge Atwell brought it in. He had constructed a large flume around the side of the mountain to pipe water to the mill. A waterwheel was used first; but not being successful, it was changed to a steam engine the next year. Atwell used oxen in his logging business; after the oxen, he brought in a donkey engine from a mine at Mineral King and anchored it to a tree stump. Log skids were laid up on the hillsides and greased to move the logs more easily.[19]

An old letter from William Hengst tells about his employment at Atwell Mill in 1909 when he was 19; he said he worked there for one year as the operator of the gang saws. At that time, the operators of the mill were Mr. Wright and Mr. Mazarett, who had come from Stockton where they had a lumber mill. Hengst stated that the year he was working for this company, the mill used downed redwood lumber only; no redwood trees being cut that year for use in the mill. The entire product from the mill at that time was pencil tablets. Pencil tablets were redwood slabs from

---

19   Ibid.

which pencils were made. Each slab was 6" long, 2" wide and 1/4" thick. These slabs were packed into boxes and carried by a four-horse wagon to Visalia where they were shipped to another location to be completed into pencils.[20] In an article from the *Daily Californian,* the headlines read: "Tulare Shipping Pencil Wood to Old World. Car Load Goes from Exeter and its Destination is France."

> Henry Alles was here from Atwell Mill on the Mineral King [R]oad Tuesday. He stated that he was about ready to ship a carload of pencil wood from Exeter and that the car would probably leave that station today for New York. The destination of the wood is France where it will be used in the manufacture of lead pencils of a cheap variety. It is redwood and is used as a substitute for cedar, which is becoming scarce. The wood is shipped in boxes about 5 feet long, 3 feet wide and 18 inches deep. Shipments of pencil wood have been made from Sanger for several years, but the shipment being made by Mr. Alles today is the first carload to go forward from this county.[21]

Atwell Mill. *Photo from Author's Collection.*

---

20   *Los Tulares* Quarterly Bulletin; September 1987.
21   *Daily Californian,* February 2, 1905, pg. 3.

Bahwell Store and Saloon

The Bahwell Store and Saloon was located just west of the Bequette house and the Three Rivers Museum. It was operated by Adam Bahwell from 1874 to 1895. The saloon, the first "public house" of Three Rivers, was located on a small, flat spot of land above a dugout below the Bahwell Ditch, next to the old Mineral King Road (just west of the Three Rivers Historical Museum). This location was important because of its proximity to the then-traveled road and the availability of spring water (this was before construction of the Bahwell Ditch in 1896) to keep the beer and liquor cool.

After the Bahwell family left the business, the saloon continued to operate under other owners including the Carters about 1910. The late Forest Grunigen remembered visiting the local watering hole during its "Grand Closing" ceremony on the eve of Prohibition, July 1, 1919.

The saloon never reopened after Prohibition was repealed in 1933. Jessie Bequette, owner of the property from 1926–1990, remembered that the place had a "cooler room" below, with steps leading up to the small wood frame building that housed the saloon.

The Bahwell Saloon occupied the site from 1874-1919. It is unknown when the building was actually removed. Some foundation stones are still visible that were used for the walls in the cooling room.[22]

---

22   John Elliott, National Register of Historic Places, Registration Form.

Philip Alles in front of Dave Carters
Saloon, first saloon in Three Rivers.
Now Bequette property.   1907

Phil Alles in front of Bahwell Saloon. *Photo from Author's Collection.*

There is not much information available and unfortunately, little is known of this family's life and history. The Bahwells did own several pieces of property in Three Rivers, where the saloon stood and also more adjoining property to the east and west, as well. Charles Bahwell donated the land for the Sequoia Hall, enjoyed by the community for many years. Although it is not known when or why the family left Three Rivers, census records record that in 1900 they were living in the Visalia area and in 1910 Adam's son Charles Bahwell had moved to Lemon Cove. Charles Bahwell died in 1915 and is buried in the Three Rivers Cemetery.

According to the US Census of 1870, Adam Bahwell was born in 1832 in Hesse Darmstadt, Prussia, but was living in Three Rivers at the time this census was taken. His wife was Nancy Bahwell, who had been born in 1846 in Missouri. At that time [1870], their children were Charles Franklin, age 7, Benjamin, age 4, and Jackson, age 1. Adam's wife, Nancy, passed away November 1882 and in the census of 1900, Adam is listed as a widower with two daughters, Maud and Bertha, as well as another son, Hade Bahwell. Adam Bahwell died March 1901; both he and his wife Nancy are buried in the Visalia Cemetery.

Broom Handle Factory

For a short time, Three Rivers had an interesting industry; it was a broom handle factory and was it located on the South Fork about 1000 yards from the Conley and South Fork bridges. It was owned by Alfred Curtis, who was the son of a Mrs. Laura Curtis, sister of Chris Devoe, who had owned the old Blossom homestead.

Mr. Curtis had acquired an old steam engine from the Kaweah Cooperative Colony as part of his factory equipment. Several thousand broom handles were made, consisting of alder and sycamore woods; however, it proved to have too many knots and many of the handles turned out to be too crooked to use. Several people worked in the sawmill and took handles as pay.

The materials were used in various ways as well, such as railings for stairways. The old Alles home at Three Rivers had these railings and the Thorn family used some in flooring their original home.

The sawmill soon went broke and was sold to a firm [name unknown] who tried making pencil boxes using redwood that they had obtained from Henry Alles under a contract. These boxes were sent to France for grooving but proved too brittle and soft so another business failure was recorded.

Conrad Alles attempted to start another sawmill with the milling equipment when he tried to cut lumber there, but that also failed. Then he moved the equipment down to the Kaweah River's main fork below the present site of the Three Rivers Golf Course and operated there for a time.

All remnants of the sawmill finally were taken in the 1955 flood, removing every trace of the history of a broom handle factory, pencil box maker and lumber concern.

However, part of the machinery for the sawmill venture, after the broom handle venture, was removed to Mendocino County. This location was found to be a better and more profitable one, since it was in an area where materials were more suitable to this industry.[23]

23   "Remember When", by Pauline Grunigen, *Three Rivers Sequoia Sentinel*, Feb. 15, 1974.

Thus ends the tale of the little-known industry of the Three Rivers Broom Handle Factory.

Kaweah Fish Hatchery

The planting of fish for the trout fishing enthusiast was begun quite early in the Three Rivers area. There is an ad from the *Visalia Daily Delta Times* of September 15, 1893, advertising "More Trout and 10,000 Bass for our Streams. Over 40,000 fish will be Planted in Our Mountain Streams."

The *Visalia Daily Morning Delta* of 1894 gives the following account:

Through the enterprise of two fishing clubs, The Tule River Fishing and Shooting Association and the Visalia Sportsman's Club, the streams of Tulare County have been well stocked with trout, and the people of this county have these two clubs to thank for this boon. During the past year, nearly 40,000 fish were planted in the Kaweah and Tule Rivers, and 20,000 extra fish, consisting of black bass and New Hampshire Brook Trout, have been apportioned to the Visalia Club, and they will be planted during the coming summer.

The fish that were planted last year have grown very rapidly, and there will be good fishing this year all along the Kaweah Rivers; every branch of the Kaweah is now stocked with fish.

The article continues:

Soon after the organization of the Visalia Sportsman's Club, a requisition was sent to the State Fish Commission for 10,000 rainbow trout. After carefully reading the fish and game ordinance, the fish were brought to Visalia by E. W. Hunt of the Fish Commission. The fish were taken to Sub Johnson's Pumpkin Hollow Ranch, thirty-five miles east of this city, and successfully planted in the Kaweah River.

A few weeks afterward, Mr. Hunt again arrived in this city, this time with 20,000 Independence Lake Trout. This consignment of fish was placed in the headwaters of the North and Marble Forks of the Kaweah. Captain James Parker of Troop B, Fourth U.S. Cavalry, aided the representatives of the club in placing the fish in the higher branches of the river.

The club expects to get 10,000 New Hampshire Brook Trout this summer, and it is the intention to place the same in the Kaweah River nearer Mineral King than the Pumpkin Hollow Ranch.

The Visalia club proposes to erect a club house this summer on the Pumpkin Hollow Ranch. J. Sub Johnson, the owner, has kindly offered to donate a reservation of ten acres for a site and ground. The club controls six miles along the river banks for its fishing ground, and the members and their friends will have a wide territory to cover in pursuing their piscatorial pleasures.

The club house will be a rough building but will undoubtedly be comfortable and well provided with camping conveniences. With such a house the club will be well prepared to entertain guests.[24]

Again, in the same paper on July 22, 1901, the following note:

Charles F. Johnson received a telegram from the state fish commissioners this morning announcing that 25,000 fish would arrive here this evening. Mr. Johnson will take the trout to the hills tonight, planting some of them at Pumpkin Hollow, some at the Mt. Whitney power house, and another lot at the Mineral King bridge. Johnny Broder will meet Mr. Johnson at Britten's store and take some of the trout to the South Fork of the Kaweah, near Broder's cabin. The fish were secured by the Visalia Rod and Gun Club.[25]

---

24   *Visalia Daily Morning Delta*, Jan. 21, 1894.
25   Ibid, Jan.21, 1894

Early in the spring of 1919, a hatchery to stock the streams of Fresno and Tulare Counties and a portion of Kern County was built on the Kaweah River near Hammond, Tulare County. The location was on the main highway to General Grant and Sequoia National Parks.

Frankie Welch's column to the *Fresno Bee* June 14, 1924, states, "Visit to Kaweah Fish Hatchery is Well Worth While," and she gives a description of the facilities that were in place at that time, telling the reader that:

> [I]t will mean a sliding scramble down a short steep trail, but it is delightfully cool when you get there and maybe you will find Ed Clessen, who operates the hatchery for the Fish and Game Commission, feeding the little fishes their meals of milk and beef liver. [I]f you are fortunate enough to arrive when hatching is in process, you will see the small golden eggs in wire baskets in the ends of the troughs, with the tiny fish as they come to life looking like polly-wogs, wiggling through the bottom of the basket and starting gaily on their water way. They are about 1.5 inches long when they are planted . . . .

That season alone, the estimated fingerling release was 350,000 and most were destined to be released in the South Fork inside Sequoia Park.

Frankie wrote about the different seasons and the amounts of fish fry that were released. In 1925, the pipe from Power House No. 1 was clogged and many fish died before the screens were cleaned and the water started flowing again. In February 1926, construction of a flume line to carry water to the then-renamed Hammond Fish Hatchery was begun; this was the first step for building a larger hatchery at the site. A hatchery with capacity for about 4,000,000 fry annually was contemplated in the Commission's plans, if the water supply was approved. The flume plans called for water to be diverted into it for the hatchery above the plant and then turned in again below it, returning the water to the Kaweah River.

By July 1926, the Kaweah Hatchery was supplying fry to other locations: 95,000 to Giant Forest lakes, rivers and streams; 50,000 went to the Tule River and that release was followed by another 60,000 later on in the month.

In the fall of 1927, work was commenced to the building of a new and expanded Hammond Fish Hatchery. The old plant with its temporary quarters was abandoned and closed; however, according to manager Ed Clessen, more than 300,000 trout fry were hatched there and sent out to stock the streams in the mountain areas. The new hatchery was planned to have a capacity of 1,500,000 fry at one time; Clessen again was to manage the plant facilities.

A report in 1928 states that work was progressing rapidly and that foundations for the various buildings were completed and the work of framing and sidings was well under way. The plant was to consist of the hatchery, which was forty feet wide by eighty feet in length; in addition, plans included two cottages, one with a garage underneath. A unique feature of the hatchery was its floor, which was laid of two by fours placed one inch apart so that, in the event of high water, the floor would drain out quickly afterward. The hatchery was very close to the river and during large storms, water would lap against the foundation. As a safeguard, sturdy cement piers reaching far into the ground were placed at close intervals in the foundation and the building was bolted to these piers.

These measures worked until November 1950, when flood waters shifted the buildings from their foundations and sand filled in, causing tremendous damage to the facility. The decision was made to close it permanently and any salvageable material was sent to other hatcheries across the state.

FIGURE 16. Kaweah Hatchery, 1935. Kaweah River in flood stage. Photograph by J. H. Wales.

Kaweah Fish Hatchery. *Photo from Author's Collection.*

Motion Picture Making

Did you know that Three Rivers was once a "hot spot" for the motion picture industry? Between 1925 and 1929, a number of films were made here and in the nearby Parks. The following are excerpts from Visalia papers:

> The first contingent of a company of twenty-three motion picture people headed by Paul Hurst of the Paul Hurst Productions Company of Hollywood, arrived in Giant Forest, Sequoia National Park yesterday to start the filming of James Oliver Curwood's novel of the Canadian Rockies, *The Gold Hunters.* The remainder of the company is expected today and Thursday. Several Alaskan dogs accompany the outfit.
>
> The picture will be made in Tokopah Valley, a rugged upland region to the northeast of Giant Forest at the very head of the Marble Fork [of the Kaweah] River. There are five lakes in the valley and it is surrounded by precipitous cliffs. The motion picture people expect to be camped in the valley for two weeks.[26]

Then, the following year:

> **"Three Rivers is Movie Producing Scene for Films"**
>
> Filming of a series of western pictures for the Bud Barsky Productions Company, under supervision of Paul Hurst, has started here with the company making their headquarters on the old Guy Hopping Ranch, now leased by Ord Loverin and working out to the many picturesque locations selected in this vicinity. Barsky himself is with the company and will watch the progress of the pictures during the coming month.
>
> Featured in these pictures will be the promising young actor, Al Hoxie, who is a "reel" western man, having been born

26   *Visalia Times Delta,* July 21, 1925

and reared on the Nez Percé Reservation in Idaho and served as a forest ranger there. He is supported by Ione Reed, [born in Hanford, CA] who came into motion pictures through winning a beauty contest in Dallas, Texas two years ago and who has worked opposite several of the western stars during the past year. She is a splendid horsewoman and makes a perfect support for Hoxie. Others in the supporting cast are Cliff Lyons, dare-devil rider of Medicine, South Dakota and champion rider of the state who has doubled for many big stars in horse stunts too dangerous for them; also Roy Watson and Floyd Amers, character men well known in motion pictures having twelve years before the camera. There will also be about a dozen other actors of lesser prominence.

Some of the locations which will be used by the company are the Dean Ranch, Britten Ranch and Store, Hengst Ranch, Kaweah Bridge, Power House No. 2 bridge and dam, old Sequoia Park control road and many beautiful spots along the rivers. Cattle are to be gathered from the ranges for use in the pictures.

Barsky, who is one of the largest independent producers in the country, is highly enthusiastic over Three Rivers as a motion picture locale and if conditions prove as satisfactory as he thinks, he will seriously consider building a studio here and doing the bulk of his western stuff in this locality.[27]

Even more exciting stories from the newspapers:

"Three Rivers Folk See Wild Ride; Woman Displays Nerve, Rider Falls On Head; Movie People Produce Thrillers"

Thrilling and spectacular stunts, many of them charged with unforeseen elements of danger, are daily being enacted by members of the motion picture company working here on a group of western pictures.

---

27   Ibid. July 8, 1926.

Ione Reed, the leading woman, seated atop a rickety, wildly-careening buckboard, guided a runaway team down a precipitous mountain road and it was only by the exercise of a steady nerve and a cool head that she managed to keep the outfit from going off the grade when a wheel cut over the bank in rounding a turn.

[This scene actually used a local boy, John Britten, Sr.; he was the stuntman for the actress. He later said that the director got mad at him since he had to use his buggy whip to get the horses to even run!]

The leading man, Al Hoxie, did a stunt the other day not called for by the director but which nevertheless will be "good stuff" on the screen. When his mount stumbled and his clothes caught on the saddle horn, horse and rider pivoted for an instant on their heads, heels pointing wildly to the sky. Supposedly shot, Hoxie fell from a swiftly galloping horse and rolled thirty-five feet over and over down a steep rough embankment.

A bonus was offered for some man to jump off a forty-foot cliff into the river. When no one came forward, the director, Paul Hurst, [and a former Dinuba boy], did it himself and then climbed a dangling rope back up the face of the cliff.

One of the most picturesque scenes enacted was when 100 head of cattle were driven pell mell into the river, horses and riders plunging after them. Many "shots" have been made about the local stores, hotel and post office the past week. This always draws a crowd of onlookers and tourists lining the highways to watch.[28]

The final article leads the reader to expect more:

---

28   Ibid., July 28, 1926.

"Three Rivers Has Proven Splendid Film Colony Set; Bud Barsky Productions Company Finishes Very Interesting Picture There"

Previews of the motion pictures filmed here by the Bud Barsky Productions during the past month are so highly pleasing and conditions for work in the locality have proved so satisfactory that Barsky plans to return sometime in September with a large company of perhaps fifty people and spend twenty weeks here making a wild horse picture, which he has recently signed a contract to do.

This picture will call for a great number of horses which will be shipped in by the carload. It was originally planned to make the picture in Arizona where horses are more easily available, but the beautiful scenery of this locality is drawing the producer back here. Headquarters will be made in Three Rivers as before, but the work will extend over a larger territory this time, many of the shots being made back in the Sierras. It is likely that there will be two directors, one working here and one in the mountains.

A street of a western town will be erected, and probably other buildings put up - in fact, it is the plan of Barsky to make a movie town of Three Rivers if he receives cooperation from the local people. The quiet, unobtrusive behavior of the present company has gone a long way to remove any prejudice entertained by the community against movie people.

Barsky returned to Hollywood with his company this week to make the interiors of the eight pictures they have been working on here. Unusual interest is felt in these pictures, not only because of the local scenes but the local people used in them. Among those in this locality who will appear on the screen alongside of the professionals, are Ernest John Britten, a fifteen-year-old lad, who takes rather a prominent part as the young brother of the heroine through one picture; Ernest Britten, Sr., who is a bandit in one scene and a wounded pioneer in another; also Craig Thorn, Ord Loverin, Miss Marjorie Fry, O.C. Bennett, "Shorty" Hengst and a number of riders from the valley.

Western Movie Star Al Hoxie. *Photo from Author's Collection.*

Special arrangements have been made to show these pictures in Visalia sometime in November for the benefit of those who have watched the making. One scene of unusual beauty and breathless interest is when the hero and heroine, Al Hoxie and Ione Reed, gliding down the river in a picturesque canoe past the face of a dark cliff, barely miss annihilation, when a great boulder is shoved off the top of the cliff and strikes the water just back of them, drenching them to the skin with its mighty splash. Another interesting shot is when Hoxie makes his escape at the old Britten [Bros.] Store, landmark in this place for thirty years. He slips into the garret of the building, climbs out a window, edges along the roof of the porch, clambers up the face of the battlement front and swings into the top of the old sycamore tree leaning over the store, thus reaching the ground and his horse by way of the tree, and eluding the "bandits" who are hunting for him inside. The stunt was so strenuous that Hoxie used a ladder in going back for a "still." [At the time this book was originally written, the sycamore tree was still there, still leaning toward the place where the Britten Brothers Store stood. It has since been cut down to the stump – the remainder carved into a likeness of an eagle.]

One of the scenes appeared so beautiful in the preview that the producer enthusiastically declared it was worthy of a painting - it depicted a covered wagon unhitched by the river, horses grazing at the side, a pioneer group around the camp fire. The covered wagon in the picture was one used in the Three Rivers' famous emigrant train last spring.[29]

Many more newspaper accounts exist of these exciting western movies filmed here in the 1920s. For many years, Three Rivers has continued to beckon movie producers, directors and actors to exhibit their screen talents in such a magical western setting; some have even decided to make their homes here in these canyons.

---

29   *Visalia Morning Times*, August 5,1926.

The Old Redwood Shop and Souvenir Business

The Three Rivers Redwood Shop and souvenir business had originally been established about 1927 by H. C. Balch. Balch came to Three Rivers from Lemon Cove to set up a wood shop where he could supply the demand for genuine souvenirs of the "big trees" to the tourists who came through on their way to and from the Park.

His first shop was in the Britten blacksmith building across the road from the Britten Brothers Store and Post Office in Old Three Rivers, since at that time the main route to the Park was via that road. When his shop was destroyed by fire, Mr. Balch put up a galvanized iron building a short distance away and remained there until 1930 when he passed away.

H. C. Balch in his studio. *Photo from Author's Collection.*

About that time, Maurice and Etta Macy arrived in Three Rivers and became interested in the souvenir business. Maurice had done woodworking in Dinuba and Tulare and had brought much of his machinery with him. After renting the business from the widowed Mrs. Balch for a year, he decided to buy it in 1931.

When the present highway to the Parks was completed in 1933, it left their redwood shop high and dry on the old road. Since the business had been thriving despite the financial depression of that time, they immediately began searching for a suitable plot of ground on the new highway and finally purchased an acre and a half from Mrs. Noel Britten, where they built a new shop.

To build the display room, which was used from that time until it was demolished after a fire in 1960, Macy used redwood staves salvaged from a 30,000-gallon water tank and tower which was a landmark at the old brick hotel building in Traver. This hotel, which had been destroyed by an earlier fire, was actually the childhood home of Mrs. Macy. The staves, which were re-sawed at their new shop, furnished enough lumber for the sales room and much of their residence which they built next door, having spent their first winter living in the new display building.

TIMES HAVE CHANGED since this photo was taken of the Redwood Shop built by Maurice Macy with his partially finished house on the left. Photo courtesy M. S. Macy

Macy House and Redwood Shop *Woodlake Echo, Nov. 17, 1960.*

In 1938, the original shop was torn down and a larger one of adobe was built. This was a more complete woodworking shop with several rooms for machinery, a dry kiln room and a shipping room. Later on, many additions were made on the outside building, the Macy's house, and two more small homes that had been constructed higher up on the property. By this time, the property and holdings had gradually increased to include three acres. The sawmill, which was at first directly behind the shop, was moved up the hill in order to allow more room to handle the large logs that were used there.

The source of the redwood lumber during the years is an interesting story. Balch first used the driftwood which was plentiful on the South Fork at that time, since it had been brought down from the redwood groves during the massive 1867 flood. Macy also got his material from this source for a while, then procured some from the old scrap pile at Atwell's Mill. A two-year supply was furnished by a single tree which had fallen near Oriole Lake one winter. Other sources were Whittaker Forest and the Balch Park area. [No connection with the H.C. Balch Family.]

The large redwood logs were usually quartered and hauled down to the Three Rivers mill to be sawed. One time they brought a log which was 14 feet in diameter and 36 feet long and contained 40,000 board feet of lumber. From just one quarter of this log, they made enough shakes to cover both the new wings of the Community Presbyterian Church and at the same time furnished siding and shakes for their newer home in Alta Acres.

While the Macys operated the shop, all their products were sold to the Park concessionaire, or in their own shop on the highway. Maurice remembered that when they first started, about 600 items were sold during a season and when he retired from the business, that figure had increased to 28,000 for one season. They made many articles according to popular demand. In fact, if anyone came in requesting something they didn't already carry, they always made an attempt to fill the order. Salt shakers, earrings, bookends, all sizes of bowls, etc., were made; items costing 25 cents to 6 dollars were turned out for the souvenir hunter.

Mrs. Macy worked right along with her husband and to her came many of the unusual requests. She recalled a woman asking her if she would carve something out of redwood suitable for favors for the officers of the State Republican Women's Convention. Mrs. Macy suggested an elephant and it turned out to be so successful that the following year she was asked to make more for the National Convention.

One year during a winter storm, a small branch fell from the Sherman Tree and park officials brought it down to Macy to use in his shop. From this, he made a gavel which he presented to Judge Walter Fry, US Commissioner of the Park at that time. Col. John R. White, the Park Superintendent, requested several gavels be sent to him while he was in Washington, D. C. on a business trip. One of these gavels made from the same limb off the Sherman Tree eventually found its way to the Smithsonian Institute, and in 1954, when the Macys were visiting there, they were pleasantly surprised to find the gavel they had made in such a place of honor.

Although his wife worked with him, it was also necessary for Macy to employ extra help. He hired a deaf boy, Gordon Lincoln, from the School for the Deaf in Colorado, and he proved to be such an excellent worker that more deaf boys were hired who were friends of Lincoln. Another employee was Jim Atwell, a deaf boy whose parents were employed in Sequoia. It was Gordon Lincoln who bought the business in 1944 when the Macys decided to retire. Gordon took his brother, Howard Kunkel, into partnership with him in 1947, purchasing the land and buildings.

Another deaf boy from the Colorado school was Archie Chaboude; he worked in the Redwood Shop for a while. When he found that Lincoln wanted to sell, he suggested that perhaps his brother Virgil might like to buy it. Subsequently, in 1954, Virgil Chaboude and a cousin, Louis Costly, purchased the business. Virgil eventually bought out Costly; however, the shop was destroyed by a fire in 1960. According to Chaboude, immediate plans were being made to rebuild a bigger and better shop and the business continued for a number of years.[30]

---

30   *Woodlake Echo*, November 17, 1960.

And where was this shop? The display room can still be seen; although at the time of this book, it is occupied by Nadi Spencer as her art gallery! She is painting and selling wonderful scenes of the Three Rivers country; lovely mementos are still being sold in the same location.

Interesting Note:

Coffee Catered Courtesy Crosbys

Not always are the firemen as lucky as they were the other night. That night in Three Rivers when they were working to put out the blaze in the Redwood Shop, they had coffee served to them from the tailgate of a station wagon courtesy of the Hunter Crosbys and Helen Ady. The Crosbys happened by just as the road was completely blocked by fire trucks and they just happened to have their big coffee maker in the car. Helen Ady took it over to Noisy Water, made coffee and she began serving the hot liquid. Business was good as everyone enjoyed the hot coffee whether working or just by-standing.[31]

---

31   Ibid.

The River Inn Hotel

The River Inn was a large hotel constructed on the North Fork Road just beyond the Main River Bridge on land owned by Jason Barton. The builders were Frank Stousland and Jason Barton; A. R. Carney was an additional owner. Frank Stousland was also the manager of the Palace Hotel in Visalia; he appointed Ernest McAdams as the clerk/manager of the River Inn.

Completed in May 1910, the Inn was constructed in a split-level style; it was finished inside with tongue and groove ceiling lumber from the San Joaquin Valley. The basement area was used for storage; the first floor was reached from an outside entrance and contained a dining room for tourists, the kitchen and a large club room where Sunday Schools, fraternal and community meetings were held. The second floor held the guest rooms and the attic rooms were for hotel employees.

The stage line to the hotel consisted of a four-horse stagecoach running from Lemon Cove to the Inn; during the summer months, the line was extended up into Giant Forest via the Colony Mill Road. Since the road had many very steep grades, there was a change of horse teams at Rocky Gulch. The stage went up to the redwoods one day and then back down to Lemon Cove the next. The stagecoach driver was Jesse Hoyt. Eventually, motor vehicles replaced the daily stage between Lemon Cove to the Inn; at that time, Shorty Lovelace was the driver.

In addition, Barton and Stousland secured the concession to operate the tourist trade in the Giant Forest, constructing an additional building there. In the early 1900s, they purchased a tourist camp in the forest from John Broder and Ralph Hopping. However, the tourist trade did not bring in the returns for which they had anticipated and the decision was made to sell their interest to Ed Demasters of Lemon Cove. The bad news was that shortly after the transfer, the hotel caught fire and burned completely to the ground September 1911.

Photo from Author's Collection.

Photo from Author's Collection.

[Ed Note: The River Inn Bridge that crossed the main fork was built under a contract with Healy, Tibbetts & Co, and was finished September

10, 1897 for $1547.00. However, this did not include the trestles, the approaches or areas to be filled in.] This bridge was demolished during the flood of December 11, 1937.[32]

1937 Flood just before the old trestle bridge went out. *Photo from Author's Collection.*

---

32   Frankie Welch's Notes

Stock Packing Industry

Nowadays, when one thinks of a business in the "packing" industry, it usually involves fruit, citrus and vegetables. But in the 1920s and earlier, "packing" meant the opportunity for tourists to view the beauties of the Sierra from the back of a horse or mule. This gave access to the wonders of the "back country" to those persons who did not care to tote their gear on their backs, stumbling along, watching their step instead of enjoying the scenery. Riding a mule or horse also provided access for those persons who were not physically able to do high altitude hiking.

The commercial packing business of the Three Rivers country was started in 1898 by John Broder, who had his headquarters at what is now known as the "Wells" Ranch on the South Fork.

An attorney from San Francisco by the last name of Thornton engaged Broder to pack him and his party into the Giant Forest area. Thornton's main idea at that time was to look over the timber in that locality, thinking that it might be possible for him to acquire some of it. But his schemes were blocked when he found that this timber was in the area that had been set aside by the federal government in 1890 for a national park, even though not much was done to develop it for tourism until 1899.

Broder made this trip with ten or twelve animals and decided that the packing business could be made to pay. In 1899, Ralph Hopping went into partnership with him and their business commenced under the name "Broder and Hopping." They purchased and rented more animals and established a camp consisting of three tents in Giant Forest.

In 1900, they added ten tents and a cook house to their camp. This same year, the government made the first appropriation for improvement work in the Park. This helped to advertise the mountains and encouraged the public to take trips to see the beauties of the forest. Broder and Hopping continued to run the packing business, adding more stock and equipment until they had about eighty-five head of pack and saddle animals. They soon discovered that they had tried to expand too fast and, in order to avoid paying his back wages, Jim Griffin, an employee, was added in as a partner.

John Broder died about 1907; Hopping and Griffin found themselves badly in debt; their entire business, including animals and equipment, was sold at a Sheriff's Sale.

However, in 1908, Chester Wright began with his pack outfit in the Giant Forest area. He started with a small number of animals and continued to operate and build up his business until about 1919, when he sold to the Kings River Park Company. In those years he had accumulated nearly sixty animals. The Kings River Park Company operated until 1924, when Ord Loverin purchased it.

Loverin had started packing early in life; at the age of 18, he was one of the packers for the 1903 Mt. Whitney Club High Sierra Trip. In 1916 he had a small outfit and at the time he purchased the Kings River Company, he had built his stock up to about 20 head. He continued on until his herd consisted of eighty head of horses and mules.

Other Ventures

In 1901, Clarence Fry and Earl McKee started to do commercial packing, each with a small outfit of about 10 animals. Fry continued to operate, adding to his outfit until he had some 30 head, when he quit the business in 1918. McKee kept on operating, using from 10 to 80 animals.

In 1920, Eugene Davis established his packing headquarters in Mineral King, operating successfully until 1924 when he sold to his brother, Phil. Phil Davis, who at one time operated about 160 head of animals, subsequently sold about 80 head to Buckman and Eggers.

Between 1914–1918, Fred Maxon, Onis Brown, Tom Phipps and Bill Canfield started commercial packing and built their herds up to about 20 animals each.

In 1927, Phipps sold one-half interest in his outfit to Roland Ross. Phipps and Ross established their headquarters in Mineral King and increased their stock to 80 animals. In October 1929, Phipps sold his half entirely to Ross.

The year of 1923 was when Roy Davis began packing with about 20 animals, and in 1924, Lawrence Davis bought a small outfit from Bert Smith at Mineral King.

Then in 1929, Craig Thorn entered the same business and took out his permit for twenty animals, establishing his headquarters at Silver City above Atwell Mill.

At its very beginning in 1898, the packing business did not have more than 12 head of commercial animals and the amount Broder received for Thornton's trip did not exceed $600. In 1928, one of the most profitable in the early history of the packing industry, there were at least 480 head of stock in use and at that time the gross receipts for the local packers totaled over $100,000.[33]

The Atwood Party. *Photo from Author's Collection*

---

33   Manuscript from Edna McKee and Oral Interview of Ord Loverin.

A newspaper article gives more detail:

Notables Start Pack Trips Into High Mountains

The season for pack trips into the high Sierra is in full swing now and many people of prominence from all over the United States are outfitting here and in Giant Forest.

A party of twenty-two, with four packers, two cooks and forty-five head of stock, was sent out from here this week by McKee and Britten, local packers and guides, for a thirty-day trip through Kern River, Mt. Whitney, Roaring River and Elizabeth Pass. Dr. and Mrs. Van Dalsem and Mr. and Mrs. A. D. Curtner of San Jose headed this party, which included a large number of Berkeley students. McKee and Britten are also taking out Mr. and Mrs. Dundan McDuffie, Fred Torrey and Lincoln Hutchinson of Berkeley and Colonel and Mrs. Chetham and party from Chicago for a thirty-five-day trip into the Roaring River country.

Dr. Henry Van Dyke, noted author and traveler, and Will H. Dige, president of the Isaac Walton League, both of New York, will arrive in Giant Forest about July 15th to be taken out by O.W. Loverin, packing under government concession, for a thirty-day trip in the back country.

James Simpson, president of Marshall Field, Chicago, with a party of nine, will be met by Loverin with thirty-two head of stock at Huntington Lake and brought across the mountains to Giant Forest.

Other people of note making extended trips through the mountains are: Dr. B. M. Rastall of Californians, Inc, John F. Grant and party of Houston, Texas on a six-week trip from Giant Forest to Yosemite and Frederick J. Swartz of New York, now in the Kern River and Black Rock Pass Country.[34]

---

34   *Fresno Bee*, July 5, 1924.

Ernest Britten, Ora Britten Welch & Maud Britten on a pack trip. *Photo from Author's Collection.*

Stock party on trail from Mt. Whitney to Lone Pine, 1910. *Photo from Author's Collection.*

Going over Glenn Pass with Stock Party. *Photo from Author's Collection.*

Three Rivers Airport

Although it's just a memory to old-timers, the Three Rivers Airport was actually a working and usable field for many years. Located on what is now North Kaweah Drive below the Lion's Roping Arena, it currently is used as a large parking lot for participants at that event. In 1935, Captain P.O. Brewer, Army Air Corp Reserve Commander of the Yucca Creek CCC Camp in Sequoia National Park, said that the airport possessed a greater advantage as an Army Air Base than any other mountain field in California. An inspecting board was unanimous in its praise of the field as a defense base. Since the airport consisted of a 4,000-foot runway, 400 feet wide and almost hidden by the surrounding hills, they declared that offensive enemy planes would be powerless in attacking the field if it were properly fortified and used as a first-class operating base in time of war.

The Three Rivers Airport was originally named "Jefferson Davis Field." The dedication ceremony took place on June 9, 1935, and was promoted by the Three Rivers Chamber of Commerce, Sequoia National Park, the Associated Chambers of Commerce Council, and the U.S. Army Air Corps.

The late John Holden, first president of the Three Rivers Historical Society, wrote the story of the dedication this way:

This summer was a thrilling time for Three Rivers and for pilots in Tulare County. The Three Rivers airport—to be known as Jefferson Davis Field—had its grand opening on June 9. A spectacular air show drew some 300 people to the strip. People crowded the bleachers on both sides of the field, and the long series of dedicatory events began at noon. The well-known local radio personality Stanley S. Simpson, explained the varied schedule of the program, which began with aerial acrobatics by Edeson E. [Monte] Mouton. After that came a polo game, in which Sequoia Park Superintendent Colonel John R. White played. Next were the Hawke Crop Dusters of Modesto who gave an amazing demonstration, which became quite tense when one plane became trapped in the branches of a tree and crashed.

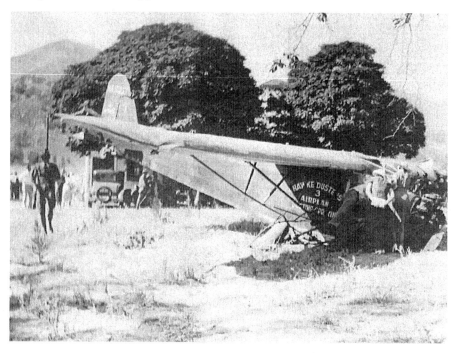

Photo Courtesy of the *Three Rivers Museum*.

Next item was a ball game between the Park staff and the Civilian Conservation Corps, and a demonstration by the Forest Service. Later there was a band concert and a stunt show by the Henderson Motorcycle Club.

But it was the flying events that generated the most excitement: an exhibition of stunts by Pansy Bowen, our local lady flyer who also worked for the State Board of Equalization. Then, a surprising get-away race between D. O. Kinnie, driving a Chevrolet Master Sedan, and Mouton, piloting a Beech Craft Cabin Plane, in which the Chevy won by a hair.

John went on to say:

The Junior Birdmen of America with some local plane builders showed model planes and did some mimic stunt-flying, and Coalinga's Margaret Vining did balloon busting in a Pusher plane. Even more exciting was a "dog fight" in the air between Mouton and Harry Sham, an Oakland racing pilot and aeronautics teacher. Next came an aerial duel between Eugene Hilton, commanding officer of the Potwisha CCC Camp, and F. H. Barber, Commanding officer of the Schreiber Flat CCC, in Pusher planes. Also, John Maggi of San Francisco did his death-defying "delayed drop" parachute jump. But the climax came with some breath-taking stunts performed by Barber at 500 feet. Between events there was skywriting.

Many celebrities were on hand, from State assemblyman Roscoe Patterson, to the famous upside-down flier Bernardine King, to movie queen Jean Parker, to stunt virtuoso Milo Burchen to Chief Ranger Ford Spigelmyre. Chairman of the executive committee for the big event was Tulare County's No. 1 Airman, Sol Sweet.[35]

The air strip was the namesake of Lt. Jefferson Davis, Jr., of the U.S. Army Air Corps, who was stationed with the 91st Observation Squadron at Crissey Field. While there, he won the highest score in the observation and attack pilots' match held at Langley Field, Hampton, VA. The eleven pilots entered in the event were the nation's leading flyers from the Army, Navy and Marine Corps Aviation services. After winning national honors and recognition for his prowess and skill in the Army Air Corps, Jefferson Davis was to work under contract for the Chinese government as an air instructor.

Returning one evening after a photographic mission in Sequoia Park, in an Army airplane piloted by a Lt. Robert Merrick, Davis met his death

---

35   *The Valley Voice*, November, 1987.

in the obscuring fog of San Francisco when his plane crashed into the sea.
Don Blanding wrote the following poem September 1932 in memory:

> They failed, those man-made wings!
> Then down the graying sky
> a living meteor fell with cruel speed.
> A cry, part fear, but greater part
> farewell to all dear things.
> Joined with the screaming of wind-tortured wings
> Farewell to clouds and clean high places of the blue;
> Farewell to sunlight, gallant daring flight
> He knew the hurt of treachery when trusted
> pinions turned to futile webs of tattered gauze
> He learned in those swift seconds <u>all</u> that
> man may hope to know of grandeur and sorrow.
> This I feel is so that are death's anaesthesia blurred away.
> All consciousness of hope, regret, dismay
> He looked into his heart and visioned there
> only a thankfulness for answered prayer
> That a crusader of blue unconquered sky
> Having so bravely lived, so might he bravely die.

The work of clearing the strip which was to be named for Davis began
in 1934. It took county workers over a year to prepare the strip prior to its
dedication. Teams of horses were used to drag out the rocks.

Airport Dedication. *Photo from Author's Collection.*

Soon after the dedication, problems developed with the air strip's name. Apparently, some northerners objected to naming the strip after the president of the southern Confederacy, since it was only seventy years after the close of the Civil War.

Sol Sweet and Earl Davis of Three Rivers were frequent users of the Three Rivers strip, but there were many others who used it as well. Sweet had a flying service in Visalia, and he often flew in to Three Rivers, using not only the North Fork strip, but also another at Big Oak Flat off the South Fork near Potato Mountain.

The strip was often clear when fog covered the valley and it served occasionally for emergency landings. Some houses were built adjacent to the airport after 1935, and at the opposite end, the Lions established their roping arena.

One major incident during the 1960s created another reason for concern about the safety of the landing field. A vice-president of Levi Strauss flew into Three Rivers to meet a real estate agent. Although he was warned about the hazardous weather conditions before his flight, this flight cost him his life in a crash after what some claimed was only one hour of air time in this particular plane. His twin-engine Cherokee wrecked not far from the Sulphur Springs schoolhouse.

From that point on, the county began to question the safety of the field and in 1967, it was stipulated in a formal resolution that the area was dangerous for flying in and out. It was "exx-ed" out on sectional flying maps and landings were discouraged, although this writer and her family landed and took off safely from time to time in a Beech Craft single engine Bonanza with no problems (and a good pilot).

Finally, in 1976, Tulare County formally closed down the Three Rivers Airport and the 1700-foot asphalt strip was ripped up and plowed under. About seven years later, rocks were mysteriously planted in the ground to discourage any further landings and to return the area to its near-original condition.

CHAPTER VI

Government Programs

California Conservation Corps (CCC)

The California Conservation Corps, or CCC as it was known, began in 1933. This organization was formed under President Franklin Delano Roosevelt's New Deal to overcome the effects of the Great Depression that followed the 1929 stock market crash. Not only did it give employment to many young men, it also achieved public works whose benefits have lasted to this day. Here in the Three Rivers District and in Sequoia National Park, the CCC were very busy and made many improvements that are still visible and enjoyed by many today.

The following is from a news story from the *Exeter Sun*:

> Putting the finishing touches on the Generals Highway and building other roads, trails, and telephone lines, hundreds of CCC enrollees are on the job in Sequoia National Park and adjacent areas this season.

Five CCC camps are under the direction of Sequoia Park administration with Forester Frank Been in charge of all projects. Men from the Potwisha camp are employed in improving the High Sierra Trail from Hamilton Lake to Kaweah Gap, a distance of about five miles; improving the Generals Highway from Ash Mountain to Giant Forest and landscaping around Ash Mountain park headquarters. A fireproof gas storage tank and pump have also been installed at Ash Mountain.

Building of a truck trail along the west boundary of the Park is the major project of the Old Colony Mill camp from the Park line to Colony Mill, eight miles, and the construction of a new trail between Heather Lake and Watchtower is also to be accomplished.

Camp Marble Fork, which was the name given to the Ash Mountain camp when it was moved to Giant Forest, will build a metallic telephone line from Lodge Pole to Lost Grove, 12 miles, and will also be employed on campground improvement. Men from Camp Buckeye, many of whom have been moved to a stub camp at Red Fir beyond Giant Forest, are building a two-mile road off the Generals Highway at Dorst Creek to open up a virgin area for campers. One thousand camp sites are planned; water and sanitation will be developed and fireplaces and tables built.

Camp Salt Creek men are employed in building a section of the Ponderosa Way fire suppression trail across the mountains south to meet the unit being constructed out of Camp Maxon. The making of adobe brick for a fire guard and patrol station at Lookout Point on the Mineral King Road is another part of the Salt Creek work for the season.

Camp Maxon Ranch on the South Fork, which is not administrated by the Park but is under the State Division of Forestry, is engaged primarily in the construction of a road to Clough's Cave. The work is progressing rapidly according to the new foreman, Byron Lovelace, and is expected to be completed by fall. This will make accessible one of the largest and best-known limestone caves in the region which heretofore has only been reached by long arduous hikes or on horseback.

Six of the eight miles between Camp Maxon and Clough's Cave have been completed and the grade does not exceed 7 percent and the road bed is 12 feet wide.

A road into Grouse Valley connecting the road from Springville has been completed by the Camp Maxon group and is being used by ranchers in the mountain district, although primarily intended as a truck trail.

A spur from the Clough's Cave road starting two miles above Maxon's is being built to meet Ponderosa Way coming across from Salt Creek.

Construction of a 45 by 100-foot swimming pool at Whitaker Forest in General Grant National Park has been completed by the Maxon Ranch men and a fire suppression station camp is being built at Badger.[36]

Toward the end of 1932, Park Superintendent Colonel White lamented the fact that although the Generals Highway to the Park had been completed and the number of visitors had increased, there was a large need for reforestation and restoration as well as conservation and landscaping, among others. The yearly amount budgeted for these projects was severely lacking. Therefore, on May 13, 1933, an advance group made up of a captain, one enlisted man and 24 enrollees of the CCC arrived to make their base at the Potwisha Camp. By May 27, fully constructed wood buildings were completed and occupied by 212 men. According to the Park, this was the first fully constructed CCC camp completed in the West.

Thus, Potwisha served as a base camp from which small details of workers were sent out to prepare the sites for the other camps. As soon as the beginning of June, four other camps were occupied by details and ready for Army cadres. These were: Marble Fork Camp, near where the bridge crosses the Crystal Cave Road; the Wolverton Camp; the Atwell

36   *Exeter Sun*, July 18, 1935.

Mill Camp and Yucca Creek camp, where the present North Fork Drive ends. Within a few weeks, a maximum personnel of 35 Army, 60 Park supervisory personnel and 1096 enrollees called these areas their home.

Life in the CCC camps afforded the enrollees wholesome food, clothing, and a token amount of expense money which was about $5.00 per month. The CCC was operated largely by commissioned officers, although many civilians were employed to provide the expertise needed in directing the various projects.

A letter from the late Don Raybourn to Pauline Grunigen appeared in Three Rivers' *Sequoia Sentinel* "Remember When" column, and he told her of some of his experiences in the Yucca Creek Camp. He said:

> John Grunigen was the superintendent and I remember that Bruce Bequette was one of the foremen. I can't tell you when the camp was built but I remember the enrollees had tents and the only frame buildings were the officer's quarters, the mess hall and the tool house where the superintendent had his office.
>
> I was first sent up to Yucca Creek in 1936 and took a crew of men up to Marble Fork Camp as a stub camp to do some work in Giant Forest. We were there most of the summer and then moved back to Yucca Creek in the fall.
>
> The enrollees did a lot of work on the Colony Mill road making it more suitable for Park use in case of fires. They also worked on the North Fork road between Yucca Creek and Schreiber Flat, as I remember.
>
> I also remember that John Grunigen had a bad sick spell and I had charge of the camp while he was sick; I think it was jaundice that he had. We had a lot of good men in both camps as well as in all the camps we had in the Park. I am sure a lot of the foremen and supervisors learned a lot about human beings and psychology during their dealings with the enrollees. I know I

did. I believe that most of the enrollees ended up better men than when they enrolled, some of them better educated.[37]

During the years of the CCCs, they published a dozen-plus camp newspapers—either regularly or sporadically—by mimeograph. These papers kept all the camp informed of their activities, comings and goings of camp personnel and enrollees; updates on projects and improvements, announcements of recreational activities and accounts of the event. They were interspersed with lots of camp humor. Some of the names of these publications were *Times of Company 992* and *Marble Fork News* from the Marble Fork Camp; Cain Flat Camp put out two papers as well: *Dog House* and *The Green Light*. *Yucca Leader* and *The Yucca Post* came from the Yucca Creek group. Up at Salt Creek, newspapers included *The Pow Wow* and *Salt Creeker*. Camp Maxon published *The Payoff*, and at Potwisha Camp, their newspaper was called, appropriately, *The Sequoian*.[38]

Camp Salt Creek. *Photo Courtesy of the Three Rivers Museum.*

37   *Three Rivers Sequoia Sentinel*, date unknown.
38   *Kaweah Commonwealth*, May 29, 1999.

These papers furnish a great deal of information that would remain unknown today if not for their contents. For instance, we learn that in the Spring 1936 issue of *The Sequoian*, local resident Jim Livingston was the civilian Project Superintendent and the foremen included Lon Oldham, who was the camp blacksmith.

Sport activities played a large part in the enrollee's spare time. Rivalry between the camps kept everyone interested and spirits high. *The Sequoian* reported that the "Potwisha Indians" were undefeated against Cain Flat, Yucca Creek and Buckeye camps. "They have yet to play Salt Creek, and you can bet your last dime they will give the Salt Creekers some strong competition."

Humor in these camp papers gave the reader a glimpse of how the camaraderie of the enrollees was close and energetic, tying them together in their common quests and projects. Rookies were often the target of jokes but many times the humor was aimed at certain individuals' well-known character traits. One columnist poked fun at his instructor, at that time a well-known NPS ranger, claiming that "Lon's class seems to be getting a little more than natural history. Yours truly recommends sending Mr. Garrison to the next National Liars Association Contest."[39]

Other recreation activities included first-run Hollywood movies that were enjoyed by the CCCs as well as many local residents from Three Rivers. Milton Savage of Three Rivers recalled "going up to Salt Creek quite a bit to go to the movies and [we] went up to the Maxon Ranch a few times." Also, Barbara Carter Milbradt remembered attending movies at Camp Maxon as did Garry Kenwood who said, "It only cost us 10 cents."

Dances were another way that the CCCs and local residents became acquainted. Again, Barbara Carter Milbradt said of the dances, "I was just a young girl, but used to accompany my aunt and uncle Della and Byron Allen to the dances at the old Dance Hall near the North Fork Bridge. My aunt told me that if any of the [CCC] boys asked me to dance, that I should. Well, they were young, and a long way from home, and there weren't too many partners available; so I did dance!" The *Salt Creeker*

39   Ibid.

camp newspaper reported that "it was a good place to get acquainted with some swell people." Clarence Searcy, a local enrollee stationed at the Cain Flat Camp, remembered walking all the way from "up there, seven miles up the Mineral King Road, to a dance . . . ."

Very little trouble was ever reported in connection with any of these events. That over 1,000 young men in their late teens and early 20s could coexist so harmoniously within a small community seems remarkable in our time; things were quite different then. As one local old-timer recalled, "[T]he moral fiber of our society was pretty strong, so these young guys knew they had an opportunity. I think that is probably part of the reason you had so little trouble . . . ."

One public statistic stated that as many as half of the enrollees in the Civilian Conservation Corps had not received an education beyond grammar school, and only one in five had completed high school. The need for education programs soon became apparent and although the Corps was criticized that education was never the most successful CCC undertaking, nonetheless it offered a wonderful opportunity for countless young men during the Great Depression. The County Office of Education assumed responsibility for CCC camp education and a majority of the enrollees took advantage of the courses offered at the camps. Education programs included on-the-job training by technical staff in the field and food preparation by camp chefs. The courses were held outside of work hours, with both Army and technical service personnel aiding the advisors. The Cain Flat newspaper urged their enrollees thus:

> The camp educational program offers to you the same opportunity as California offers you for golden sunshine - plenty of it. In grammar school, in high school, and in vocational school for better workmen, we have a fully accredited California State school. Men, you can not stand still. You either go forward, or you go backward. If you do not utilize your spare time to better yourself, you slide backward. Who wants to do that?

Most of the camps had an Army educational advisor but also state-accredited teachers to run the classrooms. One such teacher from Three Rivers received a "Vote of Thanks" in the 1936 issue of the Salt Creek *Pow Wow*:

> For a long time now, we have had a very charming little lady in our camp, who has been doing some very valuable work. We refer, of course, to Mrs. [Julia] Pierce. I think everyone appreciates the time and effort Mrs. Pierce, our favorite teacher, has expended here at Camp Salt Creek; we owe our teacher a big red apple of thanks. She has been a sweet and patient mother to us all, and it is about time we said, "Mrs. Pierce, we love and honor you."

The Visalia *Times-Delta* in 1937 reported that diplomas were presented at the Yucca Creek Camp to eleven enrollees who had successfully passed the eighth grade. According to the story, it was "the first elementary graduation exercise ever held in a CCC camp in the United States." Nationwide, nearly 8,500 CCC boys learned to read and write in fiscal year 1938-39 alone.

War veterans from World War I brought older enrollees to the CCC ranks. Camp Maxon on the South Fork was the home of these war veterans and at the average age of forty, these men were nearly twice as old as the younger CCC boys.

Located on a neatly kept tract of 97 acres leased from the old Maxon Ranch, "Maxonia"—as some of the Company 1918 veterans called it—regularly won commendations for high standards from the district inspectors. The ruins today of Camp Maxon are the most preserved of any of the area CCC camps, with numerous foundations, chimneys and stone work still present on the site. But these ruins are not the true legacy left behind by the Maxon men.

Camp Maxon. *Photo Courtesy of the Three Rivers Museum.*

Closeup View of Camp Maxon. *Photo Courtesy of the Three Rivers Museum.*

They built the road to Clough Cave (last six miles of South Fork Road) as well as the 11-mile road to Blue Ridge Lookout and a portion of the truck trail over Cinnamon Gap that connects with the Salt Creek Truck Trail. The project at Whitaker Forest was accomplished by the Maxon group. This was not too great a distance for them to travel. Indeed, Company 1918 was first and foremost a firefighting unit and regularly, they headed as far south as Los Angeles County, or as far west as San Luis Obispo to fight fires. During the summer of 1936, nearly 90 percent of the fires they fought were 150 miles or more from their camp.

In addition, Company 1918 maintained satellite camps at Badger and Squaw Valley from where they constructed miles of truck trails and telephone lines.

During the summer seasons of 1939 through 1941, the California Conservation Corps made Crystal Cave an attraction accessible to Park visitors, as well as paving more than 1,000 feet of the cave, and installing the electric lights. They built the road connecting the cave to the Generals Highway, the parking lot and the steep trail down to the entrance to the cave.[40]

At its peak in 1937, the CCC mustered 502,000 members in over 2,500 camps across the USA, while nearly three million young and not-so-young men served in the nine years of the Corps' existence.

The story of the CCCs was one of many that resulted from the efforts of the New Deal administration to put men to work on public works projects. Three Rivers and surrounding areas are indeed indebted to these men and to the crews that accomplished this near-herculean feat of projects.[41]

---

40   Kaweah Commonwealth, April, 9, 1999–August 6, 1999
41   Joe Doctor, June, 1987

Kaweah Kidde Kamp

The Kaweah Kidde Kamp was established in 1920 by the Tulare County Tuberculosis Association as a demonstration to show that good food, cleanliness, rest and recreation would aid and enrich those children in the county who were considered to be at the greatest risk of tuberculosis. These were children deemed to be undernourished and from backgrounds or families with very little income. Its purpose was to feed them with nourishing meals, teach them personal hygiene, give them plenty of exercise and promote a general sense of team spirit through games, swimming, etc.

The Kamp was located on property on the river side of Highway 198 and across from the Hammond Fire Station. This site was some six miles above Three Rivers on the bank of the river with about eight acres of sand flat on which to run. The 14.2-acre property was purchased from Mr. Sub Johnson of Visalia by the County Tuberculosis Society for $1,000. Money for on-going projects was raised by various organizations and towns in the county, among those the Three Rivers Woman's Club, the Red Cross and Cobb Drug of Porterville, California. Southern California Edison installed the wiring and lighting to the constructed buildings; waterlines were brought in and boardwalks were built from the dining room to the sleeping rooms.

The Kidde Kamp was open from July 1 - August 29. Girls attended one month and boys the other. Children were ages 7-12, as that age group was the one considered most at risk of contracting tuberculosis. Attendees were first examined and tested by physicians at the Tulare County Health Clinic in Visalia before coming to Three Rivers. All the children admitted were underweight for their age and malnourished. Dr. D.D. Nice of Three Rivers was the physician in attendance at the Kamp. He examined each member as they entered and kept a record of the gain made in weight by each child and was on hand in case any sickness occurred. The directors of the operation were Mr. and Mrs. J.C. Haines.

During the first year of operation, only simple equipment was used. A single building, 50x18 feet, served as the mess hall and kitchen. Tents were loaned by Southern California Edison for the dressing rooms. Cots were set up in regulation pattern under the sycamore trees on the property. As the years of operation progressed, more buildings were added, and in 1926, a large swimming pool (60 x 120 feet) was constructed.

Daily activities were strictly regulated, since it was felt that the children benefitted greatly from schedules consisting of exercise, rest, relaxation and three balanced meals. Instructions were given in personal cleanliness, neatness and manners. Fun activities included swimming, team play, fishing, story time, etc.

The children were organized in squads of about fifteen, each group having a leader who led them in their daily activities.

Photo from Author's Collection.

The schedule for the summer of 1922 used as a sample was:

6:00AM   Squad leaders arise and dress.

6:30   Children arise and dress; wash hands and face; wash teeth and drink a reasonable amount of water from the faucets - not from the drinking fountain. Unit A wash on the south side and Unit B on the north side.

7:00   Staff eat breakfast.
         Children have flag salute during flag raising - sitting up exercises directed by Mrs. Blair - short rest before breakfast.

7:30   Children eat breakfast - squad leaders at the tables to help children. Leaders, please insist on proper table manners and table conduct. Children, please pass in and out quietly and orderly.

8:00   Make beds - sweep and clean around units - wash clothes at the washing sinks. Squads take turns in picking up papers and all such litter on the grounds.

9:00   Inspection by Nurse and Superintendent:
         Assembly - Scripture reading - story reading - story telling by leaders and children. [on Fridays this part of the schedule will be brief as these are weighing days.]

9:30   Library and reading time - writing time - write to your folks but leave your letter unsealed. Put letters in the box on outside of office.

10:00   Mid-morning milk and graham crackers at the table outside.

10:15   Rest period - lie on beds - keep quiet - sleep if possible.

10:45   Swimming and sand bathing

11:15   Recreation and play.

11:30   Staff dinner time - one squad leader with children. Children wash and get ready for dinner.

12:00PM Children eat dinner - wash teeth, leaders oversee.

1:00   Rest period - on beds, quiet, sleep if possible.

2:15   Swimming and sand bathing

3:00   Get out of the water and dress

3:25   Milk and graham crackers
3:30   Rest period - lie on beds - talk, stories - but on beds.
4:00   Recreation
5:00   Staff eat supper; one leader out with children
5:30   Children eat supper - wash teeth, leaders oversee. Recreation - plays - pageants, etc. Short hikes.
7:00   Lower flag.
7:15   Hospital call.
7:45   Ready for bed
8:00   Lights out - children stop talking - camp quiet.

This regimen proved very successful over the years; the average weight gain per child was 6 lbs.

A report for 1924 revealed that the average weight gain for girls that year was 4.1 pounds and 1.5 inches in chest expansion. The boy's average weight gain was 4.17 pounds. The highest gain in the girls for that year was 9.25 pounds; one child who entered was 29 pounds underweight; she gained 8.5 pounds and follow up work in her home added a gain of 3 pounds. The State Inspector stated that the Kaweah Kiddie Kamp made the best showing in the State of all these experimental camps for weight gain in the camp's children.

Costs of caring and feeding these children was very low by today's standards. A 1927 report revealed total expenditures of $2825.31, including food and maintenance, resulting in an average of $1.10 cost per child per day.

In 1929, the Tulare County Tuberculosis Association issued a notice that Kaweah Kidde Kamp would be closed. In the report, it stated that during its history, more than 800 undernourished children had been given a month of care and health training. This resulted in more than 90% whose weight was raised to normal. The facilities were then consolidated and transferred to Springville, thus closing the operation for the Kaweah Kiddie Kamp.

Photo from Author's Collection.

CHAPTER VII

Nearby Communities and Settlements

Big Oak Flat

Big Oak Flat is an area little known to most residents of Three Rivers. Nevertheless, it played an important role in the settlement and the contribution to the society of our community. The information contained here is edited from a manuscript by Arthur Wells, given to the late Frankie Welch in 1959. Arthur was the son of one of Big Oak Flat's pioneer families and his memories tell us with his words how life in those days must have been. The following is also comprised of notes written by Frankie Welch and this author's personal knowledge of the area.

Lying about six miles south of Three Rivers, nestled among the Sierra foothills is a beautiful mountain valley long known as "Big Oak Flat." The valley floor has an elevation of approximately 2000 feet and an area of about 8 miles. The foothills surrounding the valley are 500 to 1000 feet higher. One of these peaks, Potato Hill—2800 feet in elevation—can be seen from many places in the mountains and the San Joaquin Valley, as well as from Highway 198 driving around Lake Kaweah.

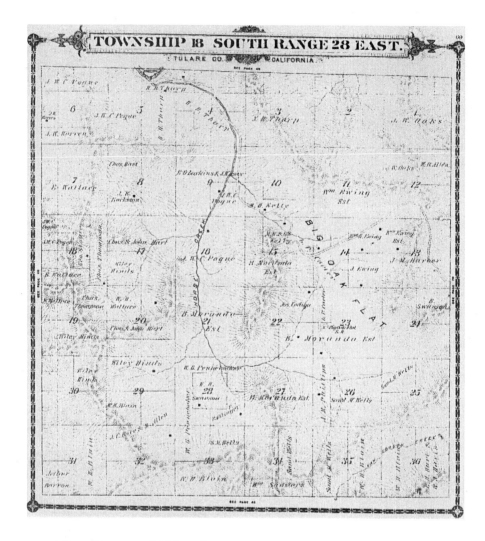

Photo Courtesy of Mike Whitney.

Approximately 113 years ago, the valley teemed with wildlife of all kinds found in the California hills. Squirrels and rabbits were everywhere; raccoons, foxes, wildcats, coyotes, badgers, skunks and rattlesnakes. Deer in large herds roamed freely through the valley. Numerous species of birds—wild canaries to eagles—were present as well as quail, doves and pigeons in numbers that seemed to be in the thousands.

Before the advent of the "white" man, a tribe of Native American Indians lived there or came from outside the area to gather buckeyes and acorns for food. The only record they left was one small burying ground and many mortar holes drilled into the granite rocks and an occasional pestle site in the hardest granite, perfectly formed and smooth as ice, some measuring 16 inches in length.

Equally unknown is the date of the first white settlement there. Arthur Wells' father, Dr. Samuel M. Wells and family moved into the Joseph Homer house in the fall of 1882. His mother's name was Ida; sisters Cora and Alice, a babe in arms; sons Albert, Arthur and Frank. Born in the valley later were sons Clarence and Clement and daughters Helen and Avis, twins who arrived on Easter Sunday, April 14, 1895.

Besides the four-room frame house in which they lived, there was a much older log house beside a giant fig tree that may have been at least twenty or more years old at the time of the arrival of the Wells family. Arthur was never able to learn who built the log house and planted the tree.

In 1882, there were three neighboring families: Ewing, Carter and Kelly. The Kelly family did not live in the valley, but down at Little Oak Flat at the foot of the first long grade on the road to Lemon Cove. Kelly was a brother of Sam Kelly of Three Rivers. The Kelly family consisted of Kelly, his wife and three grown sons, Monroe, Alvin and Lester.

The L.P. Carter family consisted of the parents and daughters Julia, Maggie, Alice, Mary, Minnie and a son, William.

Grandpa and Grandma Ewing lived in an old log cabin in a lonely meadow near the north end of Blue Ridge. Arthur never saw them and his only memory of them is that one snowy winter night, a rider came for his father to go to the old man's bedside. Despite the storm and the lateness of the hour, Dr. Wells answered the call but it was too late to save the patient.

Their nearest neighbor was John Ewing who with his wife Rachel, sons William, John Jr. and Howard, and daughter Myra, lived about a mile from the Wells' home.

The only other family was that of Bill Ewing, his wife Mattie, son Henry and daughter Maggie. Verbally, Bill was quite a scrapper. His favorite attack upon his imaginary opponent was to "give him one swift kick" in his four-letter-word meaning abdomen. The value of this strategy he impressed on his son Henry who tried to use it on Arthur's person, sometimes to his sorrow. One day, Bill dropped dead of a heart attack; his widow married a man named Bolton who owned a ranch on the South Fork of the Kaweah River, to which the family subsequently moved.

For several years, these six families were the sole residents of the valley. They made their living by raising a few cattle and hogs, keeping a few milk cows and making their own butter. They raised chickens and turkeys and hunted wild game. The Carters had a family orchard and a vegetable garden where potatoes, beans, tomatoes and some green vegetables were raised, providing there was a good rainy season. Often, the families had to cover everything with burlap bags to protect them from frost. Mr. Kelly kept bees; once trying to "hive" a swarm, the queen bee settled in his hair and in an instant his entire head and shoulders were covered with bees. He panicked and rolled over and over in a dense patch of nettles. Dr. Wells finally got all the bee stings out, and eventually his head and face returned to normal shape.

Romances among the old-timers were few. Monroe Kelly married Myra Ewing; Alvin Kelly married Alice Carter and young Bill Ewing married a school teacher from San Francisco, named Janette Hatch.

In those early years, access to the valley was difficult. A round trip to the nearest store at Lemon Cove with team and wagon took a full day's journey. A visitor from the outside world was a rare occurrence. There was no community life there at all, except for occasional visiting among the women; not even so much as a community picnic.

The only institution that enjoyed a semblance of community interest was the school. Appropriations were meager, permitting the payment of a teacher's salary of $60 per month for only six or seven months, depending on the average daily attendance during the previous school year.

The school district was created about 1880. The first teacher reported by the county superintendent's office was E. R. DuBrutz, who taught a summer session from July to September. Following him in order were W.

S. Chrisman, J. E. Buckman, Jennie Pogue, Eva M. Coburn, Mattie B. Blair, Etta B. Dean, Helen Hausch, Lulu I. Smithson, V. M. Clarke, Carrie Barnett, Janette T. March, Lyda Carroll, Cora Wells, Thirsa Linnell, Helen Osborn, A. E. Ainsworth, F. B. Howard, A. M. Wells, Phoebe Barton, Carolyn E. Gregory and Mrs. C. F. Brandon who taught the 1904-1905 term, after which the district merged with Cinnamon Creek School.

As a kindergarten pupil, Arthur went to Eva M. Coburn in 1884-1885 and to her successors as named above until 1895-1896 when Thirsa Linnell was the teacher. The first four listed above came from Visalia or vicinity as were Helen Hausch and Carrie Barnett. Jennie Pogue came from Lemon Cove, Etta B. Dean was the wife of W. F. Dean of Three Rivers; Phoebe Barton was also from Three Rivers. Of all of the ones who left a permanent influence on Arthur's life, he remembered Carrie Barnett the most vividly.

The first schoolhouse was a small frame building covered, roof and sides, with shakes. It had four small windows and one door. The furniture consisted of a small table and two straight-backed chairs for the teacher's use and a dozen hard, double desks for the pupils. The floor of the room sloped to the north; any round object, such as a ball or an apple, if dropped anywhere in the room, would roll to the north wall and sometimes out through a hole and down the hill.

The building was located at the head of a canyon beside a trail and about midway between the homes belonging to the Wells' and John Ewing, far from the only traveled road. About the year 1886, this building was abandoned and a new schoolhouse was built near the road, midway between the Carter's and Wells' homes. This building was destroyed by fire in 1893. The following year, school was held in the old log house near the Wells' home.

Listed below are the names of the pupils of the Big Oak Flat School in 1898 taught by A. Edwin Ainsworth. School board members were: John Ewing, W. T. Jobe, Clerk, Tom Wilkinson. Mr. Ainsworth died at Big Oak Flat before the term was finished. The pupils by age were: Ellen Jobe, Tillie Maxon, Ray Maxon, Mamie Maxon, Alice Wells, Helen Wells, Malissa

Eslinger, Howard Ewing, Frank Wells, Clarence Wells, Clem Wells, Willie Jobe, Willie Eslinger, Don Maxon, and Harrison Maxon.

Meanwhile, some new neighbors appeared. In 1888, one Baptista Moranda located a homestead and started a dairy ranch. His family consisted of his wife Christine, sons Walter and Florence, and daughters Lucy, Fanny and Lelia. His younger brother Joe Moranda also lived with him. Baptista Moranda was brutal to his family, and overbearing to everyone else. A blustering, gun-toting bully, he seemed to expect everyone to fear him. Eventually, he started a feud with little old man Carter whom he cursed out at every opportunity. Mr. Carter eventually began carrying his 45-70 caliber rifle whenever he was riding the range. One fine, sunny morning, Moranda met him in Carter's own pasture and began cursing and making threats, to which the old man replied with a bullet, thereby ending Moranda's career. This was the only act of violence that ever occurred in the valley. Poor old Mr. Carter; instead of receiving a medal for his action, he was arrested and tried for murder. Eventually, he was acquitted but lost his ranch to his lawyers. His family moved from the valley; the Carter Ranch was purchased by Nancy Swanson of Grouse Valley and on her death passed to her two surviving sons, Wallace and John Serby, together with a homestead adjoining the Wells Ranch, which she had acquired from Joe Moranda.

In 1893, two new families arrived; W. T. Jobe bought the Kelly Ranch and moved there with his brother Zack, daughters Rebecca, Lily and Ellen, and sons John and Will. Ellen and Will became pupils of the Oak Flat School in 1893-1894 as pupils of Cora Wells. The Jobes were a family of good American citizens; kindly, friendly folk, highly esteemed by all who knew them.

In April 1893, George Eslinger, his wife Alice, son Will and small daughter Malissa came to the valley. They lived for some time in the old log cabin on Dr. Wells' place. The next year, the George Eslinger family moved to a cabin located on a homestead Eslinger had previously filed on. George's brother Frank, who had been living at Dr. Wells' ranch, moved with them and lived there also until his death in 1902. The family left the valley in 1904.

Old Apple Still Growing on a Big Oak Flat Homestead. *Photo Courtesy of Mike Whitney.*

The Fred Maxon family lived in a valley lying south of a pass in the hills that bordered the valley on the south. The Maxon children attended the Big Oak Flat School. They were Tillie, Ray, Mamie, Don, Sophia and Harrison. The first three attended the school for several terms, later moving to the old Alles Ranch on the South Fork of the Kaweah River.

In September 1913, Wallace Serby, his wife Ida and daughter Laura May moved from Granville, Illinois to the Carter Ranch, which by that time had been purchased by his mother, Nancy Swanson. The Carter house burned in 1915, after which the family moved to the Joe Moranda homestead. Wallace Serby passed away in 1933. His widow moved to Visalia in 1935 and later became the wife of Axel Anderson, a well-known cattleman. Daughter Laura May married Charles Castle in 1920 and resided in Tulare.

Arthur Wells later sent this letter to Frankie Welch in 1960:

Of those old timers who lived in the valley in the early 1880s, I believe that I, Arthur Wells, am the sole survivor. No one lives in the valley now, nor in Little Oak Flat. Over-grazing of cattle for many years has diminished the number of wild flowers, but still in early April and up to June, can be found the same wild flowers that grew in such profusion eighty years ago. Buckeye trees with their dark green leaves and fragrant white blossoms stand out in sharp relief against the background of pale green grass. The higher hillsides are dotted with the scarlet [yellow?] bloom of Fremontia. The air everywhere is filled with the perfume of wild thorny currant and manzanita blossoms. Only a few species of the wild birds that lived there in those long past years can be found today, and those are few in number. Returning to the valley after an absence of half a century, I missed many things that were a part of my boyhood memories. The air was just as balmy, the sunshine just as warm, but somehow the glory that once hovered benignly over meadow and cliff and over the rolling valley and the waiting hills had passed away, leaving in its stead a somber stillness, a brooding quietness as profound and all-pervading as the silence that reigns in the fabled valley of Eternal Sleep.

Arthur continued in his letter to Frankie Welch:

I regret that my story of Big Oak Flat is so lacking in interest to the casual reader. I suppose the different families on the Flat lived interesting lives considered by themselves, but as a community that place was dead. As one woman wrote, replying to my inquiry for information, "I am unable to help you, for we lived there 21 years practically alone!" Had we had a civic leader like your Uncle Frank Britten we might have developed a community spirit.

The Valley is drained by Wells Creek and its many tributaries. Wells Creek flows from east to west about through the center of the valley and just a few feet from our old home. Its main tributary crosses the valley about two miles to the north and joins the main stream at the west boundary of the valley proper. About a mile further west the creek flows into Horse Creek which you cross on Highway 198 at the end of the curve west from Cobble Stone Lodge [this is now lake bottom]. When I was a boy those creeks flowed year round and after very heavy rains were raging torrents.

In the early days, my brother Frank and I trapped squirrels for the bounty, but we stayed on our own ranch with one exception, when we worked the Jordan Flat country west of the headwaters of Horse Creek. We also trapped foxes, wildcats, raccoons, skunks and coyotes. The money received for these went into the family coffers. We kids kept our earnings only after we were of legal age.

I doubt whether you will be able to get the matter of school teachers straightened out. I think that in the early days, the superintendent's office must have filed their records in a barrel. About Professor W. F. Dean, peace to his memory, that old boy had a way with school trustees. As I noted, he taught Oak Flat School one summer term subsequent to 1886, but not reported to the Superintendent's list. Confidentially, I use the word "taught" as a matter of courtesy, for he read library books during school hours and often slept with his head down on his desk. Cora and I used to draw cartoons of him on our slates while the younger pupils threw spit balls at his bald spot.

Besides the permanent residents, there were, or had been, homesteaders, some of whom had left the valley before our arrival or shortly after. To this day, their names are still used to designate the location of their homesteads. The Lloyd place, Davis camp, the Joe Moranda place, Tenny flat, the Whiteside place, etc. to name a few.

I rather vaguely remember having seen Davis and remember Tenny quite well, because he was incredibly dirty. His fingernails were exceedingly long and black; his skin, where visible, was caked with grime and his clothes were stiff with filth. It was a common belief that he hadn't had a bath since his mother last dunked him in the dishpan. There was a story current in those days that one summer day, a quail hunter met Tenny on the bank of a canal, and forced him at gun point to strip and bathe himself from hair roots to toenails. The story ended with the statement that hundreds of fish were killed for miles downstream from the scene of Tenny's bath!

The man Davis, it seems, was an itinerant preacher who had absconded with some lucky fellow's wife and headed for the hills. My father bought his homestead and he went away, leaving his pet sheep at our house, promising to return for her in a week's time. He never returned and that rowdy sheep became more unruly every day. She ate my mother's flowers, she chased the chickens, bounded stiff-legged through the open hallway and finally jumped through a closed window. That same day, her skin was observed tacked on the barn door.

Arthur Wells concluded his narrative to Frankie Welch with the following:

> ... I enjoyed your own articles .... They called up memories of the close-knit character of Three Rivers community, the wholehearted cooperation in public projects: The annual Christmas Tree; the Fourth of July picnic, the building of a dance hall, the Three Rivers vocal chorus promoted and directed by Frank Britten. One of the entertainers enjoyed by audiences was Al Redstone of the Colony Mill group. He was a skillful juggler, turned back-somersaults and with Ray Barnard did a mother-and-son black face act.
>
> My arm is about all in, so good by now. Cheerio to you - Arthur Wells

Big Oak Flat, looking southeast. *Photo Courtesy of Mike Whitney.*

CHAPTER VIII

Three Rivers Schools

Three Rivers Schools - A Short History

Formal education of Three Rivers children started in 1873 when the first school was built, although some of the "old-timers" claimed it was actually built in the 1860s. The earliest recorded date was September 9, 1873 and the school was called "Cove School." It was built originally as a log cabin and located on a flat piece of land on the South Fork, about one-half mile above the old South Fork Bridge crossing. This area is now known as Cherokee Oaks, although at the time it was called Cherokee Flat. For many years, a stone chimney marked the spot where the school had been, until development of the area removed any trace of this landmark.

Students attending this school must have been greatly motivated, since much of the time, many of them had to ford the South Fork by one means or another, due to the fact there was no bridge. According to the old school register, the following entry was recorded: "February 6th, 7th and 8th and February 11th, 12th [1884]—lost on account of rain and high water."

Not surprisingly, the next year in 1885, the school was moved across the South Fork to the intersection of Blossom and Old Three Rivers Drives; the site was donated by Sam Kelly. In 1910, the name was changed to Three Rivers School. From 1885 to 1917, classes were held there in a rough, clapboard one-room building, at which time a newer school was constructed over the old. This building was used until all the schools in the district were consolidated into one in 1928. The home that is there now is where the school was located.

1st row: Nate Lovelace, Mattie Washburn, Grace Mullenix Alles, Albert Griffes, Mary Washburn.
2nd Row: Byron Lovelace, Mabel Griffes, Bertha Bahwell, Ethel Loverin, John Washburn.
3rd Row: Hade Bahwell, Frank Brown, Bertha Griffes, Rose Mullenix Vaughn, Walter Lovelace, Oren Griffes.
4th Row: Edgar Washburn, Mrs. J. P. Carter, Teacher, Maude Bahwell
Photo from Author's Collection.

Before the time of district consolidation, there were several other schools in the area as well as one which was located up the South Fork just northeast of the junction of South Fork Drive and Cinnamon Creek. This was the Cinnamon School, organized in 1888. It operated until about 1903 when it was destroyed by a fire and never rebuilt. Cinnamon Creek students then had to travel down to Cove School for their lessons.

Cinnamon Creek School
1st Row: Grandpa Bolton, Clarence Fry, Pansy Cahoon, Bessie Fry, Rose Busby, Maggie Ewing, Lafe Kirkpatrick, unknown, unknown.
Row 2: P.C. Kirkpatrick, Trustee, Jim Cahoon, George Cahoon, Charlie Bolton, Cora Wells, Teacher, Eva Kirkpatrick, Fred Kirkpatrick. *Photo from Author's Collection.*

Another school in the area was the Big Oak Flat School. This was opened in 1881 and students living in that area attended until 1905, when it too was destroyed by fire. It was annexed to the Cove School in 1906.

The Sulphur Springs School, named for the springs south of the Middle Fork, was established May 14, 1880. It was first located on the Clarence Fry property, burned and was rebuilt on land across the road owned by Charles Bahwell. This schoolhouse also burned and was rebuilt on land donated by A. G. Ogilvie at a site on the north side of the river near the Ogilvie home. Years later, this building was converted into a dwelling and for a time was the home of Mr. and Mrs. Rollie Cowle. According to the late Grace Alles, Mrs. Marion Griffes regularly rowed her children across the river where the Kaweah River Bridge to the North Fork now stands so they could attend Sulphur Springs School; high water made this endeavor somewhat of a hazardous feat in a small boat. Sulphur Springs School operated until 1928 when it merged with Three Rivers Union.

The Kaweah Colony had a school at the colonists' headquarters on the North Fork during the 1880s. Students were taught in a tent by a Mrs. Miles. Later it was moved to the Taylor Ranch in Kaweah and then to Redstone Park, another Kaweah Colonist settlement.

There was a seasonal school at Atwell Mill on the Mineral King Road. Judge Atwell, who operated a sawmill there from early May to late November, established a school and hired a teacher for the workmen's children during the seasons of 1887-89.

Children came to these first schools on foot, some walking several miles, while others came on horse or donkey. Youngsters from one family drove an old-fashioned two-wheeled cart. Some walked across a swinging bridge to the Sulphur Springs School. Grace Alles remembered that when she was a little girl just starting to school, she was carried across that bridge by the male school teacher who boarded at her home.

In 1928, the Three Rivers Union School District was formed, a new building was constructed on Highway 198 and all the other school districts were combined into this one. Since the present school building was constructed, classrooms have been added and extensive remodeling has been done to meet the demands of Three Rivers' growing population.

Cove School after move to new location.

Pupils of the Cove School, 1894:

Teacher: Kate Smith

<u>Lower Row, Left to Right</u>: Dan Alles, Frank Devoe, Frankie Welch, Hattie Loverin.

<u>Second Row, Left to Right</u>: Clark Rice, Madge Flag, Adam Alles, Harry Britten, Della Carter, Olie Carter.

<u>Top Row, Left to Right</u>: Bert Carter, Carl Rice, Ora Carter, Lizzie Alles, Julie Loverin, Ray Barnard. *Photo from Author's Collection.*

Three Rivers School. *Photo from Author's Collection*

CHAPTER IX

Community Services

History of Phone Service in Three Rivers

The first telephones in Three Rivers were installed 1903-1904, initially by the old Mt. Whitney Power Company. Although the number of phones put in was quite small, they were placed in strategic locations throughout the community. One of these designated locations was "naturally" installed at the Bahwell Saloon (near the present-day Museum) and one at the Britten Brothers Store (now the entrance to South Fork Estates); some accounts list another installation at the Marion Carter residence on Old Three Rivers Drive. Bob Barton told of Noel Britten's improvised switch board in the store, where several of the lines came in. Noel would listen or look to see which line was ringing and then switch his phone on to answer that particular line. [42]

Since this arrangement was not satisfactory, a number of Three Rivers citizens took it upon themselves to construct their own phone lines. They used what materials were available to them at the time and strung their

---

42   From Frankie Welch's notes.

lines on trees, fence posts and along bridges in the area. Cows would sometimes rub against the fence posts and break the lines or the drop wire material would deteriorate over a short span of time. To repair it meant taking hot tar and rolling it on the wires; thereby creating the insulation and protection at the same time. In 1909, there were 32 subscribers to the Three Rivers Telephone Company; by 1965 it had increased to 497.[43]

Telephones for sale at the Britten Brothers Store. *Photo from Author's Collection.*

Eventually the switchboard at the Britten Store was moved to the Conrad Alles home and an actual phone exchange was maintained there for years by Pacific Telephone and Telegraph Company, with Conrad Alles named as their agent. However, the building subsequently caught fire and burned, causing the exchange to move across the road. Before

---

43   *Visalia Times-Delta*, January 26, 1966.

the conversion to dial telephones, Fredna Eggers operated the exchange in a house on Blossom Drive. In 1946, Fern and Russel Doherty operated the exchange for nine years until the dial system came in. At that time there were 222 subscribers. The Doherty family was given a citation of appreciation for their years of service by the Chamber of Commerce.[44] Dial service commenced April 2, 1955, thus ending the era of cranking the phone to reach "Central" and asking for a particular number. Before dial service, one had to listen for their own specific number of rings to know who was getting a call and even sometimes listening(!) in to see what was happening with their neighbors.

Grace Alles told that in the earliest days of phone service, when there were only two or three phones in the community, she was pregnant with her soon-to-be-born daughter Rena Alles Ogilvie; her labor pains had started and her father, Isham Dykes Mullenix, tried to phone for help but the phone line was "out." Out of necessity, he was forced to hitch his horse to the buggy and drive to Lemon Cove to fetch Dr. Robert Bruce Montgomery. As one can imagine, this was only one of many similar occurrences for the Three Rivers community.[45]

The Park Service had their own phone service installed in June 1928. Pacific Telephone & Telegraph Company strung six miles of wire from Three Rivers to the Park, connecting with a line being built concurrently by the government. The construction crew and their families were housed during this time at the Three Rivers Lodge.[46] [Now the entrance to South Fork Estates.]

In March 1950, the office of the Three Rivers *Current* was given their own phone line, using Farmer's Line #9 which was undergoing extensive remodeling at the time by A. A. Hardison. They were given telephone number 9F11. Before the job began, Line #9 had carried eighteen phones, but was improved and further split into three separate lines with no one line carrying more than ten phones. According to the article, Line #9 had

44   Ibid., March 1955.
45   Frankie Welch's notes.
46   Ibid. 8 June, 1928.

been in business for over forty years and had been known as the Three Rivers Home Telephone Company. This line was originally formed by thirty-three residents who joined and built the utility for themselves since phone service was not available.[47]

---

47   *Three Rivers Current*, March 3, 1950.

Kaweah Post Office

The Kaweah Post Office on the North Fork of the Kaweah River is one of Tulare County's famous landmarks that is still in use in 2012. Its origins began May 17, 1890 when a grant was given to the Kaweah Colonists. This first post office was located in a tent cabin at "Advance," the site of the Colony several miles up the river from its present location. In December of that same year, the name was changed from "Advance" to Kaweah. For several successive years, the post office was moved from cabin to cabin in the Colony as different members served as postmasters. In succeeding years, the Colony ceased to exist and their dream of a utopian society collapsed. However, many of the colonists elected to stay on in the area and eventually became farmers, stock raisers and members of the surrounding community.

By 1910, it was obvious that a new post office was needed to serve those living on the North Fork. Accordingly, the patrons of the post office, at their own expense and labor, donated about $2.50 each for enough rough lumber to build the 10x12 structure. At that time, it didn't have any post office boxes and patrons got their mail via general delivery through a window opening onto the porch.

Kaweah Post Office, Original Location. *Photo Courtesy of the Three Rivers Museum.*

Eventually, the window was replaced with a grilled opening inside and 40 interior locking mail boxes were installed; however, the rest of the tiny building is almost exactly like the original. Postmasters continued to take turns until Mrs. Ida Purdy (who had been postmaster several times already), agreed to take the job on a permanent basis, providing the building be moved closer to her home. Neighbors obligingly hoisted it up on log rollers and dragged it about 700 feet south to its present location.

Kaweah Post Office. *Photo from Author's Collection.*

In 1948, the Tulare County Historical Society dedicated the State Registered Landmark #389 at the Kaweah Post Office. A special first day cover was designed for stamp collectors and 5,000 cachets were mailed in commemoration of the dedication.

Perhaps another delivery service would be more convenient, but it is doubtful if the patrons of this picturesque little building would accept it. Although the little post office isn't safe from being sold, torn down or used for other purposes in the future, the Kaweah Post Office remains an institution to which the patrons are attached with strong ties of loyalty and devotion.

Three Rivers Post Office. *Photo from Author's Collection.*

Mail Delivery In Three Rivers

When Three Rivers was first settled, mail service was non-existent. The early day families were forced to go all the way to Visalia for their mail, and as more and more people moved into the area, the need for a post office became obvious. In the 1920s, Mrs. Clara Conley Barry, 85 years old at the time, was visiting Mrs. Eva Barnard, and she told about her father, T. J. Conley. He had moved to this area in 1874 and settled on land in the vicinity of the Jordan and Spotts places. Mr. Conley brought mail by horseback from Visalia and kept the "post office" in his home. In 1879, the closest official mail delivery location was at Lime Kiln, near what was to become Lemon Cove. Isham Dykes Mullenix, father of the late Grace Alles, served as postmaster there.

Since it was still a distance for Three Rivers folks to travel, a group of people met in the fall of 1879 at the home of James Butz and discussed the possibility of a local post office. The Post Office Department asked the settlers to send in a number of suggested names and the one submitted by Mrs. Louisa Rockwell—that of "Three Rivers"—was selected.

Soon after this meeting, December 23, 1879, to be exact, the first Three Rivers Post Office was established. The first postmaster was Laura E. Grove.

Laura Grove. *Photo from Author's Collection.*

Succeeding postmasters from Post Office Department records were Francis N. Grove, December 30, 1880; Samuel W. Kelly, April 18, 1881; Henry Alles, February 11, 1895; Catherine C. Clayton, September 16, 1898; Rhoda Finch, August 7, 1903; Abram Dinkins, June 29, 1907; Noel Britten, October 20, 1909; Mrs. Nellie A. Britten, July 8, 1935; John F. Buchholz, October 1, 1945; Willis Beutler, March 1, 1969, and many others since then; Noel Britten held the office for 26 years, the longest of any of the postmasters.

The location of the first post office is not definitely known; the Thompson Tulare County Atlas of 1892 shows it located on the north side of Old Three Rivers Drive, slightly east of the old South Fork crossing. In 1903, the post office was located in the Britten Brothers Store on South Fork Drive and remained there until 1945, when the new Britten Store was built on Highway 198 (the site of the present Three Rivers Market). In December 1963, the post office moved into newer quarters west of the Three Rivers Market. In February 1983, it was moved to its present location.

Mail from the valley was transported to Three Rivers by almost every conceivable means: by spring wagon, buggy, stagecoach and motor vehicle. Some of the early mail carriers were Bart Smith, Charley Lawless, a Mr. Beville and S. M. Wells. According to the late Frankie Welch, one of the early mail carriers brought the mail pouches in a two-wheeled cart. Occasionally, this particular carrier was known to drive his cart in an inebriated condition, and at one time he ran completely off the grade; horse, cart and man rolled down to the river. The horse waited patiently until his driver was sober enough to complete the trip to Three Rivers.

In the early days, requirements for mail delivery were not very strict. Grace Alles told of one of the early postmasters who could not read or write; he would dump the mail pouch on a table and tell the post office patrons to pick out their letters. She recalled that her father, Isham Mullenix, had to make out the reports for this illiterate postmaster, even though he served for nearly fourteen years.

In October 1905, a post office at Hammond, located at the Mount Whitney Power Plant No. 1, was established. Members of the operating staff there acted as postmasters. The mail for Hammond was taken by stage from the Three Rivers office. Ira Blossom drove the mail stage from October 6, 1906 to December 1, 1916; W. A. "Bill" Swanson was the driver until June 30, 1922; E. J. Briggs served until November 1, 1928 when service to Hammond was discontinued.

Before the Advance post office was established by the Kaweah Colony in 1890, there was an earlier Kaweah post office. Mail service began there October 9, 1879 and T. J. Conley was appointed postmaster; it was discontinued March 5, 1880. The Advance post office operated from May 17, 1890 to December 22, 1890 when the name was changed to Kaweah. It served the families in that area until Nov. 30, 1925 when service was discontinued and post office patrons had to come to Three Rivers for their mail. On May 15, 1926, the Kaweah post office was re-established once again and continues to this day.

Although there are times now that we think our mail service is too slow and we are occasionally frustrated with all the "red tape," it certainly beats what folks around here in the early days had to contend with; at least our mail carriers today are dependable, conscientious and certainly sober!

Three Rivers Libraries

The history of the Three Rivers libraries began about 1910. The earliest one appears to have been the Three Rivers Branch that was located in the River Inn, on the north side of the main river (approximately where the Three Rivers Arts Center stands today in 2012). The library came into being, evidently at the written request of ten Three Rivers residents.

According to Tulare County records, it was established December 19, 1910; it housed fifty-one books and six magazines. The custodian [librarian] was originally Ernest McAdams; he was succeeded by Mrs. E. J. DeMasters. Unfortunately, the entire collection was destroyed when the River Inn succumbed to fire September 15, 1911.

The Three Rivers branch re-opened December 15, 1912 at the home of Ora Britten Welch and Frankie Welch on South Fork Drive, across from what was then the Britten Brothers Store (west of the entrance to South Fork Estates). The librarian was Frankie Welch. At the time, Frankie said that placing a single case of fifty books in a home constituted a branch library! The hours for the library were 9 a.m. – 2 p.m., Monday, Wednesday and Saturday; however, from 1922-1959, the library was open daily. The library was housed in Frankie's home until June 1959, when it was moved to Highway 198, in what was then called the "Wylie" building (the current home of the *Kaweah Commonwealth*). At the time of the library's relocation, it had accumulated 3,000 books. The library was in its new location in August 1959, with Ester Peck as the librarian until construction was completed on the present library; it opened August 1, 1977 with Neil Fernbaugh as librarian.

Kaweah Branch Library:

This branch opened December 15, 1912, again with fifty books and six magazines. It was located in the home of its librarian, Laura Hopping on the North Fork Road, and she was paid $2.50 per month, the going rate for library custodians at the time. She was succeeded by Ida Purdy, and subsequently, Viva May; Ida Purdy resumed duties as librarian until the collection was merged with the Three Rivers Branch in June 1959 when it was moved to the Wylie Building on Highway 198.

Hammond Branch Library:

Established December 31, 1918 with 107 books, this branch was located in the homes of its succeeding custodians. The first custodian was Lawrence Hough. In 1921, Mrs. Phoebe Wells housed it in her home and in 1924, it moved to the home of Mrs. Linnie Blick. This branch was closed October 31, 1928, when the home at the Hammond Power House was shut down.

The community of Three Rivers seems to have been unique in its citizenry and their quest for knowledge and appreciation of the written word. This is just another reminder of the mystery and uniqueness of the surrounding canyons in which it is located.

HAMMOND - TULARE COUNTY'S FIRST WATER POWER

Kaweah Power House No. 1

June 29, 1899 was an important milestone in Tulare County; that was the day that long distance transmission of electrical power was transmitted along electrical lines to Visalia from the Kaweah River's first power house. This had long been a dream of three visionary men that finally came true on that special day.

These three men—A. G. Wishon, William H. Hammond and Ben Maddox—believed they had a workable plan for using the Kaweah River to generate power, but at that time they needed about $250,000 to finance this venture. Since local contacts failed to produce enough capital, Hammond tried to find investors in the Bay Area with no success; investors there were putting their funds elsewhere at the time. One financier decided his money would furnish a better return in passenger ships running to and from the Klondike gold fields.

Disheartened, Hammond thought of one last person: his wealthy brother John Hays Hammond, who at that time was the world's most noted civil engineer, living in England. Subsequently, passage was raised and William Hammond set sail for London. He soon wired back that he had the necessary funds; his brother put up half of the amount and a friend, Leopold Hirsch, the balance.

On Mr. Hammond's return from London in 1898, work was immediately started, and necessary franchises and deeds were obtained to complete the project. Thus was formed the corporation of the Mt. Whitney Power Company: Mr. Wm. H. Hammond, president; A. G. Wishon, vice president; R.P. Hammond, secretary; John Broder, asst. secretary; Robert Doble, consulting engineer; D. L. Wishon, civil engineer and Donald H. Frye, electrician.

Their plan was thus: to take water from the East Fork of the Kaweah River near the bridge on the present Mineral King Road, route the water along the mountainside in a flume where it would finally be dropped 1,400 feet through a penstock to a powerhouse on the banks of the Middle Fork and then released back into the river channel.

It was a tremendous undertaking especially in those days, because it all had to be done from "scratch" or by hand. They couldn't call a lumber yard and order the materials, so they leased the Atwell Mill below Mineral King and hired a crew to cut and haul the redwood timbers and boards needed for the flume.

There was no road on the south side of the canyon where the flume was to be built, and a crew of as many as 600 men at times built the flume along the precipitous, rocky mountain face by floating the lumber and timbers down the flume itself as it was being constructed.

The cut lumber was hauled by 4- and 6-horse teams down the steep, twisting road from Atwell Mill to a wooden chute suspended on cables which was used to slide the lumber down to the head works of the flume in the river.

The flume was started in 1898 and completed in 1899. When it was finished, it was 30,771 feet long with an elevation at the intake of 2,581 feet and at the forebay (the pool at the end of the flume where the water enters the penstock), at 2,425 feet elevation. The flume carried 23.6 second feet of water at a gradient of 26 feet per 1,000. The steel penstock was 3,320 feet in length and the pressure at the power house at the bottom was 565 pounds per square inch, corresponding to a 1,300 ft. head; the velocity of the water issuing from the nozzle was over three miles per minute.

Kaweah No. 1 Flume Construction. *Photo Courtesy of the Three Rivers Museum.*

Robert Doble, a San Francisco engineer who later became an officer in the company, was in charge of planning the power plant itself, and work started October 1, 1898. All the heavy machinery for Powerhouse No.1 had to be hauled in by wagon and parts of the road changed to eliminate the steepest grades. The water wheels in the generator were originally cast-iron buckets, but they were soon replaced with bronze ones. The main transmission line carrying 1.8-kilowatts was suspended on square redwood posts 35 feet long. The insulators were a glass pin type with one crossarm carrying two conductors and the other pinned to the top of the pole.

Hauling the Turbine for Kaweah No. 1. *Photo from Author's Collection.*

The water wheels were of the tangential type and were the first to be
equipped with ellipsoidal buckets. They were driven by a single jet of water
at a speed of 514 revolutions per minute, and were regulated by means of
a hand-operated deflector, deflecting a part of the jet away from the water
wheel buckets as conditions required.

There were three 440-volt, 3-phase 60-hertz generators rated at
450-kilowatts each and two 125-volt exciter units, rated at 15-kilowatts
each at 1,050 revolutions per minute. The exciter units were belt-driven
from pulleys on the outer ends of the generator shafts.

Current was carried from the generators in ducts, beneath the floor
to the Marble Fork switching board and then to the 500-kilowatt, oil
insulated, air cooled, static transformers which stepped up the voltage,
from 440-volts to 17.3-kilovolts for transmission. The high-tension wires
passed through fused air-break switches to the lightning arresters, which
were in a separate building, and then to the valley below.

In 1902, the transformers were moved from within the corrugated iron
power house to a row of separate concrete cells outside, to guard against
possible accident or fire. These transformers were abandoned in 1921 and
the outdoor type installed in their place.

The company built dams across the canyons at the outlets of several
lakes in the high regions above Mineral King; these were to store water for
use during the low water period before the winter snows. These dams hold
back the runoff and increase the depth of the water to the height which
they are built. The water thus stored is turned directly into the stream
through hand-controlled gate valves. These valves are opened in the fall
when the water in the river drops to such an extent that the head of the
flume is below normal. These valves are left open until all surplus water
is drained from the lakes and then closed, which generally occurs about
December 1st of each year. The first dam was completed in 1903 and the
last in 1905. The amount of water thus stored in Monarch Lake is 314 acre
feet; Silver Lake (renamed Crystal Lake), 162 acre feet; Franklin Lake, 467
acre feet and Eagle Lake, 210.

Lady Franklin Lake and Florence Peak, 12405 ft. Elevation, Mineral King, California.

Franklin Lake and Storage Dam. *Photo from Author's Collection.*

Since the transmitting of energy through thirty miles of line was still in the experimental stage, the fledgling company was far from perfect. Storms blasted the porcelain arresters and knocked out the power, and landslides would rip out sections of flume. The transformers were also vulnerable in their metal tanks with wood plank covers.

The Mt. Whitney Power and Electric Company was taken over by the Southern California Edison Company about 1916, and in 1929, the old Mt. Whitney Power House No. 1 was torn down with only the flume and the penstock kept in use as it is today. A new, fully automatic power plant was built within 150 feet of the old power house. Of the generator units from the old power plant, one was left standing as a monument to the original site.

In spite of all the problems, Kaweah Power House and Flume No. 1 began an era that continued—two more flumes and powerhouses were subsequently built—this time on the Middle Fork of the Kaweah River. Homes, businesses and agriculture in the San Joaquin Valley flourished with the electricity they provided.

An interesting post script from the *Visalia Times*, dated Aug 20, 1926: "That for which Three Rivers has waited, 'Lo, these may years' became an actuality yesterday when 'juice' was turned into the distribution line just completed by the Southern California Edison Company and the first electric light switched on in Three Rivers. Ever since Power House No. 1 of the old Mt. Whitney Company started operation in 1899, electric power has flowed past the doors of the residents of this community but never until now have they had any use of it. . . ."]

Interior of Kaweah Power House No. 1. *Photo from Author's Collection.*

Power Houses 2 and 3

Power House No. 2 of the Mount Whitney Power Company was built February 1905. The water for this plant was diverted from the main Kaweah River just below the Sequoia National Park line and was carried to the forebay by means of concrete ditches and wooden flumes, about four miles in length, and then by a steel penstock 1,011 feet long to the power house. Water entered the power house under a static head of 369 feet and was delivered to three turbines of the Girard type, driving three 60-hertz, 3-phase, General Electric generators. The normal output of the generators was 500-kilowatts each, at a terminal pressure of 2,300-volts. There were two exciters, 30-kilowatts each, driven by a directly connected Girard water wheel.

The main transformers, seven in number for this station, were placed in separate concrete compartments outside of the main corrugated iron building, and stepped up the voltage from 2.3-kilovoltz to either 17.3-kilovoltz or 34.6-kilovolts.

In 1912, two of the water wheel generator units were removed and a single Belton-Francis turbine installed in their place. This new unit had a normal capacity of 1.5-kilovolts. This change was found to be necessary due to the low efficiency of the Girard turbine.

In 1922, the plant was converted to semi-automatic use by the proper installation of relays and controls. Under this system, it was not necessary to keep an operator on a shift in the power house. If major trouble occurred, the plant would relay and clear itself from the line, at the same time giving an alarm in the operator's cottage, who would then synchronize the plant back to the line when the trouble was ended. This was the same scenario in the case of problems with the actual apparatus or water supply.

In 1925, the voltage was raised to 66-kilovoltz and at the same time, the high-tension oil switch, lightning arresters and transformers of the outdoor type were installed. By July 1926, transformers were installed and an 11-kilovolt transmission line was built to supply Three Rivers with light and power. The plant became fully automatic by 1929, with the installation of a Belton-Francis turbine, replacing the Girard water wheel that was in place at the time. The automatic control line of Power House No. 2 was extended in order that the unit could be shut down and started from the office room at Power House No. 1. It was so arranged that if either plant shut down, an alarm would be given at the other plant as well.

Power House No. 3 was the third to be built in the Three Rivers district and began operation May 1913. The water for this plant was diverted from the Middle and Marble Forks of the Kaweah River. The water from the Marble Fork was conveyed through a concrete conduit, 6,000 feet long, crossing the Middle Fork through an inverted steel syphon 1,085 feet in length, joining the Middle Fork concrete conduit, a little less than 4 miles in length, then on to the forebay. The steel penstock carrying the water from the forebay to the power house below is 3,151 feet in length, with a static head of 775 feet.

The original transformer equipment of this plant consisted of three units and a spare and stepped the voltage up from 23-kilovoltz to 34.6-kilovoltz. These transformers were removed from the reinforced concrete powerhouse building and the outdoor type installed in their place in 1925. At the same time, the main oil circuit breaker and lightning arresters were replaced by those of the outdoor type, thus raising the voltage on the transmission line to 66-kilovoltz. The necessary alarm systems, relays and controls were installed in 1922 and the plant became semi-automatic.48

---

48   From notes by Margaret Stoppel.

CHAPTER X

Hazards of Nature

Flood of 1867

Much has been written about this major catastrophe that occurred in December 1867 and its effect on the Visalia area and west as far as Tulare Lake. Judge Fry wrote an expanded manuscript in the February 1933 *Sierra Club Bulletin*; he titled it "The Great Sequoia Avalanche."

And, avalanche indeed was what it was. The following is taken from accounts by Bob Barton and Muriel Kenwood that gives one a sense of what it was like during that enormous flood:

In the late 1850s, two large families came to Three Rivers, the first white people to settle here. They transported their household articles on sleds from the Hale Tharp ranch to Horse Creek by way of Big Oak Flat and over what is now the Seaborn Ranch [Wells] on the South Fork.

Ira Blossom, with his large family along with a family friend, Joe Palmer, built log houses in the river bottom, near the spot where Hopkins Work and his wife, sons, daughters and grandchildren had settled. This was on land at the mouth of the South Fork where the Weavers, Nunnelees and several other families have recently lived. At that time, the surrounding lands were flat and very fertile, not sandy and filled with river rocks as they are now.

Before Christmas 1867, the weather turned warm and a heavy rain started falling; it rained steadily over four days and four nights. There had been an abundance of rain in November and again in December, thus accumulating a heavier than normal snow pack in the high mountains. The warm rain, falling on all this snow December 23rd, melted it and raised the levels of the rivers to flood stage. Sometime early that day, the settlers on the South Fork noted that although it was still raining hard, the river was dropping rapidly and had receded to a low level. They knew that something drastic had happened up the canyon and that disaster was imminent. They immediately started moving their belongings to higher ground.

Sometime during that night, an unbelievable torrent of water came rushing down the South Fork, demolishing everything it its path and leaving nothing but devastation in its wake.

Although the settlers all escaped with their lives, they lost almost all of their buildings, fruit trees, fences, livestock and land. Joe Palmer, a large man, had carried several of the Blossom children along with their mother to safety through waist-deep flood waters.

It was later determined that the Garfield Grove of Giant Sequoias, on the slopes of Mt. Dennison, had formed a landslide that had slid into the South Fork Canyon, causing a temporary dam that had shut off most of the water in the river. When the pressure behind this dam grew too great, it released; subsequently, all the redwood logs, pine trees, and debris of an unmeasurable quantity swept down the canyon, wiping out all in its path and even scouring out new canyon walls that can still be seen today.

Where once flat fertile land had been, nothing was left but sand, boulders, and driftwood, including huge chunks and logs of mangled redwood trees. This debris was even carried to the Visalia area and beyond. The flood waters filled Tulare Lake to where it overflowed into the San Joaquin River and the streets of Visalia were under water for six weeks.

Hopkins Work and his family were so discouraged by this catastrophe that they just moved out and left Three Rivers for good. However, the Blossoms stayed on, rebuilt their home on higher ground, planted new trees and started again. Their new home was constructed of poles, shakes and clapboard, all made from the huge redwood logs brought down by the flood.

Joe Palmer made a statement to Judge Fry October 5, 1890:

It had been raining in the Three Rivers district almost steadily for 41 days and nights with heavy snows above the 5,000-foot level. All the rivers were very high. On the morning of December 20, the weather became warmer and a hard rain fell all day, even at high elevations. It was still raining when I went to bed that night, and a strong wind blew down the canyon. Just before midnight, I was aroused by a heavy rumbling sound such as I had never heard before, and which lasted for an hour or more. Then a great calm set in, and even the roaring of the river ceased.

On leaving my cabin in the morning, I found that despite the heavy rain flow, the river was unusually low. From this I knew that a great slide had blocked the canyon above, and that later the dam would give way and cause a flood. I went up the river to Bennett Creek but saw nothing wrong; returned and watched all day, but no flood came, so I went to bed at 10 p.m.

About 1:30 a.m. I was aroused by a tremendous thundering and rumbling sound which made my hair stand on end. I jumped out of bed, grabbed my clothing and ran for safety up the mountainside some 200 yards from the river. In a few minutes, the flood came, along with a crest of water some 40 feet in depth that extended across the canyon, carrying with it broken-up trees, which were crashing end-over-end in every direction with terrific force and sound. The river remained high for several days and all the while timber was going down and being swept clear out to the valley.

From an article written by Frankie Welch:

The recent cloudburst at Horse Creek, which swept a torrent of water four feet deep across the highway in front of the Barney Mehrten ranch, stalling cars and making it impossible to get to and from Three Rivers for a long time, brought recollections of the big flood of 1867 to the mind of Mrs. Mehrten. A little 6-year-old at the time, she was living with her parents, the well-known pioneer Hale Tharp and his wife in a log cabin by the Kaweah not far from her present home. [Ed. Note: this is the area that is usually covered by Lake Kaweah, where Horse Creek flows into the Kaweah River.]

It had rained steadily for nearly two weeks. Suddenly, the swollen waters of the river began to rise and soon a widespread roaring torrent was sweeping past. Great logs and trees tossed like chaff upon its surface.

Higher and higher the mad waters climbed toward the Tharp's little cabin. Their Indian helper began carrying provisions up from the cellar and piling them on the table. Presently, the roof of a house belonging to a neighbor four miles up the river floated by with an Indian clinging to it. Then Mrs. Tharp, staunch pioneer woman though she was, fainted. Mrs. Mehrten remembers climbing on to the clock shelf for the camphor which her father then used to revive her mother. The flood waters reached the doorstep of the cabin and then began to recede.

The Tharp's first thought was for the neighbors up the river. Loading a pack animal with food and bedding, they took a trail across the mountain and found the family in dire need of their aid.

The family's name was Work, and their house had stood where the state highway now crosses the South Fork just below Three Rivers. [This is where Cherokee Oaks Drive makes a sharp right-hand turn; the old road went straight ahead at that point. The old bridge abutments are still visible there.] Mrs. Work and the six children were saved by an Indian called Cherokee Nelson (or Nels), who waded waist deep through the swirling waters and carried them out. Mitch Work (the husband/father) was in Visalia at the time and did not get back for two weeks.

On the other side of the river lived the children's grandparents. Across the tree-lined roaring flood, there seemed to be no way to communicate to them that the family had been saved. But Cherokee Nelson, with Indian ingenuity, found a way. Taking the mother and children to a treeless hilltop near, he stood them in a row across its bald crest. Seven figures silhouetted against the skyline told the anxious watchers on the other side of the raging waters that all had been saved. [Note: could this hill have been the same hill of the current Crystal Drive fame?]

To this day, evidence of the big flood can be seen all the way from the high canyon in the South Fork, to where a landslide held back the gathering waters until they broke loose with a rush, to the fields about Visalia where great redwood logs can be found buried in the sand. Fences made of these logs are still to be seen. Above Three Rivers are great redwood logs lying on top of boulders twenty feet high. In other places the reverse is seen—huge boulders resting on fallen Sequoias.

The streets of Visalia ran like rivers during the flood; the citizens went about in boats. Much livestock was lost; Mrs. Mehrten's father lost 80 head of goats—all the band but one little fellow who managed to ride a log to safety.[49]

---

49   *The Fresno Bee*, October 18, 1924.

Judge Fry later interviewed some older valley settlers about their memories of the great flood. Here is one the reader might find amusing. Betty Townsend (January 31, 1926):

> I was living out near Cutler Park at the time of the '67 flood. The flood occurred on the evening of December 23rd. Mr. & Mrs. S. C. Brown, Mr. & Mrs. Dinely, Frank Kellenberg with his son Frank Jr, and four other people sought refuge in my home that night and remained as refugee guests for a week. Our Christmas dinner, in part, consisted of a turkey feast. The turkey was captured by one of the party from a bale of hay which was being swept down the torrent. A pig was similarly rescued and consumed.

* * * * *

Subsequent floods that followed the "Great One" of '67 are noted here, although some may have been omitted due to lack of material or actual accounts.

The Flood of 1893 was described thus in the *Daily Morning Delta*:

A Great Storm; crashing sounds like the discharge of artillery; bridges washed away - roads badly damaged; narrow escapes from drowning.

The inhabitants of Three Rivers have been rained in, except those who during the late storm were flooded out. Beginning in early evening of the 7th, the rainfall continued for forty-eight hours. The South Fork rose rapidly, and on the 9th at 4PM had attained its greatest height.

The muddy water tumbled along with a constant roar, accompanied by the booming of the boulders as they were hurled upon each other; frequently being heard was the heavy thud of some large log, which had been caught up and carried along by the furious water and then, as if tired of its burden, would throw it headlong anyway and anywhere to be rid of it. Occasionally would be heard a quick succession of rumbling, cracking and crashing sounds, like the roll and scattering discharge of artillery, as a tall, heavy tree became uprooted and fell through branches of surrounding trees into the fast accumulating driftwood and debris. The scent of phosphorous ground out by the tumbling rocks was disagreeably noticeable.

By the morning of the 10th, the storm had ceased and the level of the river fell, revealing much damage. Foot bridges had been carried away and there were many impediments to travel over former trails. The new bridge at "Kirkpatrick's Crossing" was slightly damaged but was easily repaired.

Charlie Blossom, Alfred Curtis and Henry Alles were among those who were away from home during this time and were subsequently flooded out and unable to return home. They drove from Visalia in a buckboard about 10AM, not reaching Ira Blossom's barn until nightfall. They had to camp on the opposite side of the river until morning, when they found the foot log put there by Mr. Blossom. After tending to their horses, they arrived at the house in time for breakfast.

Fred Clough walked from Ira Blossom's to the Three Rivers post office starting on the morning of the 10th and did not get home until near night, having to climb over the mountainside on a new trail as there was no place to cross the river safely.[50]

Through the years, many more floods were to raise the waters of the Kaweah, wash out bridges, strand families and change the flow of the rivers.

---

50   *Daily Morning Delta*, Feb. 17, 1893.

Flood of 1955

The following is an account written in part by the late Frankie Luella Welch and is presented here as an edited version:

Three Rivers is digging out of one of the worst floods known to old-timers.

Mrs. Mary Barton, 91 years, who came here in 1885, can recall nothing like it.

The flood came swiftly and with little warning after midnight Thursday [this was Dec. 23,1955]. Practically all the bridges in the area were swept away or the approaches washed out. Long stretches of highway were torn up, isolating Three Rivers from the outside world and marooning many separate areas within. The North Fork, upper North Fork, Middle Fork, main Three Rivers and the South Fork were all shut off from each other as well as from any communication with the outside communities.

Homes were washed away, businesses wrecked. On the state highway above the Sequoia Cider Mill, Wayne Haapala, the Pete Nourses, Mrs. Reena Soske, the K. Hartlerodes and Mr. and Mrs. Jim Kindred lost their homes, swept away completely and all so quickly that practically no belongings were saved.

The Dunlap Motel in this same area was also claimed by the river. Further up in the Three Rivers village, the Post Office, the Three Rivers Market, Noisy Water Lodge, garage and filling station were flooded. The Sierra Hardware was completely wrecked and gutted. Contrary to early reports, Noisy Water Lodge was not washed away. The river came across the highway in front of the business houses and washed out the road. Broken Sequoia trees, three feet in diameter which have come down from the high mountains, are strewn along the river bank and roadway.

When the water was at its height, the waves leaped 10 feet above the railings of the big cement and steel Kaweah bridge; finally it gave way and one span was swept down with the torrent; the roar was deafening. The Miller Motel was taken by the flood waters and the houses along Weckert Flat are filled with mud and debris. Many homes were flooded by water though not completely washed away.

Frankie's article continues:

Families fled and stayed with neighbors, telephone communications and electric power were cut off. People used candles and cooked over their fireplaces if they were fortunate enough to have one as well as dry wood.

Archie McDowell, who lives on the North Fork, lost 1,000 chickens and two poultry houses. Willie Clay, proprietor of the Moro Rock Tavern [White Horse Inn], had started driving down the road and had to abandon his car and climb a tree where he spent the night, waiting for the waters to subside.

At least two persons sat out the flood on a house top. One of these was Russell Weckert and the other was Jay Kidder who had fled to the home of Mr. and Mrs. Paul Scheerz, after Mr. Weckert was rescued from his own home; but water soon flooded into the Scheerz' home as well. When the Scheerz' car slid against the house, Russell and Mr. Kidder climbed out of the window, then to the top of the car and from there to the roof of the house. Mr. and Mrs. Scheerz clung to a telephone pole to keep from being washed away.

Mrs. Karen Johnson, who lives on the North Fork, and a woman friend stayed in Mrs. Johnson's house three days after the flood water shoved it 40 feet against the trees. They were rescued from the home late Sunday.

The battering of the trees and debris against the side of the Three Rivers Market knocked much of the goods down into the water on the floor. The receding waters left from six inches to a foot of mud there as well as in the post office. However, people came in immediately to buy things and were waited on in rubber boots.

Repairs started almost before the flood waters subsided. Edison repair men came in transported by helicopters; road equipment was put to work and as soon as the road was cleared, telephone trucks came in. The helicopters gave emergency service to the community as well as repairing the lines. They carried food and medicine to marooned areas and helped string a cable across the river for a basket ferry which the local men contrived.

Vehicle travel in and out of Three Rivers has been restored by temporary repair on the South Fork bridge on the old road to Three Rivers. However, no sightseers are allowed. George Lovett, deputy sheriff, is organizing a road patrol. Only those persons who live or have business here will be permitted to come in. The roads are still too dangerous and travel interferes with the needed repair work.

Telephone communication to the valley was restored the next evening. Electric power has been restored to much of the community, although many marooned areas are still without.

Helicopters from Bakersfield, working for the Edison company, did a fine job of spotting and bringing crews to repair broken lines.

The Airport bridge has been repaired so that North Fork residents can soon drive up the Middle Fork road and to the Park road at the Gateway Lodge bridge, which is nearly repaired. The approach was washed out and a ladder crossing had been installed.

Crews from the park on the upper end and state crews from the lower end are working on a very bad washout of the highway between Pumpkin Hollow and Gateway Lodge bridge. The North Forkers are also using two-passenger cable baskets to cross the river to the post office where the main river bridge was torn out. Mrs. Martha Warren, assistant to the postmaster, came across on this cable, and was taken back in a 'copter with the Kaweah mail. The South Fork is still marooned but Walter Wells and other residents felled a tree across Connelly Creek and walked out. They report that the residents are faring well.

Water will be a problem for a long while here; pumps from the river were washed away. These pumps serviced many of the Three Rivers homes and businesses. Ditch heads and Edison flumes also were torn out in many areas. The damage is expected to run into thousands of dollars alone to repair them.[51]

Photo from Author's Collection.

The following is by one of the "North Forkers" who didn't let the flood interfere with his father's business:

Riding The Cable Car
by Barry Bartlett

I was born and raised on my folks' dairy/chicken ranch on the North Fork, up the road from the Kaweah Post Office [the present site of the Kaweah Community Church]. In December

1955, I was 19 and home on leave after completing Army basic training.

On the night of the 23rd, Chuck Chaboude and I were returning to Three Rivers about 12:30 a.m. from our dates in Visalia. Rain was pouring down and we both knew that the river was very high.

Being young and foolhardy, I decided to see if I could drive across the main river and get home. The water was about six inches over the top of the bridge surface and we could feel the pounding of giant sequoia logs as they slammed against the bridge sides.

Chuck walked in front of the vehicle to make sure we could get across. Parked facing us on the North Fork side was a fire truck with its lights aimed at the bridge. The fireman informed us that the water was four to six feet deep a quarter mile up North Fork Drive by Barton's place and that Mankin Creek [above the Kaweah Post Office] had flooded.

We turned the vehicle around and drove back across the bridge. Chuck and I were probably the last ones on the bridge before it went out.

We picked up our friend, Jim Ady, whose family owned the Noisy Water Café and gas station. We left the café to take Chuck to his home near the Waterwheel Motel [present-day Pierce Drive at Highway 198].

About a mile downstream from the bridge, we noticed that the river was starting to get close to some houses on the river side of the highway. We woke up Bob Dunlap and told him that he'd better think about getting out.

We were only there about 15 minutes but by the time we all left, the water was flowing waist-deep on both sides of the house. We had to make a human chain to get back across. All of these houses and some others along the river were soon swept away.

After getting Chuck home, Jim and I drove back downtown where we helped put groceries up on higher shelves in the Beutler's store [Three Rivers Market]. There was no electricity and we worked by flashlight.

The water in the store was about a foot deep. When it became more than knee-deep, we decided it was time to get out of the building. We drove the car to the top of Britten's hill and parked it, then walked back to the Ady's home near the Three Rivers School and spent the night.

During the night, the Three Rivers Bridge over the Middle Fork went out, which caused the water level in the downtown section to go down. The bridge had acted as a dam because of the trees and other debris abutted against it.

The water in the river was still flowing four feet higher in the middle than it was on the sides. The logs and huge boulders were still rolling down and the noise was so impressive.

Earl McKee, Jim Livingston and a group of men were working on building a cable car to be used to cross the Middle Fork to the North Fork. Men worked on both sides of the river, each constructing a tower.

An Edison Company helicopter helped stretch a light line across from the Three Rivers side to the North Fork group. The North Fork men attached a heavier rope to the line and the rope was pulled back across.

Next, a cable was attached, then hauled to the opposite side and secured to the towers. A small wooden platform with sides, which was suspended from rollers, was hung from the cable. It took all day to finish the construction and I spent the night with Earl and Gaynor McKee.

I don't remember if I volunteered the next morning—being young, strong and invincible in my mind—but I was the first to take the cable car across. I had to pull it hand-over-hand along the cable to get it across the river while pulling a heavy rope behind me. At first it wasn't difficult as my weight stretched the cable down to within about three feet of the raging torrent in the middle of the river. But then I had to pull all that weight back up the cable to reach the other shore. I remember that my arms were so tired.

The rope was attached to the cable car on the Three Rivers side and on the North Fork side. The North Fork rope was also attached to Ken Savage's tractor, while the other end was hooked to a jeep. In this way, the little cable car could be pulled from one side or the other. People needing to cross would signal to the person volunteering on the far shore and they would haul them across.

At our North Fork ranch, there was no electricity or phone service for many days. But several days after the bridge washed out, three of our neighbors came by with a generator and plugged in our food freezer for several hours. No one called them. They were just going around the neighborhood helping where they could.

It was a blessing in disguise that I had the ranch wagon on the Three Rivers side of the river and my folks, Ted and Mauricia Bartlett, had their pickup on the North Fork side. Our business was to deliver milk and eggs so we hauled our deliveries across the river on the cable car and were able to keep most of our customers supplied on the highway side.

We delivered the North Fork route and crossed the Airport Bridge and stayed on the northeast side of the river to get to Ash Mountain. We weren't about to get out of the North Fork by vehicle until the washout below Pumpkin Hollow was repaired much later.[52]

[The road Barry refers to here was opened up by bulldozers through River Way Ranch and up to Ash Mountain, using an old road bed from

---

52   *The Kaweah Commonwealth*, December 30, 2005.

many years before. This writer can remember Laura Hall using it to deliver the mail to the Park until the large break at Pumpkin Hollow was repaired.]

Photo from Author's Collection.

Here is yet another account:

River takes family home, business
by Robert Dunlap

I was 17 at the time of the flood. My parents had left several days earlier to visit my sister in Southern California for Christmas, so I was home alone.

Our property was located between the Kaweah River and Highway 198 from the South Fork Bridge east to the Hartlerode house (my aunt and uncle). Next to them was Cooney Alles' place and across the highway were the Haapalas, Nourses, Soskes, and Kindreds.

Our home was a trailer with a bedroom/bathroom built on one side and a sun porch on the other. My dad had built a four-unit motel between the house and the highway.

It had been raining hard for a few days and the Kaweah River, which was several yards behind our house, was extremely loud and rising. During the night of December 23, the water rose and eroded away the soil until it got to the bottom of our house.

I had gone to bed early that night and several friends woke me up because they thought the river was getting too high. The possibility existed that the water might get into the house, so I removed as much of the furniture as I could and put it into my pickup truck.

I put my dresser with my clothes in it, some guns that were close to the back door, and my dog in the truck, and saw that the truck was too small to hold all that was in the house, so I decided to put everything I could carry into the motel.

While clearing out the kitchen, I heard groaning noises from the bedroom that was closest to the river. I looked into the bedroom and suddenly it fell away from the house! I leaned out the dining room door and watched it float away. I knew then that the rest of the house would be flooded so hurriedly grabbed what I could and carried it to the motel.

When I opened the door to one of the motel units, water came gushing out of the room. The river had risen at the back of the motel, had broken some windows, and was filling the rooms with water. I jumped into my truck and drove it onto the highway which was about 15 feet higher than the land on which the motel was built.

I went back to check on the Hartlerodes. The water was about waist high and Drummer, the Hartlerode's dog, came swimming by so I pushed him onto the bed of a 2½ ton flatbed truck that was parked in the driveway.

The water level was to the headlights when Charles drove it up the highway. Once on the road, I couldn't see the river or the homes due to darkness. I left and drove into Three Rivers. Water was at the bottom of the North Fork Bridge. When logs or trees would come down the river and hit the bridge, it would cause a loud ring.

As soon as it was daylight, I drove back to my house to find that the river had taken all the homes in the area, the motel, and the highway from the South Fork Bridge to the Dixons. Nothing was left except a well pipe sticking up, which meant that the river had not only taken all the dwellings, but about five feet of topsoil too.

I drove into Three Rivers and found that the bridge was gone, businesses were filled with mud, and the roadway was littered with mud and debris. I drove up the highway toward Sequoia National Park and found that several homes that had been along the river were now gone.

For days, I scouted the river downstream as far as Woodlake for any sign of my house or motel, but only found a few pieces of wood with paint that was the color of our house, some broken dishes, and some blankets.

When my parents heard about the flood, they painstakingly made their way into Three Rivers. They didn't know if I was dead or alive. My dad drove as far as he could, then walked in the rest of the way. When he saw that our house was gone, he thought maybe I was gone with it.

When I finally found my parents, they were standing on what was left of the South Fork Bridge, crying.[53]

Photo from Author's Collection.

<hr>

53 Ibid.

Photo from Author's Collection.

Photo from Author's Collection.

CHAPTER XI

Wildlife

Wildlife in Three Rivers Country - Overview

Many animals are found living in the canyons of the Kaweah. Some of them are destructive as far as man is concerned; some are not.

Deer are often found here, although they are not as plentiful as the herds were approximately fifty to 100 years ago. Their numbers seem to be dwindling, but they have learned to inhabit areas close to homes and especially gardens and family orchards. This author can remember large herds of deer grazing in clearings in the North Fork area, mainly Yucca Creek and its environs. The imposed moratorium on the hunting of the mountain lion has resulted in the increase of the lion's species and therefore, the decrease of the deer herds. The deer are beautiful and intelligent creatures but they are hard-pressed to increase their numbers due to the larger number of predators, such as the coyote and bobcat as well as the cougar.

Ground squirrels have adapted quite well to the environment and the advent of man upon their habitat has not seen their demise; quite the contrary. This is also true of pocket gophers, much to the surprise of new residents when their carefully planted crops of flowers, shrubs, etc. seem to just disappear into the ground!

Other frequent and more common species in this area include the aforementioned coyote and bobcat; the skunk also makes his presence known in most evenings when the scent of his "perfume" comes wafting down the canyons. Two kinds of foxes, the red and the smaller gray are living in Three Rivers; their little coughs or barks can be heard at night and they are often sighted crossing the road in the headlights of a car. Raccoons are a nighttime visitor and have also adapted quite well to man's environment. They are frequent raiders of local chicken coops and have learned to appreciate cat and dog food left out on patios or decks. Their charming appearance with their bandit-like masks makes them hard to dislike; however, their very sharp teeth and claws can inflict some serious wounds to any hand that feeds them.

The beautiful gray squirrel lives here as well. His safest place is high up in the oaks or cedars growing along the rivers, but his need for food and his curiosity often find him crossing the road and he makes an easy prey for a speeding auto or any of the predators that roam the area. His chatter or barking can be heard as he scolds someone or something he doesn't like.

Many species of snakes—some venomous, some not—make their dens in the Three Rivers country. Gopher snakes, diamondback rattlesnakes, water snakes, racers and the California king snakes are among the most-often spotted here.

Occasionally, muskrats can still be seen as can the California badger. Although it is not commonly known, the beaver once called these streams and rivers his home. Many rodents seem to like Three Rivers as well; species of mice, kangaroo rats, wood rats, and others. Also, several species of rabbits are frequently seen hopping around in the brush.

Three Rivers has a large and varied animal population, and there are more species not mentioned here although no less important to the area. Subsequent chapters will tell the story of other less known or more "uncommon" animals.

Extinct Animals

Within our canyons, four species of mammals have disappeared from this area. Several remain elsewhere, so the elimination of these animals is properly called *extirpation* and not *extinction*. The California Gray Wolf, California Grizzly, Jaguar, and Bison no longer exist here as wild species, and their departure is a matter of historic record. We can regret that these beasts no longer exist here, but were they to roam freely over our lands today, they would cause some serious problems, to say the least! They all demand large pieces of land, and all have habits that conflict mightily with certain aspects of human activity.

The wolf *[Canis lupus]* occurred along the eastern edge of the Central Valley and up into the Sierra. When the Hudson Britten family built their homestead cabins in Britten Cove, they related incidents of wolf predation on their livestock and small domesticated animals. These animals were quite ferocious and determined at the time to overcome any obstacles to obtain their prey. Wolves and coyotes could be distinguished from each other because of their size and color. In the early part of the nineteenth century, the State Bureau of Biological Survey paid trappers and hunters to eliminate the wolf from cattle ranges. The wolf disappeared from California about 1924; they were last seen southwest of Tule Lake in 1922. More recent reports of wolves in the Sierras and foothills are based on an animal which was of Asiatic origin, presumably an escaped captive or pet.

The California Grizzly was the New World representative of the Brown Bear *[Ursus arctos]* of the Old World. The grizzly once occurred widely throughout California and was a constant threat to humans and domestic stock. Its total lack of fear combined with its destructive habits rendered it a dangerous member of our animal population. In the 1850–1870s, the grizzly roamed the Central Valley and Sierra as well as the Coast Ranges. Generally, it reached its greatest concentrations in the Central Valley and in the chaparral at low elevations. Vivid accounts of this huge bear are to be found in *California Grizzly* by Tracey Storer and Lloyd Tevis, Jr. This bear was genuinely abundant, and there were numerous places where travelers risked meeting actual groups of them, consisting of ten to twenty or more grizzlies together. Because its centers of density coincided with ranching activities, it was persecuted whenever it was encountered. The last grizzly in our area was killed in 1924. Since there are so many interesting accounts, the author will devote a chapter to this unique animal, even though he is no longer seen and is definitely "extinct."

The Jaguar [*Felis onca*] is the largest cat in the New World, and like the grizzly, an awesome creature to have as a neighbor. A large jaguar may exceed 240-265 pounds and can easily bring down prey up to the size of a grown horse or a large bull. The occasional incidents with these animals that have recently occurred within the United States have been conspicuously destructive to domestic stock. Unlike the grizzly, however, the jaguar is rarely, if ever, a threat to human life. It is a rather shy creature and seldom to be seen without the aid of hunting dogs. Today the jaguar is found occasionally in states that border Mexico, but it is not known if these are strays or residents. Its original range was between the South Coast Ranges near San Francisco up to at least 1826 and down into old Mexico. The last known jaguar was killed in Palm Springs in 1860. It is now regarded as extremely rare throughout the United States.

Added to this list is a large bird, known as the California Condor. Although he is not technically "extinct," he is no longer seen in our area. However, there is an enormous effort by many State and Federal agencies as well as other groups to bring him back to his wild environment. In the 1980s, one condor was visible on Blossom Peak, but since that time there have been no sightings.

The California Grizzly

When you look at the California State Seal, you will see a grizzly bear, more specifically a California Grizzly Bear. This animal is now extinct, and although conservationists and environmentalists might disagree, this could be a good thing.

Yes, we know that this enormous animal is considered extinct and is no longer living in our canyons. However, history demands that he has his own chapter, since the early settlers here encountered him and therefore his story needs to be told. *Ursus horribilis,* or *Ursus californicus,* as he has been re-named, once roamed freely in this state; he was king of the valley animals. He was a huge and often fierce beast that could weigh as much as 1500 pounds and could measure eight feet tall while standing on his hind legs. He must have been a sight (fearsome or not) to behold!

The early native inhabitants of the Three Rivers District, the Yokuts Indians, had no safe way to kill this bear and at times even found themselves the preferred dinner of this omnivore. The author Frank Latta related a story of a grizzly's invasion of the Indian village at Hospital Rock. The Indians surrounded the bear, using the weapons they had: bows, arrows and spears. When the bear would chase an Indian, the others would bravely close in behind him, using their weapons to wound and harass the animal. They finally got him down and killed him, but not before this particular bear had killed two Indians.

Tulare County pioneers seldom wrote about grizzlies, and the bears that were noted inhabited the mountains for the most part. Ira Blossom, an early settler on the South Fork of the Kaweah, told Walter Fry, the first civilian superintendent at Sequoia, of hearing a disturbance in his hog pen. When he went to investigate, he saw a grizzly go over a fence carrying a 300-pound hog.

Because the grizzly was a dangerous animal unlike its little cousin, the California brown bear, the pioneers killed off the grizzlies as fast as they could. Joe Palmer, another early-day South Fork resident, killed another enormous bear as it was attacking his hogs.

Some accounts from the *Visalia Delta* in 1865 read as follows:

August 23, 1865: Frightful Accident

. . . day before yesterday, at about 2 o'clock in the afternoon, Mr. W. C. Rhodes, while herding sheep in the Yokohl Valley, was attacked by a grizzly bear and very dangerously torn about the left arm and side. His boy was also badly bitten. Dr. Sill has gone out to attend the sufferers, and upon his return we shall have all the particulars...

Then, the following:

August 30, 1865

. . . Mr. Rhodes, who was so badly torn by a grizzly bear last week, is reported rapidly recovering. It appears that Mr. Rhodes and his son, a boy of some 15 years, were going to a spring at the edge of the valley to watch for deer when attacked by the bear . . . .

Walter Fry reported another encounter with a big bear by Bernard Mehrten, an early Three Rivers rancher:

In company with Henry Mehrten and William Lusky, I camped with our sheep at Alta Meadows in what is now Sequoia

National Park during the summer of 1877. We saw some tremendous big bear tracks near our camp and decided we would get him. We used a sheep for bait and set two guns for him. Along in the night, we heard one of the guns go off. Next morning, we found the bear had been crippled, and we followed his tracks down into Hell Hole (now Buck Canyon) where we shot and killed him.

It was a monstrous male grizzly. One man guessed its weight at 1,800 pounds, but of course it did not weigh that much. However, I believe the animal would have weighed over 1,000 pounds.

On another occasion, Walter Hengst, another early resident of Three Rivers related he had seen perhaps the same animal "as big as a horse" in the vicinity of Eshom Valley.

Walter Fry's Bulletin No. 2, December 4, 1924 states the following:

Under that date of November 6, 1924, Superintendent White issued a press bulletin conveying the information that a large grizzly bear had recently been seen within the Sequoia National Park. This news aroused the interest of many a California citizen; many were proud that the California Official State Animal was still among us, but some were loath to believe it.

That a California grizzly bear is now living within Sequoia National Park or the territory thereabouts, there seems no shadow of a doubt. So convincing are the reports, and so accurate the description of the animal seen by numerous persons on various occasions, that no longer can their reports be discredited or disbelieved. The most important reports of which we have record are as follows:

On August 7, 1921, 11 park visitors reported having seen a large grey bear at the Giant Forest Bear Pit that was practically twice the size of other black and brown bears. That this particular bear had a distinct hump on the top of its shoulders, and when the animal appeared in sight the other bears hastily ran away. During the month of April 1924, Mr. James B. Small and his road working crew of several men reported on several occasions having seen a large grizzly colored bear in the vicinity of their road camp near Moro Rock. Mr. Small and some of his men had previously worked in Yellowstone National Park, where grizzly bears are numerous, and all these men pronounced the bear they saw as a grizzly. They all made mention of the hump the bear had on the top of its shoulders.

On October 13, 1924, Mr. Alfred Hengst, a cattleman at Three Rivers, came into very close contact with a huge bear near the headwaters of Cliff Creek. Undoubtedly this was the same bear seen by others for this is the description he gives: "It was the biggest bear I ever saw—bigger than any cow, and looked as though sprinkled over with snow. I had a close view of this beast which undoubtedly was a grizzly."

That same year, it was reported that a grizzly had been shot in the mountains near the Park, probably the end of the grizzly population in California.

So ends the story of the California Grizzly. Did his ancestors migrate over the Siberian Land Bridge? Do some of his distantly related cousins still reside in the regions of Alaska where their size closely matches those of our California bear? What happened to the last of these great bears? Was he shot like the others or did he die of old age in the canyons below Moro Rock? In all probability, these questions will never be answered for these animals are truly extinct; we will know them no more.

The Fisher

The fisher is one of the rarest and most valuable of California's fur-bearing animals. In size, it is the next-to-the-largest member of the weasel family. The adult male is a little over three feet in length, nearly twice as large as the female. The shape of the animal is like a dark house cat with short, powerful legs.

The overall color of the fisher ranges from a light brown to a dark, rich tan. The front half is grayish brown, with the pale color sometimes extending part way down the back. The legs and feet are black. The long, fully furred tail tapers from the body to the tip.

Irregular white spots may occur on the throat and chest, with a spot on the belly between the hind legs. The underfur is long and interspersed with glossy black guard hairs; the nearly white hairs inside are close set. The ears are half-round in shape, and the white claws mark his pelt with distinction. The fisher is a solitary animal, roaming at will over a large home territory. It is as much at home in trees as on the ground, and like other members of the weasel family, it is a tireless hunter.

Photo from BritishColumbia.com

The name "fisher" is misleading, as reports show there is no inclination toward fish in his diet. Except when hunting for mountain beaver, fishers are associated with mountain meadows and spring bogs, although they really prefer the heavily timbered ridges.

Fishers are not entirely nocturnal; they also hunt by day and because of their strength and agility, they prey easily on grey and pine squirrels that they capture in the trees. Fishers kill many other small mammals such as rabbits, marmots and other rodents for food; they are the only animal which continues successfully to prey upon porcupines.

The fisher makes its den in hollows in living and fallen trees and sometimes in holes in rock ledges. The young are born in May and June; two to four pups in a litter. They grow rapidly and by winter are nearly as large as their parents.

In the early days of California, the fisher was found from Oregon south to Marin County and throughout the Sierra Nevada to the Green Mountains in Kern County. At present, however, their population is stable but sparse and they find refuge in Tulare, Trinity and Tuolumne counties.

The fishers thrive in elevations of 3500' or higher, just below the average of their cousin, the martens. Like the martens, they prefer the environment of dense fir forests in which to live and hunt. There is no trapping or hunting season on these beautiful creatures; and because they prey on porcupines, which in their turn are somewhat destructive to trees, careful consideration needs to be given to preserving this elusive animal.

The Mountain Lion

In our canyons lives a large feline; we know him as the California Mountain Lion, although he carries many other names: *felis concolor*, Puma, Painter, Cougar, Panther, among them. He has lived here since time immemorial; he ranges from Southern South America into Canada, probably the longest range of any land mammal.[54] Each adult lion stakes out a home range by leaving markers. Along the edge of the range, a cougar will scrape together small piles of leaves, pine needles and twigs and urinate on them. These "scrapes" act as boundary markers. Generally, the cats respect each other's territorial rights. This behavior is called "mutual avoidance."

An adult male's home range often spans over 100 square miles. Females have smaller ranges-- between twenty to sixty square miles. In an ideal habitat, such as the west side of the Sierra Nevada, as many as ten adult lions may occupy the same 100 square mile area.

The adult male mountain lion can grow in length of six to eight feet, including the long tail and they closely resemble very large, tawny house cats in appearance; they can weigh up to 150 pounds. Females can be up to seven feet long and weigh from 65 to 90 pounds. They occur in two color phases, one grayish-brown and the other reddish-brown. The young kittens are spotted and have rings around their tails. The track of this big cat is large and round in shape with the pad at the rear having a characteristic three-lobed appearance that is absent in that of dogs and coyotes.

Note the obvious toenail prints for dogs that are absent for mountain lions. Also the lion track has a distinctive "M" shaped pad

Image by the Author.

54   *Mammals of California*, Lloyd Glenn Ingles, pp.81-84.

The cubs arrive most frequently in April, though they can be born during any month. A litter may contain two or three young, probably never more than four. The mountain lion's den is generally in a cave or crevice of a big rockslide at the base of a rocky cliff and is often quite inaccessible.

The diet of this animal consists mainly of deer and he is popularly supposed to kill and eat a deer each week. However, little more than 50 percent of the food of an adult mountain lion is deer meat; the rest is made up of all kinds of smaller animals, including skunks, porcupines, domestic dogs and cats. There are documented cases of mountain lions attacking human beings; yet even after the lion has killed his victim, it seems to dislike human flesh. Lions prefer venison [deer meat] to any other food and except for old or decrepit individuals who are unable to catch a swifter prey, they will seldom attack humans or livestock if deer are plentiful.[55]

The lion population in our vicinity is unknown, although in the 1990s, the estimated State population was about 6,000. It is certainly not uncommon nowadays to see a lion crossing the road in front of our headlights, or to see one sunning itself on a rock, even near the center of town. [This author has personally seen a mountain lion at least five times in the Three Rivers area.] These creatures are, like house cats, very curious and can become relaxed and unafraid in the vicinity of humans. With a decline in the local deer population, this animal begins to look for other food, domestic animals included.

The sound the lion makes is a terrifying, elongated, piercing scream, which sounds like the scream of a terrified woman. In addition to growls and hisses, they also emit bird-like whistles, which are probably used to communicate where they are and to sound instructions between a female and her kittens. One of the great mysteries about cougars is their fear of barking dogs. It is hypothesized that sometime in the cougar's evolutionary past, they were preyed upon by barking animals.

Several years ago, the voters in the State of California voted down and defeated Proposition 197, the Mountain Lion Initiative, which would have allowed limited hunting of these animals. This brings to mind how much

55   Ibid.

the public's attitude has changed in the last 80 years. In the 1930s to the 1950s, the big cats were rarely seen; this was no doubt due to the fact that there was a bounty paid on them. Or perhaps it was also because they had learned to fear humankind and took great pains to stay out of sight; lion attacks at that time were extremely rare.

As a way to illustrate this point, here is a short story about a man that many people in Three Rivers knew and liked quite well. His book, *Cougar Killer*, is interesting and well worth reading. His name was Jay C. Bruce, Sr.; he was born in 1872 at the Washington Mine, Mariposa County, California. While he was a boy, his parents evidently lived in Wawona [now in Yosemite National Park]. During that time, he earned money by catching trout in the river for the kitchen at the Wawona Hotel; he also sold rattlesnake rattles to the tourists who stayed there.

He was appointed the first official mountain lion hunter by the State of California Conservation Authority in 1918. During his career that spanned twenty-eight years, he trapped and killed nearly seven hundred cougars. His highest year was 1927; he trapped 42 that year alone. Many of his lion chases were in the Sierra from the Kern River in the south to the Merced River in the north. He was clawed many times and had many narrow escapes. Once, he lost his footing and slid down a snow bank, landing between two cougars devouring a deer they had recently killed.

Another time, Bruce crawled into a cave to rescue his hunting dogs from a cornered lion. He faced a treed lion with an empty rifle on another occasion; he was saved when one of his dogs brought him a little pouch that contained extra bullets. He and his great friend, Ord Loverin, hunted lions in California, Arizona, New Mexico and even into Old Mexico. Bruce's work in controlling the lion population in this state was credited with allowing an increase in the California deer herds and making life safer for livestock and humans in the mountains.

The following is from a newspaper article printed in 1924:

Three Rivers, Jan. 26 - Two immense lions have been killed as a result of the hunt being conducted by the state lion hunter,

Jay C. Bruce. Accompanied by Gilbert Dixon, vertebra zoologist from the University of California, and Colonel John R. White, Superintendent of Sequoia National Park, Bruce entered Giant Forest with his trained dogs by way of the Hospital Rock Trail. No lion sign was found in the vicinity of the forest and the next morning at the suggestion of Supt. White, the party, augmented by Ranger George Brooks, moved on toward Colony Mill.

Photo from Author's Collection.

At Marble Fork Bridge, a track was picked up by the dogs and followed about five miles up the canyon, where a large lion was treed and subsequently shot. The state zoologist found it to be badly scratched and torn about the head, indicating a fierce struggle with some other beast.

With the aid of Ranger Brooks, the large cat was carried out of the canyon to a place where Dixon could prepare it for a specimen and then the party continued on toward Colony Mill. They soon came upon a female lion standing guard over the body of a dead male; probably her mate and killed by the same lion just shot by Bruce. The lioness was reluctant to desert her mate though he had apparently been dead several days; but the dogs drove her up a tree and she soon lay dead beside him.

The lion hunting party will work out of the country about Colony Mill for a few days and then move camp to the Burdick Ranch on the North Fork, where some lions have committed many depredations on the cattle ranges in the black oak country above there.[56]

How times have changed in the last 70 years! California now has an estimated lion population of at least 7000 animals. This is evident in the number of lion sightings in our small community alone. With the deer herd getting smaller, the lion has learned to catch more helpless prey, domestic cats and dogs among them.

If we want our deer population to make a comeback, and at the same time provide a safe environment for our children and domestic animals, it seems only logical that the number of the mountain lion be closely managed, for the lion's sake as well as our own.

The mountain lion is a magnificent animal—rugged, strong, fearless and very, very intelligent—he deserves his place in the ecosystem. If his numbers could be reduced and his natural prey given a chance to replenish, then perhaps a balance could be re-established.

---

56   *The Fresno Bee*, January 1924.

Jay Bruce and baby lion. *Photo from Author's Collection.*

Jay Bruce, baby lion and his dog. *Photo from Author's Collection.*

Ringtail Cats - Our Elusive Neighbors

Most of us living here in Three Rivers don't even realize that there is an elusive little animal called the Ring-Tailed Cat or a Civet Cat. He remains elusive, because like his cousin the Raccoon, he is nocturnal. Although the Raccoon and Ringtail are related, they definitely have some very distinct features from one another. The raccoon can weigh in at 20 pounds while the little ringtail is only a featherweight at about two pounds! His familiar black face mask distinguishes the raccoon, while the prominent facial feature of the ringtail is his disproportionately large eyes with white rings that really seem to make his eyes even larger than they are. However, the deciding trait between these two species is their tails. The raccoon has a brown and white tail that makes up only a third of its overall length and plays a distant second to his very conspicuous facial "bandit's" mask. His little cousin the ringtail has a boldly banded black and white tail that takes up easily one-half of its total length and is strikingly prominent when illuminated by a car's headlights.

https://en.wikipedia.org/wiki/Ringtail

This little guy has been given a number of names but most people call it a ringtail cat. Since it is actually a cousin of the raccoon, it has been called a coon cat as well. In addition, it can secrete a pungent odor not unlike the skunk and because it is similar to the African civet, it is also called a civet cat. Miners sent it into mines to catch rodents and then gave it the name "miner's cat." It was said that the Aztec Indians of Mexico called it a cacomistle, which means half mountain lion, because it pounces on its prey and delivers a death-bite to the neck of its unlucky victim in the manner of the cougar. And lastly, scientists have given it a handle, *Bassariscus astutus*, which means clever fox.

The ringtail is found in rocky areas, like canyons and rock piles, and trees as well. This author has seen them in the high reaches of large oak trees. Its range extends from Oregon into Mexico, including the Sierra and throughout the southwestern United States.

The ringtail uses moss, leaves, or grasses to line its den under rocks, in crevices, or in hollow trees, stumps or logs. A gestation period of eight weeks produces two to four young in May or June. After about a month, the babes' eyes are open and they begin to eat solid food. At seven or eight weeks, they venture out with their mother for hunting practice. They travel single file behind her and learn how to hunt and consume insects, snakes, small birds, carrion, small mammals and fruit. At four months of age, the ringtail is ready to hunt on its own but it must take care, since the great-horned owl and the bobcat are its natural predators.

So, if you think you see a small raccoon, take a closer look; it could be our elusive ringtail instead.

Our Not-So-Wild "Wild" Turkeys

These beautiful, sometimes comical, sometimes aggressive animals "pecking" their way across our yards and roads are actually "foreigners." None of these birds is native to California; humans brought them here— not nature.

When Europeans journeyed to New England, they found a species of turkey in abundance there. However, when settlers came to California, they found a land that had not seen a turkey track since the last ice age. Scientists discovered a native California turkey in the tar pits of La Brea, but he had been extinct for 10,000 years! And for some reason, the turkeys of the East Coast never made it across the plains and the Great Western Divide to populate the West Coast.

Private ranchers in 1877 released turkeys in California. Later, the state bought turkeys from Mexico. Some of these were bred on farms and their offspring released into the wild; however, these farm-bred birds were not successful at living off the land. It was not until efficient methods were devised to safely capture large numbers of wild turkeys and relocate them that their populations finally began to increase and thrive in the western states.

In fact, the relocation program was a resounding success, so much so that now the population can actually be a nuisance to some "civilized" areas. Turkeys are now found in many places in Three Rivers; they can either be a nuisance to the residents or a delight to the casual observer.

https://www.fws.gov/refuges/features/WildFacts.html

When the tom puffs up his body feathers and fans his tail during springtime, his wattle turns blood red and his head turns shades of blue. If the light strikes his feathers just right, they give off an iridescent palette of bronzes, burgundies and green colors.

During spring, the toms court the hens and they travel with a small harem. Then during the summer, the hens take off on their own to raise their young. During the fall and winter, the wild turkeys sometimes form large flocks—both sexes combined.

The turkey commands a wide vocabulary with more than 30 vocalizations. The young chicks make a peeping call even before they hatch. A young turkey (or a poult) who has become lost will alert its mom of its predicament with high-pitched whistles. Mother turkey will warn her poults of danger with an alarm "putt." Turkeys who are contented will purr softly or if irritated will purr loudly. If the irritation continues, a fight might result, and combatants use the fighting rattle. Only toms gobble, and they do this to attract hens.

Relocation programs rescued the wild turkey from the disastrously low populations of the 1940s to the current abundance in much of the United States. Now, California, which lost its native turkey to another epoch, once again has a wealth of wild turkeys roaming where they will.

PART TWO

Family Histories

1850–1860s

Hopkins L. Work and Family

One of the earliest settlers to Three Rivers was the Hopkins Work family. Hopkins L. Work had been born November 14, 1809 in Roane County, Virginia, the son of Joseph Work and Nancy Ballenger Work.[57] He married Martha Ann Parker February 13, 1830. They had come across the plains with ox teams from Kentucky in 1849; their route took them through Walker Pass and down by Bakersfield, then north to the mines. They stopped at Hangtown and later were in Georgetown, eventually moving to Yolo County before coming to Tulare County about 1857. Their family consisted of four sons, Pleasant, Jonathan, James B. and Enoch C., and one daughter, Martha. They settled on the South Fork near where it meets the Middle Fork. It did not take Hopkins long to stake out his land claims and begin construction of a home for his wife and their children.[58]

In May 1857, the Works and Pemberton families had received a considerable amount of money from the sale of a cattle herd; it was rumored that they still had the money on hand. A few days after the sale transaction, a band of 80 or 90 Indians came over from the Owens River Valley and established camp just across the Kaweah River from the Works

---

57   www.findagrave.com
58   *Junep's History of Sequoia National Park & Vicinity*, p. 27

home. Many of the Indians carried firearms and among the group was one who had recently killed a white man on the Owens River without cause or provocation; he was wearing the dead man's clothes at the time.

On the 25th of the month, when the male settlers were away looking after their stock, a portion of the Indians looted the premises of Pemberton and Work. When the men returned home and saw what had happened, Joseph Palmer, Hopkins Work and Jasper Pemberton immediately started out for the camp of the Indians to "adjust" matters. While en route to the Indian camp, they met six Indians and told them of the depredations they had committed. Immediately, the Indian that had killed the man at Owens River made an attempt to draw his pistol, whereupon Joseph Palmer struck the Indian on his head with his gun, killing him instantly. Then several shots were fired at close range from both sides in which three or four Indians were killed and the whites not injured. The Indians all left the country the same evening, after which the dead Indians were buried by the whites. According to the story, this was the first, last and only trouble with the Indians.[59]

Another account of this story is from T. J. Brundage:

> While I was teaching at a school east of Visalia, a friendly Indian came to where I was boarding and informed us that the Work family who lived at the mouth of the Kaweah River was in danger of being massacred. I immediately started out on Mr. Crowley's horse about 11pm and notified the neighbors, so that next morning about 15 men armed with rifles started out to relieve the Work family. We arrived at the Work home about 10am and were informed the fight had already taken place, the Work family having successfully defended themselves, killing two Indians and the rest driven away. We were agreeably surprised to learn that the Work's daughter, Mrs. Lane, was to be married that day to a Mr. Markham, who lived south of Visalia, and we were invited

59   *History of Tulare and Kings Counties, California*, Menefee & Dodge, p. 58.

to stay for the wedding. That hit us just right, as we would rather enjoy a wedding than to be in an Indian fight.[60]

Hopkins Work and his family continued to raise cattle and horses and to farm on the homestead until the flood of 1867. Since their property was situated at the point where the South Fork joined the main river, the flood took all the buildings, stock, etc. that they had. They were lucky to have escaped with no loss of life. Understandably disheartened, they moved down to the valley, eventually near Dunlap. Their son Enoch continued on with the ranching pursuits and added a lot of acreage to their holdings. Hopkins Work passed away July 3, 1887; his wife Martha preceded him in 1878. They are both buried in the Visalia Cemetery along with many other members of their family. The Work family was a large and prolific one; they were truly some of the valley's first pioneers.

---

60   *Los Tulares*, #22, March 1955.

The Tharp/Swanson Families

During the summer of 1856, a group of Yokuts Indians were camped on the meadow near where the South Fork and Middle Fork of the Kaweah River come together. The Indians were gathered around an amazing spectacle of a man and his horse; this man was a new experience in their lives, since very few of them had ever seen a horse or a white man. The man was Hale Dixon Tharp, a native of Michigan.

Tharp was born in Michigan in 1829, the son of Nathaniel and Lucinda Zane Tharp. At that time, Michigan was on the American frontier, and Hale learned to hunt, shoot, to track animals and even human beings. At the age of 18, he became very interested in the tales of California and the gold mining possibilities there. When he was 23, he was ready to leave for California. A physical description tells the reader how this pioneer looked:

> He was rangy and stood six feet, two inches without his boots. He had black hair and a red beard. His eyes were blue and piercing. Hale always carried an 8-inch knife in a scabbard at the belt of his jeans. If anyone stepped a little out of line with him, he didn't hesitate to draw it.[61]

Hale's step-grandson, William (Bill) Swanson, later gave a story of Tharp's quick-thinking on the trail with the wagon train:

> My granddad was on scout duty ahead of the train one day when he was sitting on his horse beside the bank of a river, waiting for the wagons to cross. He spotted an Indian up to his neck in the water just below the overhanging bank. When the first team reached the bank, the Indian raised his tomahawk to kill the lead animal. My grandad raised his six-shooter and killed the Indian with a single shot.[62]

61   *The Fresno Bee*, October 3, 1954.
62   Ibid.

Hale Dixon Tharp. *Photo courtesy of the Three Rivers Museum.*

Hale joined a wagon train headed by John Swanson and with it started west. Included in the train were Edward Swanson, Jr., a nephew of the leader, and Edward's wife Chloe Ann; the family included their four boys: Julius, John, Henry and George. Along the way, Edward Swanson, Jr. succumbed to one of the diseases encountered by pioneers on the way west in those days. He left Chloe Ann and the boys to drive the wagon themselves and carry on with the train. Chloe Ann hired Tharp to help drive her wagon; evidently, they decided to make it a permanent arrangement, since they were married December 25, 1853 in El Dorado County, California. They had a son, Norton Hale Tharp and a daughter, Fanny Ann. Norton was married twice; first to Alice Myers, who died young. His second wife was Mary Work; they had no children. Fanny Ann Tharp married Bernard Mehrten.

When Hale's family reached California, he set about working in the mines but he was injured in an explosion and decided to raise cattle and horses instead; he wanted to find a peaceful place to settle his family, somewhere away from the environment of the mining camps, yet at the same time provide feed for his stock. With his friend John Swanson, Tharp came south and eventually found his way to the Kaweah River, following it up to the spot where he had earlier encountered the camp site of the Yokuts. Here at last was the perfect place to pasture his stock, especially since the Indians had proved to be so friendly. He finished his explorations and went back to El Dorado County and his family.

Two years later, he returned with John Swanson, and several miles below the junction of the three forks in the main river, he selected a site for a house and barns. The two men made their camp on a sand bar near what was later known as Cobble Lodge [now under Lake Kaweah]. In the morning, Tharp arose and told his companion, "This is the first good night's sleep I have had in two years." He was so impressed with the site that he and Swanson started construction of a crude log cabin. After a few more exploratory trips, he returned to El Dorado, leaving Swanson to guard his home. He went back to Chloe and within two years they had come to the new homestead. However, the family decided to stay in Farmersville with the children so they could attend school there while Hale continued on to their homestead on the Kaweah.

Means of communication between the two places was accomplished by a pet bulldog belonging to Tharp; he would attach a note for his wife to the dog's collar and the dog would make the 26-mile trip to Farmersville with the message, receive his meal and return to Hale with any further messages.[63]

In the meantime, Tharp had been making friends with the many Indians who camped in his vicinity. Among them was a young chieftain by the name of *Hon-hush,* or Chappo, as the name the whites later gave him. The chief had heard of this friendly pale-faced man and with his leaders he visited Tharp at his new home. Thus, a friendship was formed between the two men which was destined to last for many years. Tharp himself said, "[T]he Indians all liked me because I was good to them. I liked the Indians too, for they were honest and kind to each other. I never knew of a theft or murder among them."

Tharp added, "[T]here was an abundance of game and other animals in this country when I first came here. Deer were practically everywhere with lots of bear along the rivers; occasionally a grizzly bear too. Lions, wolves, coyote and fox were plentiful as well as many ground squirrels, cotton tails and jack rabbits; quail were in coveys of thousands."

In the meantime, Hale's stock of cattle and horses was prospering and growing. The small herd he originally owned had increased to nearly one

---

63   *Junep's History of Sequoia National Park,* pg 4 (unpublished). Note says that Tharp himself told this to Ira Clayton in an interview.

hundred head. This forced him to think of summer pasturage and since the Indians had told him of the lovely green meadows in the high Sierra and of the gigantic red trees, he was determined to investigate and find out if these stories were true. Soon, a messenger from the Indian seat of government several miles up the river arrived at the Tharp home with an invitation from Chief *Hon-Hush* to spend the night with him. Tharp readily agreed and was led up into the canyon by the guide.

Although Tharp found the way hard going, when he reached the encampment, he declared, ". . . when I arrived at the camp, Chappo and his men extended to me a cordial welcome and gave me the best his camp afforded. He called out every individual in the camp and with much dignity and very long ceremony introduced me to all. At that time, there were over 600 Indians living in the camp . . . ." Every effort was made to make this friendly white man comfortable. Chief Chappo was the gracious host and sought in every way to return the many kindnesses tendered by his white friend during the two years he had known him.

The tribe gathered for a great feast in his honor. A huge fire was made and many large baskets of acorn meal were heated. Deer, bear and fish meat was also cooked in abundance. There was no other drink but water as the Indians made no brews of any kind, except in sickness, when medicinal herbs were used. Small baskets of wild gooseberries, blackberries and wild grapes were also enjoyed by all. Everyone ate with gusto until the meal was over. Then, small cigarettes, made from bamboo-like reeds gathered near Tulare Lake, were smoked. With amazement, Tharp watched one young Indian draw one of the small pencil-shaped reeds from a hole in the lobe of his ear, stuffed it with *sho-kun*, a wild "tobacco," lit it and passed it around for a few puffs. Tharp later learned that this cigarette would be allowed to go out and cool, when it would be placed back into the pierced ear lobe and smoked from time to time; evidently the tobacco lasted for several lightings at the smoker's convenience.

Eventually, the members of the tribe began to drift to bed until nearly all were retired and in the quiet of the low burning campfire, Chief *Hon-Hush* began the tale of his race and their beginning to his white friend.

He told how:

> ... in the beginning there was the eagle *Tso-hit* and the lion *Wu-hus-pet*. These were the Great Creators who made all things as they are and who made the first man. They molded him out of mud and then gave him life by breathing upon him, which also gave him breath. But they forgot one thing: his hands. Lacking these, the man was unable to procure food and was forced to eat of the earth. Everywhere they searched to find hands for him, as they feared he would eat up *Watchumni Hill* which they thought was their heaven. At length the little lizard was chosen to give the new creature his hands. This the lizard agreed to do as he was called *kuh-cha-choo'-yuh*, or the "Fingered One." But the coyote *Kai-yu* became very jealous as he feared for his life if the man were given hands with which to hunt and kill him for food. He looked for the lizard everywhere, even trying to smoke him out of his tiny hole in the crevice of the rocks. But the wily lizard, seeing his chance, dashed to the mud man and left the imprint of his hands where they should be. Now the man was able to forage for himself. But as all animals lived together then, the Creators were afraid many would take them for food. Therefore the fox and the deer and bear were sent to diverse places in the forests, the fish to the rivers and the birds to the skies. Thus it was that all birds and animals became scattered throughout the land.[64]

Having told Tharp this legend of the creation of his race, *Hon-Hush* indicated that it was time for sleep. He led Tharp to a wigwam constructed of posts placed upright in the ground in a circle about eight feet in diameter. The tops of these leaned toward the center forming a beehive-shaped dwelling. Beginning from the top, but far enough down to leave a hole for smoke to escape, was tightly wound a long rope of tule grass as one might wind an inverted top. The spirals were tightly bound together with small lengths of wild grapevine. The whole thing was waterproof, yet so portable that the tule rope could be unwound, the stakes taken up and the entire structure moved at will. The interior was immaculate and contained

---

64   Ibid. This interview was told to Junep by Joe Poh-hot and agrees closely with all other versions by various authorities.

numerous deer and bear skins spread on the floor while a small pile of bear robes were rolled into a corner to use as blankets. It was in this place that Hale Tharp spent the night.

While Tharp was at the camp of Chief Chappo, he was shown all around the area and Chappo explained to him its many advantages over that of other camps. The houserock especially was of great interest; their supplies were all neatly stored under the rock, leaving just enough space for two beds. In one of them was a woman with a broken leg and the other a woman with a very young baby. The bed mattresses were bearskin robes and white buckskin. Nearly all the Indians were wearing buckskin suits. There were great stores of supplies under the rock and there was no smoke residue on the ceiling of the room; this was later caused by the white men camping there after the Indians had left. Tharp was shown the paintings on the rock and was asked to tell the tribe what they meant. Chappo had given orders that none of his people could touch them as they had probably been put there by some peoples before the time of his tribe and he hoped that someday some person would be able to tell him what they meant.[65]

Early the next morning, Tharp was awakened and given breakfast and supplied with food and a sort of knapsack made of a network of woven rope and straps whose fibers were made from milkweed. He found this device very handy as well as lightweight, but at the same time, it was very tough and able to carry a great weight.

After much ceremony, Tharp left with his guides and started up the Middle Fork, winding around *Hao-mou* [later named Moro Rock]; they entered a magnificent stand of virgin timber. It was then that the Indian guides led him to an unforgettable sight. One can well imagine the awe with which Tharp gazed upon the great red-barked trees that towered above him, some as high as 300 feet. The Indians called these forest monarchs *metati-tus-pungis*, which were later to be named after a Cherokee Indian called Se-quo-yah, or Sequoia. Continuing their journey, they came upon a meadow through which ran a little brook. The entire clearing was bordered with the stately red trees and there he found abundant feed and water for

---

65   Tharp in *History of Tulare County*, by Small, pp 272-273.

his stock. Numerous deer and bear paid them no more attention other than simple curiosity.

Later during another trip around the meadow, the group came upon a massive fallen Sequoia log. Due the burning of its interior in the past, the log was completely hollow and open at both ends. It measured some 56 feet in length and the diameter was large enough to allow them to walk upright inside for at least half its length, where it began to taper to a height of four feet at the rear. Taking his knife, which the Indians greatly admired, Tharp carved, "H. D. Tharp, 1858" on the outside of the log. This was to become his summer home for all the years he grazed his stock in these meadows.

Tharp made his second trip of exploration into the big tree region in the summer of 1860; on this trip he took his friend John Swanson. In the course of their journey, Swanson had one of his legs badly injured; it became so swollen that he could not walk for the pain. Tharp moved him to Hospital Rock where the Indians took care of him. They bound his leg with hot compresses of crushed, green Jimson leaves and bear fat, which soon relieved the swelling; by the third day, he was able to return home with Tharp.

In the spring of 1861, a few other settlers had come to the Three Rivers country and Tharp decided it was time for him to begin occupying the high Sierra meadows in order to hold them for his stock. So that summer he drove some horses up to Log Meadow, where he left them all summer; John Swanson, accompanied this time by Tharp's young stepson George, helped to drive them in. According to Tharp, the day after they arrived there, they all went over and climbed Moro Rock. They came back by way of Alta Meadows and the Middle Fork, seeing hundreds of deer, grouse, quail and a few bear on their trip as well as six of the mountain gray wolves.[66]

During this time, other settlers came into the area, thereby extending the wagon road begun by Tharp from the foothills up into the Three Rivers district. There seemed to be no question but that the territory of the Yokuts was now doomed, since the whites were slowly but surely usurping their primitive country with roads, trails, and settlements.

---

66   First Ascent of Moro Rock, *SNP Nature News bulletin*, by Walter Fry.

Tharp continued on at his homestead and taking his stock—cattle and horses—into the high mountain meadows of Sequoia from 1861 to 1890, when the Giant Forest became a national park. Various members of his family would go there every year as well to take care of his stock.

In 1954, the late Bill Swanson, step-grandson of Hale Tharp, gave a lengthy interview and in it he told a lot about the character of Hale Tharp. He said:

> Grandad was a very sociable fellow; always telling folks to put their team in the barn and stay all night, whenever they happened to show up. He liked to play a little poker and have the neighbors in for square dancing in the winter when there wasn't much work to do. The women would bring baskets of food and put the children to sleep in the bedroom. Then everybody would dance until 4 or 5 in the morning. Old Jason Barton did the calling and Daddy Finch played the fiddle.[67]

Tharp, though extremely generous with any neighbor who might be in trouble, had a frontiersman's impatience with those he thought might be trying to pull a fast trick. One day a local man dropped in to the home of Tharp's daughter, Fanny Mehrten, while the menfolk were away. The visitor began trying to convert Fanny to socialism and he waxed so eloquently that Fanny became alarmed and asked him to leave. He refused and Fanny called for help; Hale came running with his eight-inch knife drawn from its scabbard. Needless to say, the visitor left at once.

And how did Tharp react when the establishment of Sequoia National Park effectively put him out of business? According to Bill Swanson:

> Granddad was never one to cry about his troubles. He stuck it out, farmed his place as best he could . . . but his heart was in the cattle business. He managed to stay on his home place as an independent farmer until his death in 1912. He was 83 years old

---

67   *Fresno Bee*, October 3, 1954.

when he died and he hadn't more than three gray hairs on his head.

Hale Tharp is buried in the Hamilton Cemetery next to his wife, Chloe Ann. The late Judge Fry summed up the character of Hale Dixon Tharp this way: "Owing to his truthfulness and honor, Tharp was a man who was honored and liked by all who knew him." Apparently, he shared some of the strength and ruggedness of the great trees among which he spent so many days of his life.[68]

✶ ✶ ✶ ✶ ✶

Hale's good friend and relative, John Henry Swanson, was born April 12, 1812, the son of John Swanson. His brother was Edward Swanson, Sr., the father of Chloe Ann Swanson Tharp's first husband. John married Hannah Sherman Swanson, August 27, 1835 in Putnam County, Illinois; they had eleven children, five of them came to California on the wagon train. Evidently John Swanson previously had been to California in the gold fields and had returned to his home in Indiana where he assembled the family wagon train to come back west to the Golden State. This was the wagon train that included Hale Tharp as well as Chloe Ann Swanson.

John Swanson accompanied Hale Tharp on many of his adventures and trips of exploration. He climbed Moro Rock with Tharp and George Swanson, John's nephew; he was injured and healed by the Indians at Hospital Rock. John Swanson remained in the Three Rivers area until his death on August 12, 1863. His wife Hannah Swanson passed away May 5, 1877. Six of John and Hannah's surviving adult children became prominent citizens in Tulare County.

✶ ✶ ✶ ✶ ✶

George Wallace Swanson, Chloe Ann's youngest son and Hale Tharp's stepson, was born April 10, 1850. He married Rachel Fancher April 10, 1873 in Los Angeles. Their children were William [Bill], born 1875, Elizabeth and Ida. George and Rachel were divorced in 1885, and he

---

68   Ibid.

married Mary Sherman who died in 1920. There is no record of any children born to this marriage. George Swanson died July 24, 1924.

Charles Alexander, Jim Purington, George Swanson, Billy Austin, Henry Alles and Jackadog; picture taken about 1890. *Photo from Author's Collection.*

George Swanson's son William, or Bill as he was known, was born in 1875 and lived in Three Rivers all of his life. Like his step-grandfather, Hale D. Tharp, Bill was a cattle rancher. In an interview done some years before his death, he said he had been born in the old Tharp cabin and lived there until he was twenty years old. He had made his first trip into the Giant Forest when he was four years old, riding on the back of his mother's saddle. Then every summer, as soon as school was out, he would drive stray cattle from Hospital Rock on up the steep Middle Fork trail to Crescent Meadow where Tharp had his redwood log cabin.[69]

Bill had a varied and colorful life, which saw him doing work as a teamster, a cowboy, a deputy sheriff, a packer and a guide in the forest. He drove a stagecoach from Three Rivers to Mineral King up the old road.

69   *Fresno Bee*, April 18, 1961.

Bill told that it took four big mules to pull the stage for 25 miles. He made three round trips a week between the two points. Bill married Carrie Clara Topping; however, they had no children. Carrie Swanson was very interested in local history and wrote many articles about her family and others in Three Rivers. She passed away in 1952.

Bill Swanson was an honorary member of the Three Rivers Lions Club, an honorary deputy sheriff, and a member of the Three Rivers Chamber of Commerce. He passed away April 18, 1961. This writer can remember Bill sitting at the end of the counter at the old Noisy Water Restaurant, always wanting someone to play cribbage with him. At that time, she was just too busy doing the things that teenagers do; now she wishes she had stopped and challenged him to a game or two.

Bill Swanson, Stage Driver, Mineral King Road. *Photo from Author's Collection.*

The Clough Family

The first member of the Clough Family to impact Three Rivers did not ever live here; however, his children and subsequent generations settled and made their homes here and in the nearby Sierra.

His name was Orson Clough, the son of Benjamin and Lydia Clough. Orson was born in New York State in 1828. Orson and his wife Julia Marsh Clough lived in Hamburg, Erie County, New York in 1850.[70] Evidently, they made their way to California since Orson later gave his occupation as a mining engineer.[71] Orson and Julia must have divorced, since in 1860 Julia married Ira Blossom. Orson is shown on the 1870 Census as living with a possible cousin, Abner in Volcano, Amador County, California and later he married Jenna Herbert and remained in the Amador County area until his death in 1897.[72]

Orson Clough. *Photo courtesy of Ancestry.com*

The children of Orson and Julia were William O. (Bill) Clough, Fred Clough, Ida Clough and Evelyn Clough; they came to California with Julia Clough and her husband Ira Blossom where they homesteaded and raised their family.

---

70   1850 U. S. Census, Erie County, NY
71   1880 U. S. Census, Amador County, CA
72   www.ancestry.com

William O. (Bill) Clough

Bill was the son of Orson and Julia Marsh Clough. Bill never married; according to the late Joe Doctor, he was a good teamster and an accomplished mountaineer. A committed bachelor, he lived the majority of his life in the mountains, specifically Mineral King, during the heyday of the mining boom there.

His many eccentricities were legend; he believed that if he didn't cut his hair or his beard he would live indefinitely. This was a belief similar to the religious order of the House of David. He was deeply religious and never hesitated to spread the Gospel to those both willing and unwilling to listen. Teamsters hauling freight to Mineral King and to the mines up the old Mineral King Road often camped together and Bill frequently entertained them with his preaching of the Bible as he interpreted it to be.

He was often the butt of cruel jokes; one time, he was standing in his wagon delivering a sermon and some jokester slipped off the brake. As the wagon started to coast downhill, Bill managed to get to the brake in time to avoid disaster. Another time, someone set his coattails on fire during his sermon, but he managed to shed the garment before any harm was done to his person and finished his sermon in grand style.

According to the late Dan Alles, Bill could not be bluffed either. For instance, at one time, Professor W. F. Dean tried to put Bill out of a cabin in Mineral King. Bill just sat down in a chair and told Dean not to bother him. Dean then went on his way and did not disturb Clough, as Bill said he was reading his Bible and did not wish to be disturbed.

Bill was not easily provoked, but once riled up, he was a man to leave alone. On one occasion, someone by the name of Red Phillips called him a vile name; Bill just hauled off and knocked him flat on his back and then walked away. When he discussed the matter later, he said he was not mad but just wanted to teach Phillips a lesson.

Bill and his friends had many mining claims in Mineral King; among them the "Annie Fox," "Lady Franklin" and others. For many years, he continued working his claims and those of others. Later he made an agreement with the Edison Company to close the valves on the storage lakes in Mineral King since he was always the last man to leave the valley. In the late fall of 1917, he failed to show up in Three Rivers; a nephew, Ike Putman, and friends Don Maxon and Dan Alles went in to try to find him. No matter how hard they looked, he was nowhere to be found; however, they were able to find his diary that stated he had closed the Eagle Lake valve on November 2, but that was the last entry in the diary. By that time, the snow was too deep and the search party gave up and came home. The next spring, another search party found a shirt, some bones and even his shoes, but not enough to determine the cause of his death.

According to Dan Alles, "Bill Clough was a great, dominating man with a great character. He had many peculiar ways, but he was always willing to help his fellow man and would go a long way to do a kind deed. If ever a man deserved a place in the great beyond—Heaven—it is Bill Clough."[73] And Joe Doctor concluded his thoughts with "There are those of us who believe that someday on a wild Sierra trail you may encounter an elderly gentleman—and that he was—with flying long hair and beard, keeping the trust that if he didn't cut his hair, he would live forever. I hope so."[74]

William (Bill) Clough. *Photo courtesy of the Three Rivers Museum.*

---

73   Manuscript of Dan Alles
74   *Exeter Sun*, January 25, 1995.

Ida May Clough

Ida May Clough was born December 29, 1854 in California; she came to Three Rivers as a young girl with her two brothers, William [Bill] and Fred and one younger sister, Evelyn. Ida's first husband was C. E. Bryant; after 1877, she married Joseph Fletcher Putman and following that marriage she married a Mr. Peters. Her children were Clarence Edwin "Ed" Bryant, Allace Eli Bryant (who married Ernest Britten, first Park Ranger; they later divorced), and Maud Bryant. Ida May passed away February 6, 1932 in Downey, California in the home of her daughter, Maud.

Evelyn (Eva) Clough

Evelyn was the youngest daughter of Orson Clough and Julia Marsh Clough; she was born ca. 1860 in California. As an infant, she came to Three Rivers with her mother, Julia and stepfather Ira Blossom in company with her two older brothers and older sister Ida May. When she was sixteen, she married George Cahoon. Their children were Daisy, George and Jim Cahoon. After Mr. Cahoon was murdered by gunshot, she married Daniel Busby January 16, 1888.[75] Evelyn and Daniel's children were: Pansy, Zinnia, Rose, Violet and Forest Busby. She subsequently married John Menteer June 30, 1900; George Joseph Long, April 28, 1903 and then Delbert "Huck" Dillon. Her date of death is not known, and her burial place remains unknown as well.

---

75   Tulare County Marriage Records.

Evelyn Clough. *Photo courtesy of the Three Rivers Museum.*

The Blossom Family

Ira Blossom was one of the earliest settlers in Three Rivers. He was born in 1832 in New York State, the oldest son of Allen and Elizabeth Blossom. When he was twenty years of age, he sought his fortune in California, and for a time he stayed in San Francisco. From there he traveled further east, going to Stockton and worked there for one year.

He had a close friend and companion by the name of Joe Palmer. They had hunted together several years earlier in the Three Rivers area, and were impressed by the plentiful game and the abundance of water and good soil, causing them to believe it would be a good place for a family to settle down.

Blossom continued to live in the Stockton area for six more years and in 1860, he married Mrs. Julia Clough, who had been previously married to Orson Clough. Ira and Julia moved to Tulare County with Julia's children, William O. [Bill], Fred, Ida and Evelyn. Although they made their home on the South Fork, for a time Ira traveled to Visalia to work in a flour mill in order to supplement their living.

Julia Clough Blossom. *Photo from Author's Collection.*

According to the late Muriel Kenwood (Julia's great-granddaughter), Ira Blossom settled in Three Rivers with his family sometime between 1858-1861. Accompanying him was his wife Julia [Marsh or Marschellaux] Clough Blossom and her four children by her prior marriage. The Blossoms had four more children of their own: Charles F., Anna, and twins Emma and Lottie; however, Lottie died at the age of nine. The Blossoms built their home on property just west of the Missionary Baptist Church on Blossom Drive; here they farmed 135 acres, part of it in fruit but most of the remainder in grain. In addition, Ira raised cattle and hogs and was considered to be very successful in his endeavors.

Annie Blossom. *Photo from Author's Collection.*

The late Frankie Welch said that Julia Blossom "tamed" the local Indians who were afraid of her. When she offered them a cup of coffee, they would run and hide. Then she would set the cup on a stump and go back inside until finally, their fear overcome, they would approach closer and taste it.[76]

---

76   Notes of Frankie Luella Welch.

During his later years, in 1904-1916, Ira took the contract to drive the stage, carrying the mail from Three Rivers to Hammond. He finally sold out to William Swanson; Ira was 86 at the time and his family was afraid that the winters would be too severe for him to continue. In 1918, Ira and Julia moved to San Francisco to live with their daughter Emma, who was married to Christian Buttman. They continued to live there until their death, Julia dying in 1922, age 88 and Ira in 1924, at age 92.

Ira and Julia Blossom. *Photo from Author's Collection.*

Ira Blossom was a friend to many in the Three Rivers community who counted him as a valued friend and neighbor.[77] He never hesitated to help his neighbors or anyone in trouble. He was regarded as one of the old reliable ranchers of his district, being honored by the people of Tulare County as one of their few remaining pioneers.

Charles F. Blossom

Charles F. Blossom, son of Ira and Julia Blossom, was among the first Park rangers for Sequoia National Park. His wife was Minerva Belle (Gilstrap) Blossom and their children were Charles, Nora and May. Charles F. Blossom was tragically killed in an auto accident April 22, 1916 in Farmersville, California, and his wife and baby were severely injured. Evidently this happened when his car overturned.[78]

Charles' wife Minerva passed away in June 1961; at that time, her son Charles was living in Fresno, daughter Nora [Lowman] was living in Sebastopol and other daughter May [Knisley] in Fresno.

---

77   *Menefee's History of Tulare & Kings Counties*, California, 1913, pg 628-629.
78   *Oakland Tribune*, April 23, 1916.

Joe Palmer - Hunter, Frontiersman and Pioneer

Very little is known about Joseph Clifton Palmer, an interesting early resident of Three Rivers. He was born about 1836 in the State of Maryland. His parents were Samuel and Susan Palmer. He had an older brother, Benjamin, three younger sisters and a younger brother. In the United States Census of 1850, he was living with his family in Anderson, Texas; by 1870, he was living in Three Rivers, next to Ira Blossom's homestead.

Ira Blossom and Joe Palmer evidently were close friends and they had hunted and trapped in the Three Rivers area during the mid-1850s, finding it a good place to settle. There is no record of any marriage for Joe Palmer. Physical descriptions of him tell that he stood six feet, eight inches tall; he always carried his rifle and he knew how to use it. Joe Palmer told the following story to Walter Fry, who recorded the incident:

It was during the month of November 1865, while asleep in my cabin on the South Fork of the Kaweah River, that I was suddenly awakened by the loud squealing of my hog in a log pen that stood fifty feet away. The night was quite dark, but nevertheless I grabbed my single shot rifle, dashed out in my night clothes and jumped over into the pen. Just then I saw a large, dark animal reared up in front of me with the hog in its mouth, and attempting to climb out of the pen, which was about six feet in height. I jumped forward, jabbed the muzzle of my rifle against the animal and fired. The shot broke the animal's back a little behind its shoulders, and it fell over backwards against me with such force as to cause me to fall, and the bawling bear and squalling hog were almost on top of me. Never in my life was I so badly scared. After gaining my feet I cleared that log crib fence in one jump, ran to my cabin, where I remained the rest of the night, but further sleep for me was impossible.

On going out the next morning, I was greatly surprised to find that it was a grizzly bear that I had killed. It was a male animal and weighed 967 pounds, actual weight. The hog the bear had killed I used for food, and I kept the bear's pelt for many years thereafter as a gentle reminder of that exciting night.[79]

During the great flood and avalanche of 1867 on the upper South Fork, Ira Blossom was in Visalia working; Joe heard the avalanche and hiked up the canyon, finding the huge dam that was blocking the South Fork. Hurrying back to the Blossom home, he took Mrs. Blossom and her children up to the hillside just as the dam gave way and the flood swept down the canyon.

Joe Palmer loved flowers; he surrounded his cabin with flowers of all kinds and named his place "Rosebud." In the middle of his lily pond was a rare flower which he offered to give any woman who would pick it. One daring pioneer lady took off her shoes and stockings, and boldly though blushingly, lifted her skirts and waded in for the prize.[80]

In one of Joe Doctor's columns, he mentions Joe Palmer as being one of the guides for the Rev. F. H. Wales, who led a scientific expedition into the mountains, following the Hockett Trail to Trout Meadows. Palmer told Wales that he had been camped on the Kern River in 1868 when the avalanche that formed the Kern Lakes occurred. Palmer described the terrific crash as causing him to think the "day of judgement" might be at hand, as the avalanche filled the lake area with all kinds of debris. Palmer's account refutes the belief held by many old timers that the lakes were created by the great Owens Valley earthquake of 1872.[81]

California voter registration records show Joe Palmer living in the Three Rivers area as late as 1896; however, he must have left soon after and moved to Visalia. In 1900, he is registered as a "boarder" at the home of Mr. and Mrs. Christian Buttman. The wife, Emma Buttman, was the youngest daughter of Ira and Julia Blossom.

---

79   *History of Tulare County*, Kathleen Small, pg.276.
80   From Frankie Welch's notes.
81   *Woodlake Echo*, February 9, 1994.

In 1910 and 1920, Joseph Palmer was living in the National Military Home in Malibu, California, where evidently he spent his last days; by 1920, he was age 84.[82] And that is the last record the author can find of his life. Rest In Peace, Joe Palmer; you were a colorful part of Three Rivers history.

Only photo known to exist of Joseph C. Palmer. *Photo from Author's Collection.*

The Lovelace Family - Three Generations

John W. Lovelace and his wife Arminta (Stallard) were the parents of the Three Rivers branch of the Lovelace family. They were from North Carolina and Tennessee, respectively. John Lovelace and his family of four boys came from Texas to California as members of an ox-team train that included 75 wagons; the journey took six months to complete. The family stopped at Bakersfield in 1861 where Mr. Lovelace built a small cabin that was swept away by flood waters the following winter. He moved his family to El Monte and from there to Tulare County in 1863. John Lovelace engaged in merchandising at Farmersville, where he bought the store of Crowley and Jasper and formed a partnership with T. J. Brundage. In addition, he purchased a cattle ranch in Three Rivers in 1869 on which he made many improvements.

In an oral interview, Ellen Hill, the granddaughter of Joseph W. Lovelace said:

> . . . the first trail that was built into Mineral King, or what is Mineral King now, was built in 1871 by John Lovelace, his sons and his brother Tom Lovelace. The year earlier, they had constructed the trail into the Milk Ranch; then later that summer, they completed the trail into Mineral King.

Ellen quoted from an early manuscript of the family history, saying:

> While we were still building the trail, T. J. Brundage of Farmersville and his wife came up to our camp at Mineral King; his wife was thus the first white woman there. John Crowley and wife and their son came up some six weeks later.

She continued,

> Four prospectors from Nevada came through Mineral King and out over our trail. They were the only people seen there in 1871 and it has been recorded that Harry O'Farrell had a cabin in Mineral King. There was no cabin in Mineral King before the mines were found by O'Farrell or anyone else. I was over every foot of it in 1871, a year before the mines were found.
>
> In 1872, we drove some three hundred head of cattle into Mineral King.
>
> During the summer the mines were discovered by Belden and the Crabtrees, Jim and John. That fall a local company with John Meadows, foreman, started work on a wagon road. The road began at our ranch [Hammond] and went over the summit above Red Hill, some four miles of road. There was a toll trail up the south side of the East Fork above just opposite Cold Springs where they bridged and crossed the East Fork, then up to Lookout Point. From there, it ran below and parallel to the road that is there now.
>
> The road went to Timber Point where the trail hit the pinery on to where Atwell Mill is now. They connected with the Lovelace Trail from there to Mineral King, and followed the old Lovelace Trail.[83]

John W. Lovelace eventually returned to Texas, where he died in 1875.[84]

The children of John W. and Arminta Lovelace were Martin F., Charles P., Willis R., and Joseph W. Lovelace. Joseph was very young when his father brought the family to Tulare County. He remained in the area and finished his schooling in Visalia. For twelve years, he was engaged in cattle raising on the ranch in Three Rivers; however, in 1900 he moved into Visalia to give

83   Ellen Hill oral history, July 16, 1994.
84   *Menefee's History*, pp 631-632.

his children access to better education. Joseph married Helen Schlichting, a native of Wisconsin. They had the following children: Byron O. Lovelace, who became County Surveyor of Tulare County; Nathaniel Lovelace, who was the engineer for the Oak Grove bridge on the East Fork as well as the Pumpkin Hollow bridge on the main river. The other sons were Clay (or "Doby") Lovelace; Walter (Shorty) Lovelace and Lee Lovelace.

Joseph W. Lovelace remained in Visalia and died February 14, 1931 at the age of 72. His son Nathan Franklin "Nate" Lovelace married Viola Wilson; he was killed while building the road to Mt. Lassen. Clay "Doby" Lovelace was a druggist in Visalia; Walter "Shorty" Lovelace was the famous fur trapper of the Sierra. More or less a hermit, he spent his winters running his trap lines from October to May, traversing the length of the Sierra back country from Johnsondale in the south and then north through Sequoia National Park along the Upper Kern River into the Kings, and as far north as the south fork of the San Joaquin River.

Shorty's Cabin at Granite Basin. *Photo from Google search.*

He traveled by short ski and snowshoes, baiting and setting traps, and harvesting pelts. He built 20 or more lean-tos or primitive cabins in hidden, sheltered places, all of which were provisioned with canned food, blankets, reading material and his pelt stashes. He never changed clothes all winter; he would come out of the mountains in the spring and take his furs to San Francisco to be sold. In a good year, he could earn about $5,000. Although he would then proceed to spend some of it getting totally drunk and staying that way for days, he always put enough aside for provisions to last through the coming winter.

Each of his cabins were a day's trek apart. Experience taught him just where to locate each overnight resting place, based on the number of traps he had to check, and the difficulty of the terrain and snow conditions. He built his cabins away from the main trails and in places unlikely that animals would visit. He marked his cabins by hanging a short piece of rope from a high branch directly over his lean-to door. By positioning himself directly under this marker, he could dig down through the snow until he reached the door [which was always constructed to open inward].

In March 1940, Kings Canyon National Park was created by an act of Congress. Shorty was notified that trapping was no longer allowed. He took his traplines north and built more cabins, continuing to trap into the 1950s, living the life of a mountain man in a more modern time. In 1961, he visited for the last time one of his old camps in Roaring River. Shorty died two years later on November 25, 1963 and is buried in the Visalia Cemetery next to his brothers Byron and Lee.

The Homer Family

A long time ago, John Orth, a surveyor for the General Land Office, sat on an old log at Big Oak Flat and gazed with a speculative eye at the Sierra, silhouetted against the eastern horizon. "See that mountain?" he said to Joseph Homer, pointing to a peak at some six thousand feet above them. "That looks like your nose; I'm going to mark it on my map as Homer's Nose;" and it has been so named since 1868.[85]

The Homer family's pioneer settler who came to the Three Rivers district was Joseph William Homer. He was born February 4, 1825 in Dudley, Worcester, England. His parents were Richard Homer, born 1790 also in England; his mother was Rachel Bridgewater Homer, born 1794. Records show that all of the family was born in the same Dudley township in England.

In November 1831, Richard, Rachel and son Joseph sailed from Liverpool, England on the ship *Ajax* and landed in New York. They settled in Indiana and when father Richard died, Joseph William Homer went down the Ohio river and enlisted for service in the United States Army to serve for a while in the Mexican war. Returning to Indiana later, he met Colonel John C. Fremont and came west with him during the 1846 period of the Bear Flag Revolt, just before California became a state. According to the late Joe Doctor, Homer was among those present when General Vallejo, the Mexican governor, was captured; in addition, Homer was among the group who voted in the historic local election held under the "Charter" oak tree to make Tulare a county.

In 1848, Joe Homer returned to his old home in Indiana, riding horseback over the Oregon-California Trail but he was not content to stay there; instead, two years later, he rejoined Colonel Fremont on his Las Mariposas ranch and mined for gold at Bear Creek near Mariposa. Joseph Homer married Martha Mae Balaam April 12, 1860; she was the daughter of an established pioneer family in Tulare County. The Balaams had come

---

85   *Silver City History*, by Keesey, Gladieux & Merrill, 2009, pg.68.

to California in 1852 from Texas and settled about three miles south of Farmersville. Martha had walked all the way from Texas to California.

Joseph William Homer. *Photo from Ancestry.com.*

Joe and Martha Homer's children were Emily Josephine; Rachel Katherine, Sarah Ellen, and Truman John. Martha and Joe lived on their homestead near Farmersville until the mosquitos and the fear of malaria drove the family to move to Big Oak Flat. The last three children born were Edward Bridgewater, Thomas William, and Anne Mae Homer.

Joe Homer died in 1880, and was buried in the Deep Creek Cemetery; the family moved down closer to Three Rivers where his widow Martha operated a place for travelers on the road to Three Rivers and Mineral King to buy meals. It was on the property later owned by Legrand Ellis near Slick Rock.

While the family lived at Big Oak Flat, the children's schooling there was under the tutelage of Professor W. F. Dean; he instilled in them his love of nature and gave them a zest for learning.

Young Edward, especially, was bitten by the education bug and he continued his schooling, living with his older sister Kate, who had married and was living in Arroyo Grande; he finished his courses there at a nearby

Normal School. Edward taught his first two terms at the Cinnamon School on the South Fork. The next two terms were taught at Sulphur Springs School and then at the Antelope School [Woodlake]. He taught at other locations throughout the valley but always seemed to return to the Woodlake and Three Rivers areas.

Edward Homer married Annie Swank in 1899 at the Swank home near Twin Buttes. They made their home in the Paloma District; they had five daughters: Marjorie, Helen, Genevieve, Ione and Dorothy. Edward's wife Annie passed away 1931 and Edward married Bertha May Alexander. Later, they sold the ranch and moved to Visalia; Edward Homer passed away 1956.

Joseph's son Tom Homer gave a lengthy interview to Joe Doctor in years past and he told about their life in Big Oak Flat; going to school there, and also about the terrible drought of 1864, when thousands of head of cattle died of starvation on the plains of the San Joaquin Valley. He said that many mired in the mud in their frantic effort to get to water. Tom said that his father, Joe, gathered up a few head of cattle that survived around the water hole and took them to Big Oak Flat to the homestead. Tom said that their only neighbors there were lions, bears and a few "jackass tramps" who stayed in the hills and raised horses for the state lines.[86]

A cattleman all his life, Tom Homer recalled the so-called "Spanish cattle," the rough-looking rawboned beef animals his father raised. "[T]hey could travel 20 or 30 miles a day with no trouble," Homer recalled. "[T]hey were more than a match for lions and other predators."

Tom also told about the famous fight between Tom Fowler, the cattle baron who lost his fortune at Mineral King, and Philo St. Johns, for whom, according to Mr. Homer, the St. Johns River was named. Evidently these two men quarreled over cattle range and decided to fight it out at Bravo Lake. At each good blow delivered by the combatants, the vaqueros watching would shout "Bravo, Bravo!" Mr. Fowler was of Irish heritage and

86   *Woodlake Echo*, April 8, 1992.

quick to fight, but he lost to St. Johns because Mr. Fowler was the smaller of the two.[87]

Tom's widowed mother, Martha, moved to Dry Creek, completed the provisions of the Homestead Act of 1862 or "proved up" on her ranch; however, when she discovered that no money could be made in raising cattle, she moved to Arroyo Grande, where she died in 1887.

Tom said he grew homesick for Three Rivers country, saddled up his horse, and rode 154 miles across country without stopping to sleep, going by way of Santa Marguerita, Creston, Shandon, Cholame Valley, Cotton Pass and Stratford.

He married Tillie Mehrten in 1901 at the Presbyterian church in Visalia. They lived for a time in Lemon Cove before moving to their home on Dry Creek. Their children were Edward and Forrest. Tom and Tillie Homer lived on their Dry Creek ranch the rest of their lives. Tillie died in 1956 and Tom in 1958; they are both buried in the Hamilton Cemetery, south of Woodlake.

The other son of the pioneer James Homer was Truman Homer (or "Tru" as he was known); he married Alice Rice in 1903 in Merced. Tom and Truman Homer together bought the Hambright place adjoining their mother's property on Dry Creek and continued to raise cattle in that area. Truman and Alice had one son, Caryl and when Truman passed away 1949, Alice and Caryl continued to live on Dry Creek near Tom and Tillie Homer for many years.

---

87   Ibid.

1870s

The Lovern/Loverin Family

Wesley Norton Lovern was the pioneer member of the Lovern/ Loverin family to settle in Three Rivers. Wesley was born May 8, 1846 in Keg Creek, Macon County, Iowa to Mormon parents John and Lucinda Lovern (later changed to Loverin). The family was headed west to California and reached Salt Lake City too late in the fall, so they were forced to stay there for the winter. The following spring, they found that their team of oxen had disappeared, and they were unable to continue their travel west. Fearing that their goal of California was not to be won, and realizing that he was ill, the father, John Lovern, sent his son Wesley, nine years old at the time, on to California with another wagon train. This was in the company of a family by the name of Cole.[88]

Wesley Norton Lovern came to Stockton, California with the Coles and he was eventually employed by a Mr. Stokes.[89]

Eventually he came to the Visalia area as early as 1867 at the age of 21.[90]

---

88   Oral interview with Ord Loverin by Barry Bartlett, August, 1973.
89   Ibid.
90   Califorrnia Voter Registration, 1867.

Wesley became acquainted with Tom Homer (son of Joseph Homer) on Dry Creek, and Chris Evans; the three of them raised hogs on the Homer Ranch property north of the Kaweah River.

John Lovern. *Photo courtesy Ancestry.com*

Wesley met Mary Alice Canfield in Visalia, and they were married at Cottonwood Creek December 25, 1873. She had been born in 1854 in Utah Territory, the daughter of Cyrus and Laura Canfield. Wesley and Mary took up a homestead in Eshom Valley where four of their children were born: Laura, Orlen [Ord], Mary and John. When a diphtheria epidemic came through Eshom Valley, two of the Lovern children died within four days of each other, and were buried in the Eshom Valley Cemetery. Ord and his older sister Laura survived the illness. According to Ord, his mother Mary was so distraught by the deaths of her two children that she told her husband that she would no longer live in the mountains and that he had to move them down to the valley as soon as possible.

So Wesley moved his family to an area outside of Exeter where he purchased 160 acres for $180 at the foot of Rocky Hill. In addition to farming on his ranch, he also worked at Quail Flat for the Razzle-Dazzle Mill and other mills, cutting and hauling lumber in order to supplement his family income.

Wesley Lovern and Family, Daughter Laura, Wesley holding Baby Naomi, Mary Alice and Orlen (Ord). *Photo from Author's Collection.*

But even more bad luck followed the family, for on July 8, 1886, Wesley Lovern was in Visalia buying supplies when he was the victim of an unprovoked shooting. His assailant shot him in the chest and at the time, it was thought to be a fatal wound. After many days of suffering from the wound, he survived; however, the doctor was not able to remove the bullet lodged in his lung, so he carried the reminder of this attack the rest of his life.[91]

Eventually, Wesley had an offer to sell their Rocky Hill ranch for $3,000; he took the offer and the family moved to Three Rivers in 1895, homesteading on the North Fork in the area of what is now Sequoia RV Ranch. By that time, the family consisted of daughter Laura, Orlen W., Naomi, Cyrus E., Benjamin and baby Ira, who was born in 1896.

Son Orlen (always known as Ord), attended school at Sulphur Springs until the eighth grade. Since there were no further grades available in Three Rivers, he went to Exeter High School, where he finished the ninth grade. Then Ord decided that he had enough schooling and wanted to start being a cowboy and earning some money for his family.

Ord later said in an interview that his happiest times were when the family lived on the North Fork. His mother would tell him what she wanted to fix for dinner that day and since he was a crack shot, he would take his single shot .22 rifle and bring her whatever game she desired – whether it be quail, cottontail, or venison. He said they always had deer meat in the colder months and sometimes even a wild hog. He learned to swim in the river and dive down into the deep holes, catching some unsuspecting trout to supplement their meals. When asked what the average pioneer life was like at that time, he said first of all that every family had a garden where they grew their vegetables, a flock of chickens for fresh eggs and meat, and a milk cow. Almost every day at mealtime, they would have potatoes and gravy – what they called "poverty sop."[92]

Sometime before 1900, Wesley Lovern relinquished the homestead on the North Fork to Sam Halstead and moved his family to Lucerne, California [Kings County]; then they moved again to Farmersville. In 1904, Wesley died suddenly, evidently from the old bullet wound to his chest that had occurred in the shooting years earlier. Mary was left to raise and support the family alone. At this time in his life, Ord was the oldest boy in the family and he took his responsibilities very seriously. Since he had already left school, he felt it was his turn to support his mother and younger brothers and sisters.

He began work hauling hay for a Mr. Montgomery north of Hanford. In 1903, at 17 years old, he was one of Broder and Hopping's packers for the Sierra Club's famous High Sierra trip from Mineral King to Mr. Whitney and back through Giant Forest. In addition, he hauled lumber from Atwell Mill for construction of the flume to Kaweah Power House No.1 and in 1904-1905, he packed construction material in by mule trains to the dams on the lakes above Mineral King. In 1905, he

---

92   Oral interview, by Barry Bartlett, August 1973.

was packing stock for a surveying party in the High Sierra; he told that he had earned $300-$400 for this trip and gave all of it to his mother.[93]

Later in 1905, Ord was working for the Sanger Lumber company, hauling supplies for the lumber camp at Millwood below Lake Sequoia, over the torturous road to the logging operation near Hume Lake.

It was during this time that he received a letter from a friend and fellow teamster, Bert Belknap. Bert was inviting him to come to Johannesburg (outside Death Valley) and work as a swamper or assistant for a freighting company where Belknap was working. "It sounded interesting and the pay was $150 a month, far better than the $1.15 per day I made with the lumber company," Ord said.[94]

So he met Bert at Johannesburg and went to work for George Coffey, hauling supplies from the rail head to the various mining areas. Their freighting rig consisted of 14 mules and two horses, the latter weighing up to 1,600 pounds each, heavy enough to swing the wagon tongue and easier for the teamster to ride than the sharp-spined mules.

Ord Loverin, teaming for Sanger Lumber Co. *Photo from Author's Collection.*

---

93   Oral interview on tape.
94   *Woodlake Echo*, May 28, 1986.

Ord was not just a swamper for long; as soon as Mr. Coffey learned about his talent with the teams, he promoted him to his own rig and gave him Pete Marks, a Cherokee Indian, as a swamper; according to Ord, he was the best man he could have had for the job.

Ord's team pulled three heavy freight wagons and a lighter trailer wagon that hauled the hay and grain for the animals, as well as the gear of the teamster and swamper. Water in that dry, desert country was hauled in 42-gallon wooden barrels; four under each wagon in leather slings and the remainder on running boards that were on either side of the wagons. The horses and mules in hot weather required about ten gallons of water each per day. And water was all important; a freighter with a deficient supply was in bad trouble. Extra barrels were left at various dry camps along the way for the return trip or to allow for emergencies. "It was an unwritten law that you didn't take another man's water," Ord said. "If you ran out, you wouldn't make it the next day."[95]

Ord believed that one reason men and animals were able to survive the punishing heat was because all the drinking water was warm. "We had no ice and there was no cold water anywhere in the desert; it was a good thing."[96]

In 1918, Ord married Maud Britten, daughter of Ernest Britten and Allace Bryant Britten of Three Rivers; Maud had been born in Three Rivers in 1896. Ord and Maud had three sons; Wesley, Orlen (nicknamed Bally) and Ellsworth (often called Bud or Friday). After many years Ord and Maud divorced, and Maud married Charles "Chuck" Wallace, a Park Service Ranger; Ord later married his second wife, Irma Sophronia Cole, December 24, 1960; she was the mother of this author.

Ord had his first concession to pack stock animals for groups of tourists in 1913; by the 1920s, Ord had purchased the Kings River Parks Company, adding to his herd of pack animals; eventually his string consisted of 80 head of stock. His headquarters were in Giant Forest, about one-half mile beyond the site of the old Giant Forest Village. In the spring, he would

95   Ibid.
96   *Echo* article.

move his herd of stock by horseback into the Park, using the Colony Mill Road. During the 1924-26 summer season, several silent movies were made in Three Rivers, and also in the park; the movie companies employed Ord, many of his friends, his horses and his pack stock.

Ord's packing trips were legendary month-long trips from Mineral King or Giant Forest to Yosemite and then returning with a new party; he soon acquired a large group of loyal clientele. However, financial conditions and governmental requirements as well as the looming Depression of 1929 forced him to end his operations. Then he was hired by Park Superintendent Colonel White to supply the trail crews working in the Park and he held this job for five years. During that time, he built drift fences to enclose stock animals from Camp Nelson, and across the horse pastures up to the Kern River. In addition, he strung telephone wire to many places, even as far as to Mt. Whitney. In 1933, Ord sold his Park interests completely; he moved his business to Three Rivers where he continued to handle several large parties every season. Many of his customers had remained loyal to him over the years, such as the Simpson Family from Marshall Field in Chicago, Fuller Brush executives, Eastman Kodak and others. It was during this time that he made many friends across the country. Some of these people formed what was called the "Soarsis Club"; among whose members were Maynard Munger, Ollie Jamison, Lloyd "Sandy" Weber, Dave Peckinpah, Leon S. Peters, George L. Mauger, J. Thomas Crowe, to name just a few.

When his son, Orlen (Bally) was killed in World War II, Ord seemed to lose his taste for the good life and wanted to spend time with his little grandson Gerald, who was Bally's only son. Gerald had been born shortly after his father went to war and they were never to meet. So in 1948, Ord started another venture; he opened the riding stables at Stony Creek for day rides only. Gerald learned from his grandfather to love the mountains and the horses and they had some wonderful years together. The riding stables kept Ord busy another 7-8 years and then he turned the business over to Gerald.

In his later years, Ord Loverin contented himself with cattle raising. He and his wife Irma lived at Oak Grove and every spring, with help from his friends and members of Irma's family, they would drive the cattle from the River Way Ranch that he had leased, ending up at the old Milk Ranch, where the cows and calves would spend the summer on the meadows there. This "cattle drive" would take about three or four days, using a pickup truck out in front of the herd with hay, a point rider on her horse and several more riders with herding dogs behind. After the first year, the cows knew instinctively where they were headed and became quite cooperative and even eager to reach the high meadows with little argument.

As late as 1970 at the age of 85, he was still riding his "Old Colt," a large sorrel gelding he had purchased from his old friend Hugh Hart. It was on this horse that he rode into the area where the Shepherd Fire of May 1970 was burning and drove 37 head of his cattle to safety. The night before, he had become concerned because the fire was racing out of control; he knew his cattle, which included a registered Angus bull, were in that area. So, by 6 a.m. the next morning he had trucked his horse and dog from his home at Oak Grove, down the 12 miles to the corrals at Washburn Cove where he saddled his 18-year-old horse, and whistled for "Homer," his cow dog. They went up the steep, rocky south slope of Shepherd's Peak and around to Pocket Canyon above and west of the River Way Ranch Headquarters (at the end of Dinely Drive).

Fighting the fire at that time was a crew of 299 men, as well as three air tankers and several bulldozers. "The tankers came within 300 feet of us," Loverin said. "And my horse didn't like it; in fact, he tried to flatten himself out on the ground when they roared over us." Ord finally got the cattle together; "I almost gave out and so did the dog before we got up to where the cattle were," he said. "So I got off and coaxed Homer to go up and bring them down. He made it, and "Colt" and I crossed the gulch, got about them and brought them out over the ridge, and let them go into the corrals, where we could load and truck them to safety. The flames were all around us most of the time."[97]

---

97   *The Fresno Bee,* May 27, 1970.

Ord Loverin on his 90th birthday. *Photo from Author's Collection.*

Ord and his wife Irma spent many happy years living at Oak Grove; their home was always open to friends and family who came to visit. Irma's cooking, especially her pies, was always offered and the coffee pot was always hot with cowboy coffee.

Ord passed away in a Visalia hospital February 21, 1976, after a bout with the flu and pneumonia. He had lived 90 years, all of it extremely full and interesting; much of his life still remains untold and hopefully, soon to be written. Ord's wife Irma passed away December 29, 1990; she is buried beside the love of her life, Ord Loverin, in the Three Rivers Cemetery.

The Grunigen Family

The Grunigens originally came from Switzerland; one family member had traveled quite a bit and when visiting the Three Rivers area, found Lake Canyon and wrote back to his family in Switzerland. The father, Johann Gotlieb von Grunigen and son John came here and established a homestead on the East Fork at Lake Canyon. Then they sent for the rest of the family; the mother, Elisa, son Armin and three girls, Freda, Elisa and a younger daughter [name unknown] who died later on the North Fork.

About 1870, at Lake Canyon, they built the two-story house that is still there today and established it as a way station on the Mineral King Road to and from the mines. When the mining boom ended, the hospitable station was kept open because of the tourist traffic that braved the old Mineral King Road and the dreaded River Hill to spend cool days in the summer in the Mineral King Valley. Once the tourists reached the Grunigen house, they could enjoy home-grown, home-cooked meals and rest for the night, completing their trek the next day.

Grunigen family at Lake Canyon, 1905: Herman, John, Armin, Arnold, front: Frieda, Eliza, and Eliza. (Louise, deceased)

Photo courtesy of the Three Rivers Museum.

Grunigen Homestead and Inn at Lake Canyon.
August 2, 1918

Photo courtesy of the Three Rivers Museum.

The driver for the Mineral King Stage was Armin Grunigen, a son of John, Sr. and Elisa. When the newer, paved road on the north side of the canyon was completed in 1913, the Grunigen home gradually ceased to operate as a stopover since the automobile could make the long trip in one day.

John Senior and Elisa's son John lived mostly in Kaweah, and in 1900 he helped construct the post office building there. The late Joe Doctor told in one of his articles that John Grunigen had a major part in the building of the flume that takes water out of the East Fork at Oak Grove down to the penstock for Kaweah No. 1:

> Grunigen was engaged largely in drilling blasting holes
> to clear the way for building the flume; he had good cause to

remember the hazards of working on the steep mountain cliffs, for he nearly lost his life on the job. He said that one day, one of the other powder men (Johnny Poe) was severely injured while standing on a narrow, unprotected ledge as a blast went off; Grunigen and other workers carried Johnny to camp and as Grunigen was traversing the ledge a short time later, he slipped on the rubble left by the blast and started sliding feet first down from the almost perpendicular slope.

Grunigen landed 80 feet below and was knocked unconscious. His fellow workers carried him back to camp and when he regained consciousness, he noted a terrible pain in his fingers. He discovered he had worn his fingertips halfway through the fingernails trying to check his slide down the cliff. And just to add another chill to his disagreeable experience, workmen who picked him up found under him the crushed body of a rattlesnake that Grunigen's body had landed on at the end of his fall.[98]

John Grunigen married Jessie Hopping in 1903; Jessie had been born in Kansas in March 1881. Her father was Oscar S. Hopping, mother Susia T. Hopping. John and Jessie had the following children: Dr. Forest John Grunigen, and Ethel Berrien (von)Grunigen. John and Jessie Hopping were divorced and he married Margaret Dewitt.[99]

John Grunigen. *Photo courtesy of the Three Rivers Museum.*

98   *Exeter Sun*, Sept 14, 1988.
99   Ancestry.com.

John Grunigen entered government service with Sequoia National Park in 1901 with the road construction crews working on the Colony Mill Road. He worked intermittently on the road and trail construction until June 29, 1901, when he became a permanent park ranger, advancing to the position of assistant chief park ranger prior to his resignation November 30, 1923. On June 1, 1927 he again was appointed to a position in the Park; he worked intermittently in such capacities as CCC foreman, project superintendent and trail construction foreman. From 1939 through June 19, 1954, he worked seasonally as a fire control aid from which position he retired. He received a service citation in 1955 for his record of 31 years of service to the Park.[100] John Grunigen passed away in Porterville, March 1972 at the age of 95.

John's younger brother, Armin, came to America when he was eleven years of age; he remained a resident of Three Rivers for 70 years. He drove the first stage to Mineral King in 1899. Purchasing his property in Three Rivers in 1908, he lived there for 70 years. Armin married Ethel Dillon in 1909; she was born in Delta, Colorado in 1887, the daughter of Robert F. Dillon and Lucinda "May" Purdy. Armin and Ethel's children were Neil and Frederick Grunigen. Armin's wife Ethel died before him in 1958.

When Armin was young, he built the first wooden stairway to the top of Moro Rock in the summer of 1919. Later, he would tell how the lumber for this project was hauled on mules to the base of the rock, then raised with ropes.

Armin was one of the original members of the old Three Rivers Board of Trade which later became the Chamber of Commerce; he remained an active member up into his old age. His home was the site of the formation of the original Valley Oak Credit Union, and he was a rural star route mail carrier from Exeter to Sequoia National Park from 1945 until he retired in 1957. He died February 6, 1964.

---

100   *The Fresno Bee*, February 15, 1955.

Armin & Ethel Grunigen. *Photo courtesy of the Three Rivers Museum.*

The Griffes Family in Three Rivers

The patriarch of this family was James Walter Griffes; he was born about 1835 in New York State. His first marriage was to Nellie Porter, and they had one child, Annette; the marriage ended in divorce. He then married Eliza Fralick July 4, 1858 in Pennsylvania. They had one child, Marion Ellis Griffes (or M. E. Griffes). However, Eliza died in childbirth September 1862 with their second child. James then took his son and came west, probably about the time of the mining boom at Mineral King in 1870.

After Eliza's death, James married Rachel Talbot in 1877; they had one daughter, Nettie M. Griffes. Rachel passed away in 1897. James then married Adeline Gallaher, November 14, 1899; they later divorced. His last wife was Mary Alice [Canfield] Lovern, widow of Wesley Lovern. [Name changed to "Loverin" about this time.] Mary Alice passed away July 17, 1912.

James's son, Marion E. Griffes married Mary Ellen Allen; they had four children: Mabel, Oren, Elbert and Bertha. The family moved from the Mussel Slough area where they had been living, moving from Hanford to Three Rivers; here they purchased 280 acres of land and improvements from L. A. Rockwell. On this property was a two-story house facing east, on the west shore of the Kaweah. The house itself had probably been built in the early 1870s since, at the time of the purchase, it was already showing signs of wear.

The special feature of the kitchen was its running water accommodations. A V-shaped trough was constructed of pine and ran from the irrigating ditch over a trestle support to bring it into the kitchen to a wooden sink. The sink was constructed of 2-inch-thick redwood, about 18 inches deep; it had an outlet leading from the sink through the wall and running into a ditch leading away from the kitchen. The whole length of the trough was tightly covered to keep out insects and animals. Another useful feature of the house was the double fireplace with one chimney; one opening to the living room and the other side to the dining area. In

1895, a German carpenter was hired to add more rooms by elevating the roof and adding five bedrooms on the second floor and one on the first. In addition, Marion Griffes was the first settler to build a ditch from the river and he used it for irrigation purposes where he planted an apple orchard and garden.

In 1896, Marion and his wife Mary Ellen were divorced; she later married Jason Barton. Marion's second wife was Alcie "Kitty" Pease; unfortunately, she died soon after the marriage during an appendectomy operation. Marion's third wife was Eleanor [Nora] Ball whom he married March 15, 1904. They had three children, Calva, Marna May and Walter.

In 1904, Marion sold his home to Captain Charles Young, the Black captain of the troops in charge of Sequoia National Park at the time. Young lived there until 1905, when he was transferred out of the area; he sold the house back to Marion. Later it was sold again to John N. Wright.

Marion was killed in a road construction accident when he was involved with building the road from Badger to Sequoia Lake, August 14, 1914. His widow Eleanor moved to Visalia with her children and in later years lived with her daughter Calva Griffes Stuart in Exeter until her death in 1960.

Orlin Albert (or A. O.) Griffes

Orlin Albert Griffes (or A. O., as he preferred) was the youngest son of Orlin and Susan [Stillwell] Griffes; he was the brother of the pioneer settler to Three Rivers, James Walter Griffes. A. O. was born in New York State about 1845; he married Mary A. [Mollie] Tillotson August 11, 1875 in Erie County, Pennsylvania. They eventually made their home at Oak Grove on the East Fork where Mollie's fame at preparing wonderful meals was enjoyed by the many tourists who ventured by stage and wagon up the old Mineral King Road.

Griffes Homestead at Oak Grove. *Photo from Author's Collection.*

A. O. and Mollie Griffes adopted a small boy, Fay, when he was about four years old. He lived with them at Oak Grove for many years. He was known to many as "Freddie"; for forty years he worked for the Southern California Edison Company. His principal job was to walk the flume to Kaweah No. 1 and he walked it every day for those forty years. His walkway was a twelve-inch plank laid on top of the flume; no handrails, just the plank. In the winter, it could be very slippery when covered with ice but he never missed one day and although he had only one minor accident, it wasn't serious enough to keep him off the job. He would leave from Oak Grove at the intake of the flume and walk the 6.5 miles around the mountain, ending at the penstock above Hammond. His wife Ruby would drive down every day and pick him up at the power station below.

Freddie Griffes and his pet fox. *Photo from Author's Collection.*

At his retirement dinner in 1959, he told of a time when a bear fell into the flume and in its efforts to get out, it wallowed and plunged all the way down to the lower end, giving the flume such a good scouring that it wasn't necessary to clean it that year. It was estimated that Freddie had walked 150,000 miles patrolling the flume; that had added up to a total distance that he could have walked six times around the world.

Freddie passed away August 8, 1991; in his later years and after his wife Ruby had died, he lived with his niece, Karole Walker.

Jim Wolverton - A Short History

Although Jim Wolverton occupies a place as an early pioneer of the Three Rivers district, not much is known about him. What is known is that he was a trapper who had a cabin in the Wolverton Meadow area which bears his name. He worked for a time for Hale Tharp, the original settler of Three Rivers, who summered his stock in the Crescent Meadow area.

Wolverton served in the Union Army during the Civil War and rose to the rank of lieutenant. He served under General William Tecumseh Sherman, the fellow who made himself so unpopular with the Southerners for his triumphal march to the sea, via Atlanta.

Jim Wolverton evidently came to Sequoia National Park around 1874, long before it was an established park. He discovered the big redwood which he named after his old commanding officer. About ten years later, the members of the Kaweah Commonwealth Colony nailed a sign on the huge tree naming it the Karl Marx tree after one of their own heroes; nevertheless, it has retained its original name.

In 1893, according to a story in the 1935 *Exeter Sun*, Jim Wolverton was employed by Hale Tharp as a lookout on the Middle Fork of the Kaweah, making sure that Tharp's cattle did not graze below Hospital Rock. While he was on patrol, he fell gravely ill and the Indians at the encampment there looked after him. Tharp, who became worried when his friend and helper did not return to the Tharp ranch for provisions, went to look for him and found him still very ill at Hospital Rock. After transporting Wolverton to his own home, Tharp was unsuccessful in helping him so he had him carried to the home of Harry and Mary Trauger on the Mineral King Road; But Mary, with all her skills, could not save him. It was later reported that Wolverton had been suffering from an infection in his groin. Probably the care she was able to give the dying man was equal to or perhaps better than he would have received at what was then the county hospital and poorhouse in Visalia.

Assisting in the move to Trauger's was Dick Lane, B. W. Trauger and Hugh B. Luce. After Wolverton's death, Captain Parker, who was the commanding officer of the soldiers occupying the park that year, gave Wolverton a full military burial at the site "near the old wooden bridge" on the Mineral King Road. The site of the burial was chosen by Wolverton himself, although why he chose that particular spot has not been determined. The grave was marked by a wooden headboard which did not last many years, probably having been destroyed by fire. In 1936, members of the Boy Scout troop sponsored by the Big Tree Post of the American Legion found the grave near a moss-covered rock, again marking it and building a trail to it.[101]

---

101   *Woodlake Echo*, February 16, 1988.

The Cahoon and Busby Families

George Washington Cahoon was born in 1837, either in Indiana or Missouri. He is listed in the 1850 Census of Nodaway, Missouri as a thirteen-year-old and then appears again on the 1870 Census for Linns Valley, Kern County, CA as being 33 at the time. There he was living with a John Ford from Ireland (miner) and a James Orr. George listed his occupation as a hunter; he must have been working for the mines there.

Records show that he came to Three Rivers in 1875; in the 1880 Census he is in Three Rivers, married to Eva [Clough]; at the time of their marriage, he was 39 and she was 16. In that Census, they had one child, David, age 1. George's occupation was listed as a dairy man.

Evelyn Clough. *Photo courtesy of the Three Rivers Museum.*

George and Eva's children were Daisy, George and Jim; one child (David?) died young.

Daisy Cahoon. *Photo from Author's Collection.*

Jim Cahoon. *Photo courtesy of the Three Rivers Museum.*

According to the late historian and writer Joe Doctor, George was hunting in south Tulare County, at a place called Battle Mountain on the North Fork of the Tule River. While he was there, his burro Barney got into a fierce fight with a mountain lion. Barney came into camp torn and bloody, and George followed his tracks back to the scene of the terrific struggle. He found that the lion had been kicked and so badly bitten by the burro that it had crawled off to die, leaving the burro victorious. The burro survived and was later owned by Guy Hopping's family after George's death.

Unfortunately, George did not die a natural death; at the age of 50, he met his end at the hands of a neighbor, Daniel Busby. Since George Cahoon and Hale Tharp were close friends, George had been to see Mr. Tharp that day to tell him that things were not going well at home and that he was going to take the children and go away, leaving the ranch to his wife, Eva. When he returned home that evening, no one was there. Evidently, Mrs. Cahoon had taken the children and gone to a neighbor's; presumably this was according to arrangements with the neighbor, Daniel Busby, so that he could better carry out his plan to kill Cahoon.

Before Cahoon went down to Busby's cabin and knocked on the door, Busby had secreted himself in the bushes; he shot Cahoon in the head at the back of the ear, and powder burns revealed this fact.[102]

Evidently, then Busby went to Ira Blossom (whose wife Julia was Eva's mother) to tell about the shooting and consequently to turn himself in. The following is a newspaper account of the incident:

Last evening Ira Blossom came down from Three Rivers to procure a coffin for the remains of George W. Cahoon, who was shot yesterday by Mr. Busby. Busby came with Mr. Blossom and presented himself at the sheriff's office, where he gave himself up. Several contradictory reports are in circulation concerning this affair, but it is difficult to learn the facts at present, Mr. Blossom having returned home last night and Sheriff Parker having taken Busby to Three Rivers early this morning, where a coroner's

---

102   Notes of Frankie Welch, in her own handwriting.

inquest will be held. It is said that there was a woman at the bottom of it.

What the immediate cause of the shooting was is not learned but it is said that trouble was not unexpected. One report of the affray is to the effect that Cahoon went to Busby's house and presented a loaded shotgun at his breast intending to shoot, when the latter quickly caught up a Winchester rifle standing behind a door and fired without taking aim. The ball struck Cahoon in the neck, causing his death almost instantly. Nothing more authentic is learned up to the time of going to press.[103]

A further account says the following:

George W. Cahoon, a native of Missouri, aged about fifty years, came to his death by a gun-shot wound, the gun being fired by Daniel Busby, about 10 o'clock AM on September 14th, the bullet hitting him a little to the left on the front side of the neck, passing through, breaking his neck, killing him instantly and lodging about middle way on the right shoulder bone. A jury of twelve was appointed and the Coroner, Dr. Pendergrass and the foreman, Mr. Tharp, extricated the bullet and gave it to the sheriff. We haven't heard of any witnesses being present at the time of the killing. Mr. Busby said that Cahoon called him a _ _ _____ thieving ____ _ _ _____ and said that he would kill him, having a double-barreled shotgun cocked and pointed at the time, and that he, Busby, said to him, "For God's sake, George, don't kill me," and seizing his rifle fired with the gun pointing upwards and, as he showed the jury, without bringing it to his shoulder to take aim. George was a great hunter, a hard-worker and good provider for his family, and well known in this county. The sum of $226.25 in coin was found in his vest pocket and purse. We do not know how much of this money he had to settle with Mr. Busby. Mr. L. Davis says that he had one dollar's worth of candy for his children that he left at Mr. Swanson's the day he was shot. Mr. Busby is a stout looking young man, quite a good shot, and of a quiet disposition. He has been in this vicinity about two years and was employed by the deceased part of the time. The jury ordered the coroner to issue a warrant for the arrest of Mr. Busby, as some of the members thought the neck ought to be powder burnt at the distance of three or four feet and that the bullet ought to have gone upwards and because the evidence was not all in. These are some of the reasons why the jury could not render a verdict of killing in self defense. Feeling runs high and the excitement is great.[104]

In the same paper:

This community was shocked last week by an announcement which seems to have reached us in a mild form, that Geo. W. Cahoon, a well-known and highly respected citizen, had been foully murdered. If Busby had not desired the credit of the act it is likely suspicion would have pointed to another party.[105]

Another news item from a few days later:

Mr. Busby, the father of the man who is arrested for the killing of Cahoon on Tule [Kaweah?] River recently, came out from Kansas last Saturday and will remain until his son's trial is completed.[106]

---

104   Ibid., September 22, 1887.
105   Ibid.
106   Ibid. October 13, 1887

Then later this notice:

> Superior Court, Criminal Division: People vs. Clough [Busby?]—defendant remanded to custody of sheriff.[107]

And finally:

Tried and Acquitted:
"The Case of Daniel Busby Accused of Murder"

On the 14th of September, George W Cahoon, a farmer and stock-raiser living near Three Rivers, was shot and instantly killed by Daniel Busby, a young man who had worked for Cahoon and had lived with him a good deal of the time during the previous two years. The fatal deed was done with a rifle, in the forenoon of the day mentioned, and the bullet passed through Cahoon's neck near the front and left side, lodging in the shoulder blade on the right side. Cahoon had with him at the time a shotgun, and the plea was set up by Busby that he fired the shot in self defense. The latter alleged that Cahoon owed him money, and that his repeated demands had provoked a quarrel between them. On the person of the dead man was found the sum of $226.00, and it has been urged by his friends that he had this with him on this day for the express purpose of settling with Busby. A coroner's inquest was held which revealed facts adverse to the statements made by Busby, and he was arrested and held on the charge of murder. The trial of the case before the superior court commenced on the 8th instant, and has occupied all of the time for the past two weeks, ending yesterday afternoon. W. B. Wallace assisted District Attorney Lamberson on the side of the prosecution and the defense was conducted by Oregon Sanders and W. A. Gray. Nearly fifty witnesses have been examined on both sides and the testimony was very conflicting, but shows that

---

107   Ibid. October 27, 1887.

Busby, while partaking of Cahoon's hospitality, had been guilty of undue intimacy with the latter's wife. Domestic trouble had ensued and divorce proceedings were imminent. The prosecution endeavored to show that Busby was desirous of getting Cahoon out of the way, that he might the better gain his point and perhaps get possession of Cahoon's property. [Although George Cahoon died intestate, the inventory of his estate was valued at $2,880.45][108]

The article continues:

The shooting occurred at a little cabin which was occupied by Busby at the time, and the latter contends that Cahoon came to the door while he was kneeling on the floor inside, by the side of a trunk; that he saw Cahoon pointing his gun towards him; that he at once seized his own gun and fired, while still in a kneeling position. The evidence, however, seemed to disprove this, for the range of the bullet through the man's neck and shoulder was rather downward, when it would have been the opposite if the gun had been fired as claimed.

The body of the dead man was exhumed just previous to the commencement of the trial in order that a post-mortem examination might be held. The exact course of the bullet was ascertained and a section of the vertebrae which had been penetrated by the bullet was removed and produced in court.

The conclusion of the trial was reached yesterday, and the case was given to the jury at 3:30 in the afternoon. After being out a little over four hours, a verdict of 'not guilty' was rendered, and Busby has therefore been acquitted and discharged.[109]

---

108   Tulare County Records of Wills.
109   *Weekly Delta*, Visalia, CA , December 22,1887.

* * * * *

Daniel Boone Busby was born June 1861, in Shelby County, Illinois. He was the son of Abram Cade Busby and Susannah Leach Busby. The Busby family originally came from Londonderry, Ireland in the late 1700s. Daniel Boone Busby came from a family of four girls and six boys. He married Evelyn Clough Cahoon January 16, 1888. They were divorced about 1898. Evidently, he moved to Kansas, since he married a Minnie Ratliff there October 11, 1899. They had two children, Howard and Zoe. Daniel remained in that area and died in 1937. He is buried in the Weakley Cemetery in Wilson County, Kansas beside his second wife, Minnie.[110]

Daniel Busby Marker. *Photo from Ancestry.com*

---

110   www.ancestry.com and www.findagrave.com

Sam Kelly and Family

Another Three Rivers pioneer was Sam Kelly; he was born in Alabama about 1828. His parents were Samuel and Nancy Self Kelly; they moved to Jasper, Arkansas, and young Sam received his education there. In the early 1850s, Sam's sister Malinda and her husband Basil Parker immigrated to California; the family settled in Tulare County and sent back such glowing accounts of the area that both Sam and his brother, Greenbury Kelly, came out West to join them. Sam and his wife Celetha Hudson Kelly, whom he had married in 1853, and their small son Anderson traveled to California with brother Greenbury Kelly and his family. They were part of a wagon train drawn by oxen and the trip across the plains took seven months.

When he first arrived in Tulare County, Sam took up land in the Elbow Creek area; he built a small cabin with a hard dirt floor and, like other pioneers of the time, he raised cattle and enough garden produce to feed his family. A few years passed, then he went into the freighting business, since he realized that Visalia was the supply center of the valley and merchants had to haul freight and supplies from Stockton to the valley.

In 1867, the Kelly family made a trip back East, sailing "around the Horn" to New York, then going on to their old home place in Arkansas. Sam went to Missouri where he bought Missouri mules and once again the family made the trek west to their home in Tulare County; however, this time it only took three months with their mule-drawn wagon.

Eventually the railroads came through the valley in 1872, and although it put many teamsters out of business, Sam Kelly found ready work on the project of building the Mineral King Road; later, he was employed at Atwell Mill.

He relocated his family to Three Rivers and resumed the raising of cattle; although he kept the homestead in Visalia, he also homesteaded in Three Rivers near where the McKee ranch is today. Sam and his family lived in Three Rivers until 1894; most of that time he served as postmaster of Three Rivers.

Sam Kelly. *Photo courtesy of the Three Rivers Museum.*

Sam's daughter Mary Isabelle Sparks went to school in Three Rivers; the first schoolhouse was a log cabin across the South Fork of the Kaweah River [Cove School]. Her first teacher was Professor W. F. Dean. The local families' homesteads were so scattered at that time that there were three schools; Cinnamon, Three Rivers [Cove], and Sulphur Springs. Other teachers Mary remembered were Mr. Ellis, Mr. Brooks and Miss Swank. Later on, she went to a school located approximately on the Frank Finch place (this was the Cove School that had been moved across the river at the intersection of Blossom and Old Three Rivers Drives).

When they lived in Three Rivers, the Kelly family raised almost every supply they needed except the staples: flour, sugar and coffee. Mr. Kelly would drive to Visalia for these supplies in a spring wagon and, even with a good team, the trip took all day. Flour and sugar were bought in barrels, and coffee was bought in quantity; it was parched [a method of roasting] and ground fresh each morning in a hand mill. Butter, eggs, milk, cured and fresh meats were raised and produced on the ranch.

Recalling these times, Mary said, "While I wouldn't want to go back to that pioneer time, it was a happy, wonderful way to live. People made their own entertainment and we really enjoyed our parties and dances."[111]

In 1894, Sam and Celetha Kelly moved back to Visalia to the old home place; he lived there until he passed away in 1911; his wife died in 1915. This couple who endured the hardships of pioneer life in Tulare county will be remembered as considerate neighbors; they had the reputation of always being ready to help the other fellow.[112]

---

111   *Visalia Times Delta*, March 24, 1951.
112   Ibid.

The Mullenix Family

Isham Dykes Mullenix, or "Doc" as he was called, was born 1845 in Tennessee to James and Mary Dykes Mullenix. Doc was a Civil War veteran; he had also been a United States Marshal while living in Tennessee. He came west to join his brother John in 1875 and worked in the Hanford area until malaria, with its accompanying chills and fevers, forced him to seek higher ground on the east side of Tulare County. There he met J. W. C. Pogue, who had been stricken earlier with malaria and understood Mullenix's problem. He hired Doc to take his horse herd into summer pastures up into the Sierra.

Isham Mullenix first saw Mineral King in 1878 when he, Dan Overall, William B. Wallace and a man named Brown went there to mine for Tom Fowler at the Empire Mine. However, mining was not for the young men; Dan Overall worked one day; Wallace for two days and Mullenix for three. Later, Dan Overall became the county sheriff, developed citrus orchards in the Lemon Cove area and fathered a son [Orval] who became a great center for the University of California football team and a Hall-of-Fame pitcher for the Chicago Cubs. Mr. Wallace became an explorer of the Sierra, the planter of the first trout in the East Fork of the Kaweah River, and a judge of the Tulare County Superior Court.

In 1879, when Tom Fowler was busy at the Empire mine, the Mineral King silver boom was on in earnest and the canyon was filled with prospectors. Since Doc Mullenix was a Civil War veteran, he had a priority homestead right; he homesteaded his 160 acres along the same trail which was used by the pack trains going into Mineral King. That summer, John Crowley built the Mineral King Road, passing through the Mullenix's homestead along the present road to Mineral King. Doc began splitting shakes to roof the miners' cabins and other buildings at Harry's Bend, Beulah, Silver City and places in Mineral King, using a tool called a frow, pronounced "froe." He built his own cabin over by the "burned stump" and by 1883 had earned enough to pay off his homestead.

In 1886 with the mining boom over, Isham sold his homestead to A. J. Atwell, who was going to cut timber there; Doc reserved for himself a lot where the present ranger cabin sits. Doc traveled back to Tennessee and met Susannah Moore, a calm, handsome girl; for Doc it was love at first sight and she accepted the proposal of marriage from the ex-soldier, ex-U. S. Marshal and ex-shakes splitter. They came west to Atwell Mill but they also acquired property in Three Rivers, where the Mullenix family expanded first by the birth of Grace, then by Rose and the last child, Luther.

Mullenix Cabin at Atwell Mill. *Photo courtesy of the Three Rivers Museum.*

Although the Mullenix family spent their winters in Three Rivers, summers were spent at Atwell Mill in the Mullenix cabin there; Doc joined in the hearty good times at Mineral King by playing his fiddle for dances there. When Judge Atwell built a big split-level barn at Atwell Mill and finished the upper portion with a smooth floor, Doc played for dances there as well. His daughters Grace and Rose both learned to play the guitar. Doc also had become acquainted with the Lamberson family of Visalia; Suzannah once had to rescue little Frank Lamberson from under the hooves of cattle. The Lambersons were just one of the many families who spent the summers at Atwell Mill, many erecting cabins there.

Mullenix: Mother
with Rose, Luther and Grace,   1991

Suzannah (Moore) Mullenix and her children, Rose, Luther and Grace. *Photo from Author's Collection.*

Suzannah Mullenix died in 1895. Doc's love at first sight for her was enduring and permanent as he never re-married. He was anxious for the welfare of his children, though, and sent them off to the Good Templars school in Vallejo, where Grace, Rose and little Luther spent five years.

By the time the Mullenix children had completed their time at the Good Templars School, Grace Mullenix had become a competent young lady; she had been a valuable assistant in the school nursery and later in life she praised the school for its caring manner.

Back in her father's home, Grace met Phil Alles, brother of Henry who was running the saw at Atwell Mill. In 1902, although Grace was still a teenager, she had been matured by her responsibilities in caring for her motherless younger sister and brother. Grace and Phil were married and set up housekeeping in a cabin Phil built up on the ridge above the mill. Later, Phil quit the mill and went into the teaming business hauling freight.

Henry Alles sold out to the U.S. Government in 1916 and Atwell Mill became part of Sequoia National Park, except for a lot owned by Grace Alles. Henry retained the right to the mill and the downed and dead timber. In 1920, Phil took over the mill, which he ran until 1937, replacing the old steam engine salvaged from the Empire Mine with a Caterpillar tractor in 1929. This tractor could both haul logs and power the saw. Rena Alles Ogilvie, daughter of Phil and Grace (and later wife of Fred), took over a man's job at the mill, tending the screw that determines the thickness of the boards cut by the saw.

Isham "Doc" Mullenix remained at his cabin at Atwell until his death in 1930. His old age was quite comfortable; he had his Civil War pension, his books, and his family near him in the mountains he loved. However, in his later years, Doc had acquired a drinking problem. In an interview with the late Ray Buckman, he told Joe Doctor that when he saw Doc coming down the road in his car, he pulled off the road, as one was never sure in what condition Doc was at the time.

I. D. Mullenix and John Moore(?) Suzannah brother. *Photo from Author's Collection.*

Grace Alles not only raised her family, she also did her share of work at the mill, cooking for the millhands; she found time to feed friends who traveled up the road and to attend to the troubles of summer tourists who passed that way. Ben Harris and Billy Clough would relax by the warmth of her wood-burning kitchen stove with Ben telling the tall tales for which he was famous and Billy talking about his Christian faith.

Grace, Luther, and Rose Mullenix. *Photo from Author's Collection.*

In 1916, a tragedy occurred in the Mullenix family. After coming home from service in World War I, Doc's son Luther was shot and killed at Lake Canyon while staying in the house there. The killer was purported to be a Bert Shaffer; supposedly an intellectual rover and also a family friend. Luther's body was not discovered for two days. When he did not answer a telephone call from Atwell Mill, his brother-in-law Phil went down to check out the situation since Luther had not reported for work at the mill as scheduled. Instead, he found Luther dead in a bedroom; the rifle with which he was shot was found propped against the fireplace in the front room. The "friend" had gone and was not seen again. It was commonly thought that he had murdered Luther.

Luther's older sister Grace did not believe this, however. She always maintained that Luther had shot himself and that his friend had put the rifle where it was found and then left the country, thinking no one would believe him, although Grace said there had been reports he had been seen in the Pacific Northwest. Luther's murder (or suicide) has never been solved; although one newspaper account claimed that the supposed perpetrator had been arrested, there is no evidence of any trial or further action.[113] After news of the murder was made public, local citizens of Three Rivers held many different views of the tragedy; but no matter how high the speculation ran, the mystery has never been solved and it remains a cold case to this day.

On a happier note, Grace and Luther's sister Rose Mullenix married Frank Vaughn; they operated a store and service station in 1929 and after Frank's death in 1936, Rose continued to operate the business until 1942, when she went to work for Sequoia National Park as a fire lookout at the Cahoon Rock fire lookout. From there, she had a spectacular view of the north and south forks of the Kaweah Canyon as well as the San Joaquin Valley, Grant Grove and east to the Hockett Meadow and Atwell Mill areas. She kept this vigil every summer season for twelve years. Rose passed away in February 1955 at the age of 66 at the Exeter hospital.[114]

Grace Mullenix Alles continued to live in her house on Old Three Rivers Drive as well as in her cabin at Atwell Mill for many years. She loved the outdoors, especially the wild animals that came to her cabin and which

113   *Oakland Tribune,* August 4, 1916.
114   *Visalia Times Delta,* February 27, 1955.

she befriended in many ways. She told about a doe that often had more fawns with her than her own. According to Grace, the doe "stole" the fawns of other deer and at one time had as many as five with her.

REWARD!

EXECUTIVE DEPARTMENT,
State of California.

WHEREAS, LUTHER MULLENIX, was on Feb. 19, 1916, murdered near Three Rivers, in Tulare Co., California, by BERT SHAFFER; and

WHEREAS, the said BERT SHAFFER is still at large, although diligent effort has been made to apprehend him.

NOW, THEREFORE, I, HIRAM W. JOHNSON, as Governor of the State of California, do hereby offer a reward of Two Hundred and Fifty Dollars.

$250.00

for arrest and conviction of said BERT SHAFFER upon said charge.

IN WITNESS WHEREOF, I have hereunto set my hand and caused the Great Seal of the State of Calif. to be affixed this 5th day of April, 1916.

[SEAL]

HIRAM W. JOHNSON,
Governor.

Attest: FRANK C. JORDAN,
Secretary of State.
By FRANK H. CORY, Deputy

DESCRIPTION OF BERT SHAFFER:

Age, about forty years; height, five feet nine or ten inches; weight, about one hundred and sixty pounds; complexion, medium (inclined to be dark); hair, dark brown, slightly streaked with gray, dark mustache.

MARKS AND PECULIARITIES: The eyeball of his right eye moves and twiches constantly when he is talking. The name "B. Slater" is tattooed on one of his arms. The second finger on one of his hands is stiff.

HABITS: He is a wandering laborer, drinks heavily and is likely to be arrested for drunkenness. He frequents saloons whenever he has money. When sober he is a very industrious worker at all kinds of ordinary labor.

He was last seen at Exeter, Tulare County, California, on the morning of February, 21, 1916. At that time he took a train for the South. He wore a brown coat, gray trousers and a pair of new tan work shoes, Number 8.

71   JOHN MOE COLLECTION 2003.26, HISTORICAL MUSEUM AT
          FORT MISSOULA. USED BY PERMISSION. ALL RIGHTS RESERVED

Photo from Author's Collection.

At her home in Three Rivers, Grace was well known as a rug maker; the method she used caused them to look like the old-fashioned braided rugs but they were actually woven with a safety pin on the end of the fabric strip. She would fold in the edges of the strips and baste them so there were never any ravelings or raw edges showing. She joined her strips carefully with a bias seam, making the colors join invisibly. She became quite famous for her rug making and took orders for some as big as 9 x 12 and even 11 x 12. One rug went to Washington, DC, some to northern California and other places in the United States. Grace continued her craft and her summers at Atwell Mill for many years until ill health forced her into a nursing home in Visalia. She passed away at the age of 93.

In a conversation with the late Frankie Welch, Grace was asked what had been the most important thing in life. She replied without hesitation that her married life was the happiest; her husband Phil Alles was twenty years older than she but this was never a drawback to their 51 years of wedded life. She also told that Grandma Alles, Phil's mother, thought it was all wrong, and said, "God will punish him for marrying that little girl," but God seemed to sanction their marriage as it lasted for so many years.

Grace was a wonderful, gracious and loving person; she welcomed all who would stop and visit her, whether in Three Rivers or in her little cabin, close to the middle of the road at Atwell. This writer remembers her sweet and gracious ways with fondness. She is still thought of often and missed every time one drives by her little cabin. As the late Joe Doctor said of her in his article, "she was the Lady Who Lived in the Middle of the Road."[115]

---

115   *Heritage*, by Joe Doctor, Exeter Sun, May 21, 1986.

The Traugers - Harry and Mary

Jacob Henry [Harry] Trauger was a very early resident of the Three
Rivers district. He was born in Wayne County, Ohio on December 2, 1833,
the son of John and Mary Fisher Trauger, natives of Pennsylvania. Jacob
was their only child; he received a common school education and started to
work for himself at the age of fifteen. At the age of twenty-one, he inherited
several thousand dollars and went into the mercantile business as well as
farming in Wayne County. He continued until 1857, when he became
interested in the Frazer River mining excitement in British Columbia.
Then he left to go to San Francisco by steamer, but instead changed his
plans at the last minute and went instead to El Dorado County. There he
pursued mining operations as well as in Placer County until 1862, when he
went to Idaho. At Walla Walla, Washington, he found that "matters were
overdrawn"—he was out of funds—so he went to Griffins Gulch instead. He
next moved to Burnt River, then to Mormon Basin, then to Willow Creek
and then to the Snake River. In 1854, he returned to British Columbia, then
Idaho again and finally Montana.[116]

Evidently his wanderlust and quest for gold was satisfied, since in
1874 he returned to Ohio and married Miss Mary Holben, a native of
Stark County, Ohio in June 12, 1874.[117] In her youth, Mary had been the
playmate of William McKinley, who later became the 25th President of the
United States.[118]

After their marriage, the Traugers came to California where Harry
bought 20 acres of land for $875 per acre, but in a short time he sold it for
$500 per acre and then they went to San Francisco, where he made some
further investments, finally using the rest of their funds. They went to Inyo
Country and from there to Tulare County, where he became involved with
the Mineral King mining venture.[119]

116   *Menefee's History*, pp. 633-634.
117   www.Familysearch.org
118   *Beulah*, By Louise A. Jackson, p. 63.
119   *Menefee*.

Harry Trauger. *Photo courtesy Bruton Peterson.*

Harry came into the area with the New England Tunnel and Smelting Company before 1875. Harry and his wife Mary were in the long bunkhouse and office building of the mining company, up near the south end of the valley on Empire Mountain, when the big snow slide of that winter wiped out the bunkhouse without injury to anyone. That was the first time that Harry's wife Mary earned her title of Mineral King's "Angel," since she helped her husband locate the buried and wounded, finding one man when she heard his watch ticking underneath the snow.

Although Harry was an important figure to the history of Mineral King, he did not leave as much of an impression on the lore of the Silver

Rush as did his wife, Mary Holben Trauger. She was the first white woman to stay in Mineral King through an entire winter.

A story about her hints that when Mary came to the Mineral King area, she was in the advanced stages of pulmonary tuberculosis, and was subject to massive hemorrhages, which if they happened when she was outside, she would simply sit quietly on a log or a rock until they passed. After only several months of living in the mountains, her health came back and she lived into old age.

On right: Mary Trauger

Mary Trauger. *Photo from Author's Collection.*

She more than earned the title of "Angel of Mineral King" because of her willingness to go to the aid of ill or injured miners in times when medical help was not available or at least several days away. She and Harry were extremely poor, evidently due to his impecunious "investments" through the years, so Mary was forced to fashion her dresses out of flour sacks, which many pioneer women found useful in similar ways.[120]

Mary Trauger. *Photo courtesy Bruton Peterson.*

According to an interview Grace Alles gave to Frankie Welch, Grace told Frankie the following:

---

120   *Woodlake Echo*, December 7, 1977.

Mary Trauger had TB – [she] came from Pennsylvania or someplace East for health. Homesteaded on East Fork, called Last Chance—the last chance for regaining [her] health. She put out apples and other fruit trees and berrys [sic]. [She] came before [18]70 when Grace's father, I. D. Mullenix, came. [They] built a reservoir, collected water from the springs for summer use. The river was far below. Mrs. Trauger was aided in all these enterprises by her husband, Harry Trauger. "But she was the boss," Grace says. She was German.

Later the Traugers moved to the Bear Ranch, lower on the East Fork to the north of River Hill Bridge. Then they moved to Moffitt Crossing, below Lemon Cove. Later she lived in Hemet, California and passed away there. Mary used to write Grace from there until her blindness prevented any more correspondence.

Frankie's note of Grace Alles' interview continues:

After the Traugers moved to the Bear Ranch, Mrs. Trauger kept the toll gate at the bridge at [the] foot of River Hill—on [the] road to Mineral King. Mrs. Trauger was connected with Mineral King in [the] early days. She would walk to Mineral King from Last Chance, stopping over night at Atwell Mill with Mr. Mullenix, later with Phil Alles [when he and Grace operated the mill]. Once she came upon a bear. It went up a tree; she walked back to her home, got a gun and came back and killed the bear.[121]

Although the silver boom was financially and "minerally" bankrupt, Harry Trauger's adventuresome spirit never diminished. Previously, he had been made superintendent of the operations of the White Chief Mine and all other property of the New England Tunnel and Smelting Company. In 1884, all the properties and responsibilities were transferred to him for the sum of one hundred dollars. He continued working on the mine for years,

---

121   Handwritten note from the collection of the late Frankie Luella Welch.

expanding the tunnel and waiting, hoping another developer would come by and become interested; no one ever did. Harry was the last recorder of the Mineral King Mining District—a job with no pay. In all of their years of working there, Harry Trauger and his wife Mary had received nothing for their toil and hard work. However, they remained hospitable and willing to share with anyone who happened by Last Chance and was in need of something to eat or some other request they could fill.

There was one bright thing that happened in Mary's life and that was when her childhood friend, William McKinley, was elected to the office of the Presidency of the United States. Somehow, Mary scraped together enough money to travel to Washington, DC to see him; when the President saw her, he gave Mary hugs and they laughed together over memories from their childhood. Mary felt it was certainly worth all the money she had spent to take this trip.

Harry and Mary Trauger with friends at Three Rivers. *Photo courtesy Bruton Peterson.*

As the years passed, the Traugers moved down out of the mountains, eventually coming to the Los Angeles area where they lived in more comfortable quarters. Their son, Will, was killed in a mining accident in Alaska and then Harry passed away in 1919. Mary moved to Hemet and lived out her days there. In a statement from Louise Jackson's book, *Beulah,* Mary summed up their life together this way: "Well, such was life. We had not gotten our 30 thousand for our mining property. So we had to do the best we could. We lived just the same. Our love for each other held us together."[122]

And Mary, you and Harry are remembered every time this author drives by "Last Chance" and sees your sweet peas thriving there, still being watered from your spring.

Mary Trauger. *Photo courtesy Bruton Peterson.*

---

122   *Beulah.*

1880s

Julius "Jude" S. Glenn

Julius Glenn grew up in the pioneer land of southeastern Kansas. He was the son of a typically ambitious farmer looking for a better place to live, yet always making the best of the situation wherever he settled.

Julius's father was occupied with the building of houses and barns, clearing the woodlands and plowing the fields, as well as planting and harvesting the corn, feeding the hogs, and pasturing the cattle. All this was going on during the era when the United States was adjusting to the prosperity that followed the Civil War.

The soil in Kansas was rich, new ground. When the rains came right, the crops were enormous, if the chinch bugs and the grasshoppers didn't get there first; but when the floods came, the crops were swept away, and when the hot winds came in July or August, the cornfields withered as did the farmer's hopes of paying off the mortgage. Thus, there was always the uncertainty of how things would turn out. Man could pretty well control the factors within his reach, but the weather was always beyond his control.

After several moves in southern Kansas, the senior Glenn made the decision to go all the way west, even to California. The family conveyance for this journey in 1884 was not a covered wagon nor a Pullman car; instead, an ordinary box car on the Santa Fe tracks in Kansas City, Missouri. It was fitted up to serve the whole family as living room, dining room, kitchen, bedrooms and moving van, all at the same time.

As a guard against hunger, Mrs. Glenn prepared a great supply of cooked food; bread, pies and meats were necessary, since the train trip through the Southwest consumed more than seven days.

The end of the family's journey west was Los Angeles, and they lived in that area for two more years; then, in 1886, they moved to Visalia. The trip north was made overland with team and wagon; it took as long to make this trek as it did to come by train from Kansas City to Los Angeles.

After raising a crop of wheat near Orosi, there was another and final move; this was from the San Joaquin Valley to Three Rivers. The move took place on Christmas Day, 1886, when Jude Glenn was nineteen years of age and a very useful member of his family. The father had acquired a quit claim deed to 160 acres of land on the South Fork of the Kaweah River where they intended to settle.

To reach this attractive spot proved to be a real hardship; the damage done along the South Fork by the great flood of 1867 had not yet been cleared; logs of every size and description were scattered among the boulders, blocking their way in every conceivable position. As they made their journey to the new homestead, the Glenn family had to build their own road every step of the way.

At that time, the South Fork itself was a raging torrent too deep to wade and too swift to swim. By the use of ropes and pulleys and great persistence, on Christmas Day the family reached the side of the stream where the Glenn home was to be built.

The first major job for Julius "Jude" Glenn was to build an irrigation ditch which would bring some of the river water to the farming land on the homestead. Doing this, he learned many things that were to be very helpful to him in his subsequent jobs of building other ditches in Three Rivers.

Although Jude was 20 years old, he still wanted more schooling, so he started school in Three Rivers, commuting back and forth for the first year on foot. In his second and last year in the Three Rivers School, he lived at the home of Sam Kelly, the postmaster. Here he worked for his room and board; one of his jobs was to sort and help distribute the mail that would be brought up on Friday afternoons. It was the custom then to empty the contents of the mail bag upon the floor and then pick it up and sort the mail alphabetically into special compartments on the wall—one for each letter of the alphabet.

In the spring, Jude and a helper drove 50 head of Sam Kelly's cattle to Mineral King, where they were left to graze upon the mountain meadows in that settlement until the winter weather threatened and it was time to move the cattle out.

In the years following, Jude became an accomplished teamster, hauling machinery as well as provisions and supplies to the mills in the mountains and then returning with a load of milled lumber, bringing it down to the towns in the valley below.

In 1900, Julius "Jude" Glenn married a Miss Norma Bragg, the daughter of one of the early settlers in the Yokohl Valley; she had been a school teacher before their marriage. Two sons, Dawrence and Granger, were born to this couple as well as one daughter, Edith.

When the Mount Whitney Power Company put in the flumes and power houses along the Kaweah, Jude had a prominent part in this enterprise, since he was the teamster who assisted Jason Barton to haul in the heavy machinery that was needed for these construction projects. Jude had a six-horse team and he and Jason had the contracts for this venture. Jude said that when going up Lime Kiln Hill, he had to double up and put ten horses on one wagon; another bad place for hauling heavy loads was above Slick Rock where he used twelve horses in the team. The load of equipment for the powerhouse weighed between four and five tons, which was a very big load for the roads of those days, as well as for the methods of freighting.

For several winters, he hauled firewood out of the foothills; he also took wood to the old lime kiln operated by Dave Carter, and which is still standing on the South Fork; for this work, he received $1.00 per cord.

He often worked for J. W. C. Pogue of Lemon Cove, putting up hay and received $1.00 per day plus board.[123]

Jude bought out his brother Charley and eventually he acquired a total of 480 acres. After Jude's marriage to Norma, he moved back to the Yokohl district. He sold his South Fork property to Barney Mehrten.

After his wife's death in 1945, Julius "Jude" Glenn continued to live in their home in Exeter where he passed away October 13, 1963; he had reached the age of 96 and in his lifetime had seen the beginnings of the settlements in this area of California and watched them grow to almost the present age. Quite a life span![124]

---

123   Notes from Frankie Welch.
124   *Exeter Sun*, February 22, 1961.

Christina "Grandma" Alles and Her Family

Christina [Lyne] Alles was born in Germany, October 15, 1842. When she was eleven years old, she came with her parents and two sisters to Canada. The voyage was made in a sailing ship and it took three months. During the crossing, a heavy storm threatened to capsize the ship; all the passengers and crew gathered to pray and sing hymns. The storm soon subsided, but this experience left a profound impression on Christina that would last the remainder of her life.

She grew up in Canada and on May 31, 1864, she married Conrad Alles. In 1880, the Alleses and their eight children moved to Michigan. Their children, ten in total, were Anna, Adam, Henry, Phillip, Conrad, Christina, Catherine, Elizabeth, John and Dan. The two youngest, Adam and Dan, were born in Michigan. In 1884, the oldest son, Henry, came to northern California where he met Fred Clough, son of Julia Clough Blossom. They became friends and Fred told him of the Three Rivers country. Henry subsequently filed on a homestead on the South Fork of the Kaweah about seven miles from Three Rivers. He wrote to his parents in Michigan and they came to join him in 1887, along with seven of their children (Phil and Anna remained in Michigan for two more years).

The family traveled from Michigan to California by train, and later Adam Alles could remember the thrill of seeing their train run up and onto a boat to be ferried across Lake Michigan.

The Alles family settled on the upper South Fork on property later owned by the Maxon family. At the time, there was no road to the place and all household goods, including a stove, were carried by hand, two miles from the end of the road to the cabin. A substantial house with a rock basement was built later, with lumber hauled from Atwell Mill, which son Henry operated for a short time, until his younger brother Phil took over and continued the operation for many years.

Conrad Alles, Christina's husband, died in June 1891 and the family moved down the canyon to Three Rivers, where she lived in her home at the intersection of South Fork and Old Three Rivers Drive until her death in 1938.

Early in her life, she belonged to the German Lutheran Church. She was deeply religious and reading her Bible was a daily ritual. The dominant desire of her life was to spread the gospel. She started a little Sunday School and gathered the children of the neighborhood into her home and told them Bible stories. She played hymns on her old parlor organ [on display at the Three Rivers Museum], and taught the children how to sing them. Later she established a Sunday School in the old Three Rivers schoolhouse near the Alles home.

In 1927, Rev. Ernest Keeler, a Sunday School missionary, visited the community and held a service there; for twelve years he kept in touch with the Sunday School, which grew until it reached an attendance of 128.

Christina or "Grandma" Alles was a member of the Presbyterian Church at Lemon Cove until the time of her death. Each year at the Pioneer Dinner given by the Three Rivers Woman's Club, she would sing a hymn in German, playing her own accompaniment.

On November 5, 1939, Grandma Alles' faithfulness bore fruit in the organizing of a Three Rivers church of forty-five members. More than a hundred people gathered from Lemon Cove, Woodlake and other parts of the San Joaquin Presbytery at the Three Rivers schoolhouse to participate in the service. Among the charter members were children and grandchildren of Grandma Alles. A six-month-old great-granddaughter was baptized. When the present Presbyterian church building was dedicated more than a decade later, a picture of Grandma Alles was unveiled and the story of her dedicated life was told.

In her ninety-sixth year, she retained to a remarkable degree her physical and mental powers, raising a garden every season and doing her own housework until a few weeks before her death. She continued faithfully attending Sunday School and communion service at the Lemon Cove Church.

She died in her home in Three Rivers on a Sunday evening January 19, 1938; she had been bedfast only a few days before her death. She called her sons and daughters to her bedside, enjoined them to continue in right living and told them not to grieve for her and bade them goodbye. Her lifelong habit of thought for others persisted even on her deathbed. She was indeed the "bedrock" of the Alles and other related families that still live here today and in other locations throughout the state. Christina or "Grandma" Alles embodied the sincere pioneer spirit that is admired and remembered even in today's world.[125]

Alles family, In front, Christina Lyne Alles. L-Rt: Elizabeth, Philip, Dan, Adam, Christina, Conrad, Catherine, John, Anna and Henry. Their father, Conrad, was deceased.

In Front, Christina Lyne Alles. L to R: Elizabeth, Phillip, Dan, Adam, Christina, Conrad, Catherine, John, Adam & Henry. Their father, Conrad, was deceased. *Photo from the Three Rivers Museum.*

---

125   *Heritage,* the newsletter of the Three Rivers Historical Society, Vol IV, No. 3, September, 1955. Article by the author.

The Britten Family

Although family tradition has always told that the first Britten immigrant ancestor to America came in the form of a young boy who had been pressed into naval service in London in 1678, further research has discovered that actually the first immigrant of this family was one William Britton (earlier spelling) who came to America *before* 1678 and who settled on Staten Island, New York. His place of origin in England was probably Somersetshire, since that is where his father, Richard, died. William married Mary Stillwell sometime before 1663, when their first child was born. William and Mary were both baptized in the Flatlands Dutch Church on Staten Island July 14, 1678. William's fifth son, Benjamin, was the ancestor of the Three Rivers line of Brittens. His marriage to Maude LaTourette in 1712 began the family of this particular history.

The head of the Three Rivers branch of the family was Hudson Kinsley [or Kingsley] Britten, born April 7, 1829 in New York City, a son of Gershom Hoff Britten and Mrs. Charlotte Bashford Britten. Hudson had five older brothers: Benjamin, William, John, Hudson Kinsley I [who died young], and Richard. In 1842, the family migrated to the Territory of Wisconsin, where they settled in Lima Township, Grant County.

Hudson Kinsley had a strong urge for adventure and to seek new horizons. As a young man and before he was married, he made several trips to California, walking most of the way. On the first trip, he volunteered to be a hunter for a large wagon train that was assembling in Council Bluffs, Iowa. This oxen train left April 1850, bound for California.

En route, a group of Indians came into the camp one morning, looking for the white man's help. It seemed one of them had a rifle with a bullet stuck in the barrel. Hudson thought that he could help with their problem and was heating the barrel over a small fire to loosen the bullet when the wagon master said, "Let that d____ Indian go. We've got to be on our way."

"You go on," was Hudson's reply, "I'll catch up to you later." Hudson built a fire, and over the hot coals, softened the barrel of the rifle enough to release the lodged bullet. When the good deed was done, the Indian went on his way and Hudson eventually overtook the wagon train.

Sometime later, a member of the wagon train's company shot a squaw and the Indians became hostile. When Hudson and another man were ranging far from the train in search of game, a group of Indians saw them and gave chase, capturing the two men. They were taken to the Indian village to be tortured and killed; however, the chief recognized his one-time benefactor of the rifle-cleaning incident, smoked the pipe of peace with him and sent both men back to the wagon train with an escort of Indians.

After reaching California on this trip, Hudson Britten passed through the San Joaquin Valley, coming close to the Sierra where he later settled. In the Venice Hill area, he found the body of a man who had been shot by Indians. Fifteen arrows lay beside him that the victim had apparently pulled from his body before his death. According to the late John Britten, Sr., this happened when his grandfather Hudson and others went out to recover and bury the victims of the Woods Party massacre.

In his travels around California, Hudson mined somewhat successfully in the Yosemite area but "grub" was very high; according to Ora Britten Welch's notes, he told of a fifty-pound sack of flour that cost $15. After wandering for over a year, he returned home via the Isthmus of Panama.

Shortly after his return, Hudson was married March 18, 1852 to Parmelia Sophia Noel, daughter of Solomon Noel and Frances Johnson. Parmelia was born in Ohio in 1828, the third in a family of nine girls.

Wisconsin was the native state of all the children born to Hudson and Parmelia; first was Napoleon [or "Nap"], Zebulon M. Pike [nicknamed Frank], Eureka, Ora, Ernest [father of the late Ernest John Britten, Sr. of Three Rivers], Noel [grandfather of Larry Britten of Three Rivers and Julie Britten Bruns of Visalia]; also Jesse, who died young.

According to the late Frankie Welch, she was often told by her mother, Ora Britten Welch, that they were a lively, happy family, playing pranks on each other. When the oldest brother, Nap, began courting the girl he eventually married, his brothers and sisters set a trap—a pan full of jangling pots and pans set on the stairs and fastened with a cord to the door knob so that it would come rattling down when he opened the door and all the household would know how late he had come in!

In 1879, Hudson moved his family to Humboldt, Iowa, with Nap remaining in Wisconsin. They lived in Iowa until the fall of 1888, when they finally sold their farm and made the move to California.

At that time, Hudson and his son Ernest came to the Three Rivers area, where they filed and eventually "proved up" on homesteads on the South Fork of the Kaweah River in the area now known as "Britten Cove." This land lies northeast of the spot where Conley Creek branches off of the South Fork. Parmelia Britten came to Three Rivers and the Britten Cove the following spring, along with their son Noel. Daughter Ora had been visiting friends with her husband Ira Welch and their daughter, Frankie, at Lime Kiln (near present-day Lemon Cove). They moved with Hudson and the rest of the Brittens to Britten Cove where Ira died soon after from tuberculosis. After her husband's death, Ora continued to live on her homestead with little Frankie until the family finally moved to the main part of Three Rivers.

While living on her homestead in Britten Cove, she encountered many obstacles to raising her small family. There were wolves, coyotes, bear, lion and other predators; however, she was known as a "sure shot," and was able to defend her family in every situation. She was also able to provide their living by hunting quail and other small game with a rifle, not a shotgun.

The Brittens lived on the land at Britten Cove four years, building several homes that have long since disappeared. During that time, Hudson and his sons constructed several water ditches, cleared and planted fields with wheat, and built a corral for their stock from large native boulders and oak planks, a few of which can still be seen today.

Hudson Britten died August 27, 1892, at the age of 63. This was the same year that the family moved down from the hills and settled in Three Rivers. Parmelia died October 17, 1896, at age 68. They are both buried in the Britten family plot in the Three Rivers Cemetery.

Hudson K. Britten. *Photo from Author's Collection.*

Parmelia Britten. *Photo from Author's Collection.*

The family of Hudson and Parmelia were farmers, raising hogs, sheep, cattle, etc. The women contributed to the farm income by selling milk, eggs, cheese, and butter; even plucking their geese and selling the feathers and down. They were progressive people for their time; Parmelia had the first sewing machine in the neighborhood as well as the first set of false teeth!

The sons of Hudson—Ernest, Noel and Frank—as well as daughter Ora, lived for most of their lives in Three Rivers. The Britten Brothers Store and the Three Rivers Lodge (Hotel) were business ventures of this family.

Four Brothers - Napoleon, Frank, Ernest & Noel Britten in Front of the Britten Brothers Store. *Photo from Author's Collection.*

Ernest was to become the first Park Ranger in Sequoia National Park as well as Forest Supervisor in several National Forests, including the Inyo; Noel stayed in the Three Rivers area to manage the store and hotel; Frank eventually moved to Exeter where his family was raised and the other daughter, Eureka, lived in La Cañada, California with her husband, Anton Williams.

Although the descendants of this family have moved to different parts of the country, there are a few still living here. Until December 1995 when he passed away, Ernest John Britten, Sr., son of Ernest and grandson of Hudson, was a native-born son of Three Rivers. He operated a cattle ranch that included most of the early-day homesteads upon which his grandfather, father, uncles and aunts once filed their claims. Larry Britten, son of Dick Britten, grandson of Noel and great-grandson of Hudson, is the owner of Britten Construction of Three Rivers.

John Britten, Sr. *Photo from Author's Collection.*

The Welch Family

George W. Welch, another pioneer resident of Three Rivers, was born October 29, 1830 in Courtland County, New York. His parents were Cornelius and Sally [Lucas] Welch, prosperous farmers in their area and cousins of the Robert Taft family. George's father was a Whig and an ardent admirer of Henry Clay. George was the third son in a family of twelve children. Three of his brothers took part in the Civil War, one being mortally wounded at Gettysburg. In 1831, the family moved to Ohio, settling first in Cleveland and later in Wayne County, finally stopping in the town of Medina. Here his mother died in 1864 and his father in 1876.

George received his higher education at Oberlin College in Oberlin, Ohio where he earned a degree in engineering. He became a civil engineer and did much pioneer surveying in Michigan, Wisconsin, Illinois and Iowa. He was county surveyor in Humboldt County, Iowa and was connected with the building of railroads in that state as well as in Illinois.

In 1856, George married Miss Mary Clark in Baraboo, Wisconsin; they had one child, a son, Ira Ernest Welch. Ira Welch eventually met and married Ora Britten, daughter of Hudson Britten in 1885. Ira was suffering from consumption [tuberculosis], so he and Ora moved from Iowa to California for his health. However, Ira lived only a few years longer; he died May 9, 1889 at age 31.

George Welch, Ira's father, also came to California in 1885; he lived here with his daughter-in-law, Ora Britten Welch and granddaughter, Frankie, on the South Fork the rest of his life, except during the times he was away on engineering projects. Since surveying and engineering were his fields, he had a considerable part in the development of Tulare County. Beginning in 1887, he surveyed and supervised the construction of the old Visalia-Tulare railroad, which marked a step forward in the progress of the county. Of interest to Three Rivers residents was his job in 1900; this was the completion of the first road into Sequoia National Park. It was a continuation of the road from the point where it had been abandoned by the Kaweah Colonists, terminating at Giant Forest. He was both the locating and construction engineer on this project for five summers until it was completed; this included the construction of the first bridge over the Marble Fork.

First Bridge on the Marble Fork, engineered by George Welch. *Photo from Author's Collection.*

When the formal dedication of the second road, or the Generals Highway, into the Park was held in 1925, George was the special honored guest of Stephen T. Mather, director of the Park Service at that time. That was his first visit to Giant Forest in twenty-one years and his last to the big trees that he loved so well.

The charm of the high Sierra had cast its spell upon George soon after his arrival here in 1885. He became a familiar figure with his horse and pack animals as he explored the canyons and peaks. He was always a lover of books and magazines and displayed a keen interest in politics. As a staunch Republican, he had voted for Lincoln and witnessed Lincoln's journey through Ohio after his inauguration. George cast his first vote for Admiral Scott, who was defeated by Franklin Pierce.

Later in life, he became interested in the growing of spineless cactus and its use as feed for livestock; he planted a "cactus orchard" on the South Fork. Unfortunately, it did not prove to be a good substitute since the cattle just didn't like it, even though it was without spines. George did much corresponding with his friend, Luther Burbank, from whom he obtained starts of the cactus plants firsthand. These he planted in row upon row on the property on the South Fork where they remained for many years, even into the 1940s.

South Fork Cactus Farm. *Photo from Author's Collection.*

Welch was very active and interested in community affairs here in Three Rivers. Along with other early-day pioneers, he established the Three Rivers Cemetery, becoming its first Secretary-Treasurer in March 1909.

His obituary states that he lived a simple life, never addicted to the use of alcohol and he had given up tobacco early in his life. He believed his simple mode of living enabled him to reach nearly the century mark in age, in spite of ill health in his youth.

George Welch passed away at the home of his daughter-in-law, Ora Welch, October 1, 1926. His funeral was held at the Three Rivers Cemetery. Officiating was the Rev. W. A Sutherland of Lemon Cove. Judge Fred H. Taft of Santa Monica, husband of a niece, spoke a few words upon the integrity and sterling character of Mr. Welch, whom he had known for sixty years, characterizing him as a "gentleman of the old school." Dr. D. D. Nice of Three Rivers read a portion of the Masonic charge at the close of the service.

The pallbearers were Judge Walter Fry, A. B. Burdick, C. L. Taylor and Barney Mehrten of Three Rivers and Archibald Robertson and Robert Pool of Visalia.[126]

George Welch

George Welch. *Photo from Author's Collection.*

---

126   *Visalia Times-Delta*, October 2, 1926.

* * * * *

Ora Britten Welch was born to parents Hudson Kingsley Britten and Parmelia Noel Britten August 1, 1860 in Grant County, Wisconsin, the fifth of seven children. In September 1885, she married Ira Ernest Welch in Humboldt County, Iowa where the Britten family were living at that time. Since Ira was unwell, Ora was most eager to come west in the hopes it would cure his illness. In 1886, they came to Lime Kiln expecting only to visit friends there; however, their visit lasted longer than planned, when their daughter Frankie was born the next day. As soon as they could travel, they drove their buggy up the narrow road to Three Rivers; other members of their family met them there. A cabin had been built for them on a homestead in Britten Cove but a sled road was the only approach to the six 160-acre parcels already surveyed and filed on by Hudson K. Britten and his son Ernest in behalf of the six adults and one baby who were to live there. Although her husband Ira passed away in 1889, Ora stayed on the homestead with her small daughter and developed her frontier skills to provide for their living. In later years, she told stories about the wolves, lions and other predators that she had to deal with. She was a crack shot and she could kill quail through the eye with a rifle, not a shotgun.

Ora Welch's Homestead in Britten Cove. *Photo from Author's Collection.*

Her father, Hudson, had a homestead about one-half mile from hers; there he built a cabin with a root cellar; he dug ditches to irrigate his fields and built a corral with stones—remnants of which can be seen today. When he died in 1892, the family purchased a ranch connecting their homesteads to the South Fork of the Kaweah River. They moved out of the hills and built their homes, as well as the Britten Brothers Store and the Three Rivers Lodge, along South Fork Drive. These homes and businesses were located on what was soon to become the road into Mineral King as well as to Giant Forest and the main thoroughfare through Three Rivers in those days. Ora's home was just west of what is now the entrance to South Fork Estates.

Ora and Frankie lived in their home on the South Fork for a number of years until the 1920s when Ora built a newer home that stands today. Her brother-in-law, Anton Williams—husband of her sister Eureka—had been a developer in La Cañada, California, and his contractor built the new home for her. Ora Welch passed away there November 27, 1954 and is buried beside her husband, Ira, in the Three Rivers Cemetery.

* * * * *

Frankie Luella Welch was the daughter of Ora and Ira Welch. She was born in Lime Kiln, California November 1, 1886. She attended the Cove School and early on, she became interested in history and journalism. Her love of books prompted her to open a branch of the County Library in her home that she shared with her mother. The library remained there for 49 years; Frankie was given an award by the P.T.A. for her work with the local children.

As well as a librarian, Frankie was an active photographer, developing her own pictures of many subjects, including children, animals, family members and local scenery. She and her mother Ora often accompanied her uncle Ernest on his mountain patrols and her photographs give a good representation of the park in its pristine state at the turn of the century.

One of Frankie's Photos of the High Sierra. *Photo from Author's Collection.*

On May 20, 1978, the California Press Women came to Frankie's home and awarded her the first honorary life membership to be bestowed by that organization. Frankie was a charter member of the Three Rivers Woman's Club and for many years served as historian and publicity chairman. She was a very active reporter and journalist as well, serving as the local correspondent for the Fresno *Bee* and the Visalia *Times Delta*, beginning in 1924 to almost the date of her death in 1978. Her love of history is reflected in the many stories she wrote and the interviews she took of people living in the early days of Three Rivers development. Without all her articles and notes, this book could never have been written. She kept every one of her submissions to the newspapers and always had the goal of writing the local history of Three Rivers. On June 4, 1975, the Three Rivers Woman's Club honored Frankie at a luncheon at the St. Anthony's Retreat; nearly 200 women attended.

Frankie never married, but she was surrounded by many of her family members and friends in the community. She passed away August 11, 1978, just twenty days short of her 92nd birthday. When she was given the honorary award by the P.T.A. in 1965, the speaker who introduced her said, "Frankie's home was always open to the children of Three Rivers. They looked forward to coming there and many times she had little treats for them, a candy or a fruit from her orchard which always brought a happy smile to their faces. She gave help and encouragement to all who entered her home and she was never too busy to stop and help a child find a certain book or help with information for a report he or she might be looking for."

Frankie Luella Welch. *Photo from Author's Collection.*

The Washburn Family

The story of the pioneer Washburns begins with a short history of Mrs. Washburn, whose name was Janie Jasper.

It was fortunate for Merril Jasper and his family that their cousin Christopher "Kit" Carson left his job as a saddler's apprentice and became the celebrated scout, trapper and guide. When Merril Jasper, a Kentuckian, and his wife, Frances Crowley Jasper, a native of Clay County, Missouri, made up their minds in 1857 to turn their backs on the comforts of home and go west by oxen team to California, they sought and secured the protection of their cousin, Kit Carson. He was not only an experienced guide, but he knew the ways of the Indians and was friendly with them.

The Mountain Meadows Massacre was still fresh in the minds of the early pioneers as well as the Dred Scott Decision[127], an indication that the slavery question would soon erupt into a war. The new state of California beckoned the Jaspers as it looked like a haven of safety if it could be reached.

Their son, James Jasper, was only nine and the baby daughter Janie was two when the family left for the wide-open spaces with Carson as their guide and protector. Since he knew the ways and superstitions of the Indian tribes they would encounter, he killed coyotes and hung them on the sides and back of the covered wagons to discourage the Indians from molesting them. In spite of this, at one time a stray arrow came uncomfortably close to baby Janie as she leaned out the back of the wagon.

Eventually, the family arrived safely in Sonoma and stayed there three years before coming to Tulare County. They lived for a time near Venice Hill, and it was while they were there that James Jasper met his future wife, Margaret Blair, daughter of Rev. Jonathan Blair.

The Jaspers moved to Farmersville in 1871, where Merril Jasper owned and operated a general merchandise store which he later sold to T. J. Brundage. The mother, Frances, passed away at Farmersville June 7,

---

127   The Dred Scott Decision was a landmark decision by the Supreme Court in 1857 that people of African descent brought into the US and held as slaves (or their descendants), were not protected by the US Constitution and were not citizens.

1873. The father died July 28, 1879; his son James and wife Margaret then moved to Glenville where they made their home. Janie Jasper would ride her horse to Glenville to visit her brother and back to Antelope Valley to visit her Blair relatives. She also taught for several years at the old Visalia Normal School.

At the Crowley Hotel in Mineral King, Janie Jasper met Mason C. Washburn, son of Squire Washburn. Mason and Janie were married December 23, 1877 under an oak tree at the Crowley home in Farmersville. They made their home in Farmersville, where Mason went to work drilling water wells for irrigation and house use. He also served as constable during the time of the Mussel Slough tragedy, since that area was still part of Tulare County. Mason and Janie's children, Edgar, John and Mary were born in Hanford.

On September 12, 1884, the Washburns moved to Three Rivers, where Mason had filed on government land there. This land was later designated on the map of Tulare County as Washburn Cove. The father, Squire Washburn, made his home with them for a few years before returning to his old home at Quincy, Illinois; he passed away there at the age of 100 years. Mason and his wife had four more children after moving to Three Rivers: Mattie, Merril, Matilda, and Freda.

Squire Washburn. *Photo taken from www.ancestry.com; public photos.*

The children all attended the Sulphur Springs School and Mason Washburn served as a trustee there for many years while Professor Dean was the beloved teacher. When Dean needed to round up cattle on his ranch, he sent his wife to teach school for him; and the students loved it.

Church services were conducted in the schoolhouse by the Rev. Jonathan Blair, the pastor of the Antelope Church (and uncle of Janie Washburn). Rev. Blair would ride horseback to the schoolhouse for the service, then go on to the Washburn home to spend the night.

Teamsters on their way to Mineral King often stopped at the Washburn home as well. While Mason fed the team horses, Janie and her girls whipped up a company dinner for the hungry drivers, as well as feeding the cavalry troops of U. S. Soldiers from San Francisco who camped each summer at Washburn Cove.

Washburn Home. *Photo from Author's Collection.*

John Washburn told of driving hogs in 1894 and 1895 from Three Rivers to Taurusa (NW of Woodlake), where they were sold to Jim Hicks of that place, who finished preparing them for market. It usually took three days for the trip. The Tom Ragle place was a favorite camping spot. Three Rivers was a good place to raise hogs because of the plentiful crop of acorns each year on the oak trees.

In 1898, the Washburn family outfitted two four-horse wagons and drove to Seattle, Washington by easy stages. They stopped at Junction City, Oregon, stayed there a year and then drove on to Seattle. Their son John was married at Yakima, Washington February 25, 1903 to Mary Carpenter of Dallas, Texas; then he and his new wife returned to Three Rivers. In

1906, John Washburn laid the concrete for the Power House No. 2 ditch for the Mt. Whitney Power Company, extending it from the Park line to the power house across from the Dean ranch and across from the current Presbyterian Church.

In 1910, Mason and his wife Janie were living in Exeter with children Merril, Matilda and Freda; they were there in 1920 as well. Mason Washburn died in Exeter, July 18, 1921.

Mason and Janie Washburn. *Photo from the* Woodlake *Echo*, Dec. 17, 1954.

The Maxon Family

Harrison "Hat" Maxon has ancestral roots that go back to the Revolutionary War. Hat's grandfather was Erasmus D. Maxon; he was the son of Paul C. Maxon, whose father—another Paul—was a soldier in the Revolutionary War. Paul C. Maxon (the son), was born in New York and married Lucy Pardee. Erasmus Maxon was the third child born out of seven children in this family. Erasmus Maxon married Hannah Crouch in 1834 and over the years they produced ten children; the eighth child born was Frederick or Fred Maxon, father of Harrison or "Hat" Maxon.

Erasmus came to California in 1873, after receiving an honorable discharge from serving in the Civil War in the Union army. He homesteaded on 160 acres on what is now the Exeter Cemetery and became a pioneer wheat farmer. According to Hat Maxon, his father Fred was born on the Bigfoot Prairie Reservation in Illinois; when they came to California, it was by way of an emigrant steam train. Evidently, when the first transcontinental railroad was completed in 1869, the Union Pacific Central Railroad offered fares to the San Joaquin Valley from the Midwest for the low price of $1.00 per person, the purpose being to encourage settlement. These became known as the "emigrant trains."

Fred Maxon married Henriette Isabelle Wilkinson May 17, 1881 near Visalia; they had ten children: Tilly B., Verna R., Mamie J., Donald A., Sophie A., Harrison, Dorothy, Fredericka and Merion Maxon. The family settled on the southeast corner of Marinette and Highway 65 outside of Exeter. "Hat" or Harrison was born there on the family ranch. Fred and Isabelle operated a pack station at the Maxon Ranch on the South Fork where the road ended at that time. Fred passed away at the ranch in 1935 at the age of 82; his wife Belle died six years later.

Mr and Mrs Fred Maxon, S.Fork.
(Parents of Hap Maxon, Sophia
Maxon Cook and Mrs Freddie
Dreeman)

Mr. and Mrs. Fred Maxon. *Photo courtesy of the Three Rivers Museum.*

On May 31, 1910, Hat [Harrison] married Violet Busby, a daughter of Evelyn Clough Cahoon Busby and Daniel Busby, Evelyn's second husband. She was also the niece of Bill Clough of Clough's Cave and Mineral King fame. Hat was one of the men who searched for Bill when he failed to come out of Mineral King the winter of 1916; all he found were Bill's glasses, a religious tract and his shoes along with $8.00.

Hat had clear memories of John Broder and Ralph Hopping. He also remembered that Pat Murray was the person who drove the last horse stage into Mineral King. Hat managed Atwell Mill for the Park Service for a time;

he said that it required twelve head of horses and three riders to haul the boiler to Atwell Mill for use there.

Hat and Violet had two children; son Lon and daughter Zella. In an interview in 1973, Hat told of his many experiences and interesting life.[128] He said that he had worked for Miller and Lux in Buttonwillow; he had been the flume walker from Oak Grove for three years. He ran cattle with Earl McKee, Sr.; built the telephone line with Walter Fry from Three Rivers to Grouse Valley in 1906, and worked on the road from Colony Mill to Giant Forest. In addition, he had been employed by the Mt. Whitney Power Company and in 1918 he began working for the Associated Oil Company out of Coalinga; after working in the pipeline division for 35 years, he retired and moved to his ranch on the South Fork. Hat lived there until his death September 10, 1986. His wife, Vi, passed away in 1967. Hat had a great knowledge of the woods and animals and lived up to the reputation of being an excellent hunter and marksman with his shooting ability. Hat and Vi are both buried in the Exeter District Cemetery.

Ben Hardin, Dorothy Maxon, Ida Peters, and Fred Maxon. *Photo from Author's Collection.*

Walter Braddock

Walter Braddock came to Three Rivers about 1885. He was an English seaman who had sailed around the Horn in 1869. When docking in San Francisco, he eventually heard about the Kaweah Colony, became interested in its concept and came to Kaweah along with other colonists.

Later, Braddock and Alfred Hengst purchased the Orr Brown ranch on the North Fork and went into the cattle business as partners. During the summers, they took their herd into the Cliff Creek area via Timber Gap out of Silver City and Mineral King.

Walter Braddock died in 1941.

Mr. And Mrs. Walter Braddock. *Photo from the Three Rivers Museum.*

Braddock Ranch Cattle. *Photo from the Three Rivers Museum.*

The Redstone Family

The founder and patriarch of the Three Rivers branch of the Redstone family was John Hooper Redstone; he was born May 13, 1830 and named after his father. John Hooper Redstone I had been born in London, England and, as a young man, he booked passage on a westbound ship headed across the Atlantic. Near the East Coast of the United States, the crew encountered a terrific storm. When it became apparent that the ship would be torn apart, young Redstone was lashed to a spar. Rescuers found him the next morning, washed up on the beach unconscious; however, he soon recovered.

He had a good education in England, and in the following years he was able to build up a sizeable estate. He met and married Martha Anson; they began life in the Mohawk Valley country of New York State. During the next few years, two sons and three daughters were born. Although the daughter's names are not known, the sons were John Hooper Redstone of our story and his younger brother, Albert Ellis Redstone.

When young John was only eight years old, his father died; it soon became necessary for the older children to obtain any work they could find to help support the family. By the time he was ten years of age, John was earning small sums of money which meant he had to leave off his schooling; that was the end of his formal education. The family then moved to Ohio since one of the older sisters was living there, married to a Judge Nicholas Gilman. Though he was deprived of conventional schooling, young Redstone resolved to get a good education. In the evenings, he would read books about U. S. history; they instilled in him a lifelong admiration for the founders of our Republic. He was especially intrigued by the example of Abraham Lincoln and he resolved to emulate this lanky rail-splitter who would eventually become president.

After his day in the store where he worked, John would retire at an early hour in order to arise before dawn to study law by candlelight. His family moved again, this time to Indianapolis, Indiana. It was there that

John Hooper Redstone passed the state bar exam and began to practice law, specializing in patent procurement. With two other attorneys, he formed a partnership; their sign read Ray, Ellsworth & Redstone. In addition, John, along with his brother Albert, established a company they called The Novelty Machine Works; it manufactured many of the devices for which John had obtained patents.

John met and married Sarah Ann Griffith; in the following years they had four daughters, Dovey, Mary, Louisa and Kate. As the years passed, John H. Redstone lived a very interesting life; in 1862, he was commissioned to carry out a secret operation for the government in Washington to help the Union cause in the Civil War. Two men from the South—Mason and Sleidel—had been sent to Europe to ask for assistance for their southern cause. Through various adventures, John Redstone was able to forestall any such action on their part, while at the same time escaping several plotted assassination attempts against him. In his endeavors in Europe, he met many well-known persons of royalty and others not so royal. At a banquet in Vienna, Austria, he was introduced to the soon-to-be-named Mexican Emperor Maximilian and his wife, Carlotta; in Italy, he met Mazzini and Garibaldi, both Italian patriots of that time.

After two years of intensive activities, his mission had been accomplished and he returned home. When the country had returned to normalcy following the Civil War, the Redstone brothers became attracted to the lure of the West. In 1869, they sold The Novelty Machine Works and organized a party to head for California. With their two families, their sisters and brothers-in-law, there were 25 persons in the group.

They went by rail from Indiana to New York City and then by boat to Panama, crossing the Isthmus by rail. They boarded a ship for San Francisco; it had been twenty years since the gold rush of '49. After a brief but costly venture into gold mining, the brothers split up amicably and headed in different directions. The year after their arrival in California, John and Sarah had an addition to their family; a baby boy born November 29, 1870 in Vallejo, California. His name was Albert E. Redstone and he was the only boy in a family of four older girls.

While in San Francisco, John Redstone established a law office, again specializing in patent procurement. In 1885, there was a movement organized to exploit the milling of lumber in the Sierra Nevada mountains of central California; this, of course, was the movement that formed the Kaweah Colony. John Redstone and his family joined this group; however, this last adventure of his did not work out the way the family had hoped, as eventually the Colony was broken up and disbanded. Many of the member families had obtained ranch acreage along the North Fork of the Kaweah River. One of these became known as Redstone Park; legal title to the land was held by George W. Hopping, who at that time was still residing in the state of New Jersey. He had sent three of his sons, Ralph, Burt and Guy, to California to work on his ranch.

After the demise of the colony, John and Sarah Redstone operated a resort and staging station for Sequoia National Park at their family home; the Colony landmark known as Redstone Park, about one-half mile north of the current Lions Roping Arena and the current home of the Riata Ranch. Subsequently, Ralph Hopping was married to Kate Redstone, John and Sarah's daughter; his brother Burt Hopping married Dovey Redstone Brann, Kate's sister. Brothers married sisters; that made their children double cousins.

Redstone Park. *Photo from Author's Collection.*

After ten years of living close to each other, the families agreed to go their separate ways. Burt's family moved out of the river valley and down into the San Joaquin; however, just two years later he died of blood poisoning in Oakland following a minor operation.

A few years later, John Hooper Redstone and his wife Sarah had moved to Orosi, California to the home of his son, Albert E. Redstone. Sarah Redstone passed away in 1917; stricken with grief at her passing, John Redstone lived only another year and died June 19, 1918. In a paragraph summing up his grandfather's life, Phillip Redstone Hopping had this to say:

> He was the most unforgettable person I ever knew—and the most saintly. If anyone did him a wrong they were forgiven in advance; he never harbored a grudge. He never used alcohol or tobacco. I never heard vulgarity or profanity escape his lips. A few times, when he was severely tested, he said, with great vehemence, "my conscience"; that was the extent of his profanity.

Then Phillip added this:

> All of my grandparents were ardent Socialists; likewise my father, my older half-brother and one uncle. They held high hopes for the success of the Kaweah Colony. Witnessing the failure of Socialism in many parts of the world today, I doubt that any of the above mentioned would care to espouse that cause.[129]

John Redstone's son Albert E. was the last member of the Kaweah Colony; he was given a full membership in the Colony when he turned 21. He was also involved in the litigation between the colonists and the government over Colony timber claims which were later ruled void.

---

129   *Los Tulares*, Number 94; June, 1972; original manuscript entitled John Hooper Redstone; *My Most Unforgettable Character*, by Phillip Redstone Hopping.

Albert was employed by the Mt. Whitney Power Company in its building stage in 1900 as a mule skinner. He became a Forest Ranger in 1905, working from the Redstone Ranger Station in the Badger district. He was known at that time to be an expert amateur comedian and appeared in many of the amateur theatricals in Visalia in the early 1900s. He had a pet dog which he trained to do many tricks.

After 14 years as a ranger, he moved to See Canyon near San Luis Obispo and operated an apple ranch, with his wife, the former Daisy Martin, daughter of the Colony secretary. Together, they won many fair prizes annually with the fruit they raised on their ranch. He called his See Canyon ranch the "Daisy Dell."

Since he was an authority on the Colony, Albert was visited by many historians interested in the Kaweah Colony and the attendant labor movement on the West Coast. Albert or "Al" Redstone, as he was known, passed away April 9, 1964 in a Bakersfield hospital at the age of 93.

From left to right: Sarah Griffith Redstone, holding her grandson, Frank R Brann; Louise Redstone Ames; Kate Redstone; John Hooper Redstone; Ray Brann; Dovey Redstone Brann (later married Burt Hopping); Frank Brann, Sr.; Albert Ellis Redstone. *Photo from* Los Tulares #94.

(Professor) William F. Dean

To the residents of Three Rivers in the late 1800s, Professor Dean was a well-known and well-liked farmer, fruit grower and educator. Practically every old timer who grew up in the Three Rivers area received part of his or her schooling from Professor Dean.

He was born in Muskingum County, Ohio in 1855 and when he was about four years old his parents moved to Iowa. His father was Henry Dean, a native of West Virginia who had settled in Ohio in middle age; his mother was also born in West Virginia. A few years later, the family moved into Missouri. While in Missouri, he took courses at the State Normal School at Kirksville and was awarded a state certificate for teaching anywhere in that state.

Dean came to California in 1877 and taught in the public school in Poplar, California for three years. His abilities and his standing as an educator were recognized by then-Governor Perkins, who conferred upon him a life diploma that was the equal to the document he had received in Missouri with the same privileges of teaching anywhere in the state. Professor Dean married Etta B. Doyle in 1885, who was a native of Pennsylvania; however, she died the next year, leaving no children.

About ten years after arriving in California, Dean homesteaded land on the Kaweah River and by subsequent purchases, he acquired a total of 650 acres where he engaged in cattle raising. At his home on the Kaweah, he planted many fruit trees; a total of 14 acres of apple trees, including Winesaps, which bore the first crop in 1912.

County school records show that W. F. Dean taught eleven different terms in the Three Rivers and Sulphur Springs Schools between the years of 1881 and 1900. Old timers told tales of his being their teacher at the Cinnamon School as well, and others insisted that he also taught in the period between the organization of Three Rivers (then known as the Cove School) in 1873 and the beginning of school records-keeping that began in 1881. While teaching in many of these pioneer schools, he encountered numerous discipline problems. His most effective way of dealing with this bad behavior was to thrash the bullies and also their fathers if there was any parental objection.[130]

During the latter years of his teaching career, Professor Dean was apt to doze at his desk on a warm, spring day. Then the spit balls would fly! When a well-aimed wad made its target, Dean would rouse himself with a jerk, only to see an apparently studious group of youngsters with heads buried in their books.

All these antics aside, the children loved him because he often took them out on hiking trips to study nature, a subject that was very close to his heart. He felt that his students gained as much knowledge in their natural surroundings as they did in the classroom studying the "3 R's".

Professor Dean and Clarence Fry. *Photo from Author's Collection.*

---

130   Joe Doctor article, "The Kaweah's Springtime Toll."

Teaching was not Professor Dean's only interest; one of his hobbies was taxidermy, and he had many specimens to show for his craft. In addition, his cattle raising took up much of his time. A close friend of his, George Welch, a pioneer civil surveyor, surveyed the ditches for Dean's orchards and gardens. Since the ditch work involved a complicated system of leveling and many turns, it was a standing joke with Dean that "Welch did some crooked work for me."

Dean's home was located across from where the Presbyterian Church stands today; it extended down to the river and up the other side. The late Bob Barton said that when he was a boy, he enjoyed visiting Professor Dean and looking at his mounted animal heads, bear skins, stuffed birds and innumerable specimens all in little labeled boxes.

Barton also told this story of his taxidermist friend:

> Overhanging the precipitous old Mineral King Road, now abandoned, is a sheer cliff some 500 feet high called Swallow Rock because the swallows always nested there. Professor Dean was very anxious to get some of those swallow eggs, but there seemed no way to reach the mud nests plastered on the face of the cliff. Not to be thwarted, this adventurous man let himself down over the cliff on a rope and secured the coveted eggs.[131]

Sadly, Dean's valuable collection that had been stored in his barn was later destroyed by fire. To many residents of Three Rivers at the time, Professor Dean was certainly a hero. The following story only serves to illustrate his courage and resourcefulness:

> One Joe Carter of Three Rivers got into trouble while trying to ride his horse across the river in 1884, a year of a big spring runoff. His horse went down and left Joe stranded in midstream, hanging on to a clump of willows. In those days one did not call for a helicopter or the sheriff's rescue team; however, the

131   Notes of Frankie Welch.

pioneers were resourceful folk from necessity so Dan Clotfelter tried to ride a large horse out into the river to get Joe, but his horse also went down, and left Dan keeping company with Joe in the willows.

The Three Rivers community leader of that day was William F. Dean; he was sent to the river. He took with him a big white horse and after surveying the scene and the plight of the two men in the river, he caught up Dan's horse which had made its way out of the water. Dean went upstream to a point where the river widened and the current was not so swift. Leading Dan's horse, he rode to the center of the river and worked his way down to the men in the willows. He took one of them up behind him on his horse, and the other rode Dan's horse. Then they proceeded upstream in the middle of the river until they reached the place where they could cross safely.[132]

Professor Dean had very strong political views; as an illustration, the story is told of a very heated argument that took place between Dean and a bare-footed, bare-headed Socialist of German descent by the name of Shorty Hengst. Dean finally became so incensed that he grabbed Shorty by the back of his collar and pushed him down the path to the gate—Shorty protesting all the while: "Not so fast, Mr. Dean, not so fast—don't you see I vas a-coming."

As stated earlier, Dean lost his wife after only a short marriage; he never remarried and evidently grieved for her the rest of his life. As a couple, they had visited Clough's Cave on the South Fork and years after her death, when he again went into the cave with friends, he found that her foot prints were still there in the hardened mud. He was so overcome that his friends said he wept uncontrollably.

This pioneer and beloved professor of students in Three Rivers did not finish his days in the local area. When he became too old to live alone, some of his relatives from the Scofield branch of his family came out from

---

132   Joe Doctor, "The Kaweah's Springtime Toll."

the East and lived with him for a while; eventually, he moved to Oklahoma and died at the home of his nephew, George Dean, in 1934. He was a hero to some and a good friend to many.

The Barton Family

James and Susan [Davenport] Barton were natives of Morris County, New Jersey. James was born November 2, 1819 and his wife Susan was born October 30, 1823. James Barton crossed the plains with his family of ten children in 1865, following the North Platte River route to Salt Lake and the Austin and Walker's Lake route from there on to California. At that time, the Sioux Indian tribes were at war and caused their wagon train considerable trouble.

James brought with him a land grant for 120 acres, which had been given to his father Eleazar Barton for partial payment of services in the War of 1812. He located on the land October 24, 1868. This land was near Mud Springs Gap, west of Elderwood. His son Hudson later said, "a poorer piece of ground we couldn't have found."

James looked around and finally found a farm near Bravo Lake; the family stayed there only one summer and then sold the farm, since everyone in the family had been stricken with malaria. Barton moved his family to Auckland, [Tulare County] California, where he homesteaded more land.

The Bartons stayed in Auckland until 1880, when James bought a one-half section of land (320 acres) in Three Rivers for $800 cash. This property was on the North Fork, starting at the Barton house and to the apple house on both sides of the road to the river.

James and Susan then brought their four daughters and two younger sons, Jason and Milton Montgomery (often called Mont) to Three Rivers. They built their home at the confluence of the North Fork and the Middle Fork; this home is now known as the Pierce house. According to the late Bob Barton, it is the oldest house still standing in Three Rivers. The Bartons lived there until 1895 when James divided the ranch, giving the family home to his youngest son, Mont. Then James built another home where the Huston home is now, and they lived there the rest of their lives. James and Susan lived very long and productive lives; when they celebrated their

69th wedding anniversary, James was 92 and Susan 88. They both passed away in 1912, several months apart.

For seventeen years, James was a member of the Board of Supervisors, two terms as Supervisor at large, then as Supervisor of the 3rd District, which included Three Rivers. The first county courthouse was built under his supervision and as the building inspector, it was said that he inspected every piece of material that was used in constructing the building. He loved to walk and would walk from Three Rivers to Visalia in order to attend the Supervisor meetings. One time he walked from Mineral King to Auckland, stopping to eat in Three Rivers.

adelaide Barton Butts, Sophie Hardin Cook, Jason E. Barton, Melissa Barton Hardin, Mary E. Barton(wife of JAson) Front: Hudson D. Barton, Dorothy Hardin Hill Kroeber,Enos D. Barton ca. 1925

Barton Family. *Photo from Author's Collection.*

James built a log cabin in Mineral King long before the road was built. He was interested in the mining that was going on there; the Bartons have maintained a cabin there and continue to do so into the present generation.

Both James and his wife Susan are certainly to be honored as pioneers who braved the hardships of the overland trail to pave the way for the settling of California and the West.

* * * * *

Orlando D. Barton

Orlando D. Barton was born in LaSalle County, Illinois in 1847. It is as a writer that he is perhaps best known; his articles about the Indians and other Western subjects have been widely read. In the days of his youth, he ranched with his father and brothers, helping to build sawmills, and hauling the lumber out of the mountains. He also taught three terms of school in the Cottonwood District. Later, he settled on a ranch at Three Rivers, which was to be the site of the River Inn, raising cattle and hogs there for eight years.

In addition to these activities, he became quite interested in mining and oil and became a practical mineralogist with many years of study and experience. He was the owner of extensive oil interests in the Lost Hills and in the Devil's Den mining district of Kern and Kings Counties.

Orlando married Maggie Allen in 1880; she died in 1888, leaving two children. Their daughter Phoebe married Alexander McLennan of Visalia and their son Cornelius was employed by the then-named San Joaquin Light and Power Company.

* * * * *

Jason Barton

Jason Barton attended school in Auckland; at the age of fourteen, he started driving an ox team at Smith Comstock's Mill in the Big Stump

Basin near Grant Grove. When he was fifteen, he moved to Three Rivers with his family. He worked in the logging business with his brother, then decided to go into the cattle business in Three Rivers and in Mineral King on Forest Service land in the summer. He started a freighting business, driving a six-horse team until he had three sets of teams which hauled freight for the troops of the U. S. Cavalry stationed in Giant Forest. In addition, he hauled freight in wagons, used pack trains to Mineral King for several years, carrying material to build the dams on the high lakes for water storage.

Jason Barton married Mary Ellen [Allen] Griffes January 4, 1896; they had four children: Verna Pritchard (wife of Ray), Bob Barton (father of Jim), Myrtle Savage, and Viola Yawger. The family lived in the house that Jason had purchased from Orlando in 1890.

Jason and Frank Stousland, manager of the Palace Hotel in Visalia, went into partnership and built the River Inn Hotel. They continued its operation from 1909 to 1912 in conjunction with a hotel concession during the summer in Giant Forest. Barton also had a horse-drawn stage line to Giant Forest in the summer and a motor-driven line to Three Rivers for year-round visiting tourists.

In addition, he also farmed and planted citrus groves in 1906, including 100 acres in the Elderwood area and was active in farm real estate in Elderwood with William Fewel for many years.

Jason was an unofficial "mayor" of Three Rivers and very civic minded until his death May 9, 1938 at the age of 73. His wife, Mary Barton, died April 8, 1960 at the age of 95.

* * * * *

Montgomery (Mont) Barton

Mont Barton, the youngest child of James Barton, was born in 1867 on the Barton homestead at Auckland. He attended schools there; his first teacher was his older brother, Orlando. Mont acquired 120 acres of land from his father, James, at Three Rivers and raised cattle, hogs and fruit trees. When Giant Forest was patrolled by the U.S. Cavalry, he worked with his brother Jason freighting supplies to them from Lemon Cove. Mont married Hattie DeMasters in 1888 in Visalia.

Mont and Hattie Barton
ca. 1890

Montgomery and Hattie Barton. *Photo from the Three Rivers Museum.*

Mont worked for $1.00 per day in 1909, taking fish in cans from the streams in the Hockett Meadow area to the surrounding lakes. Nothing but pack stock was allowed in Hockett, so he made pack saddles for the two milk cows and packed them in order to have milk for their family and all campers at Hockett.

Mont and his wife bought property in Elderwood, where they built a home and planted an orchard; it had not been completed when Mont was fatally electrocuted September 16,1910 while servicing electric pumps for the Elderwood Citrus Development Company.[133]

---

133   Manuscript by the late Bob Barton, son of Jason Barton, undated.

The Hengst Family

The Hengst family originated in Germany; the first pioneer of this family was Dedo Hengst; he was from a family of twelve children. He came to Three Rivers about 1888 after learning about the Kaweah Colony. Upon arriving here, he was so impressed that he wrote enthusiastic letters to his brothers in Germany and soon they had followed him to Kaweah. Brother Frank Hengst and his wife Anna came to the Colony in the fall of 1888; while there, they had one son, George. After two years, they became discouraged with conditions there; after moving to other places in California, they finally came back to Three Rivers and took up a homestead on the North Fork above Yucca Creek.

Hengst place and barn. *Photo from Author's Collection.*

Another brother, Alfred, joined them and helped to build their adobe home where they lived for the next six years. Sons William, Walter and

Herman were all born there. In 1897, Frank moved his family to a ranch north of Exeter, three miles west of Merryman; there they had three more children: Freda, Elsa, (who eventually married Floyd Jones of Three Rivers), and Ada. Frank and Anna remained in the Exeter area for the remainder of their lives. Frank and Anna's daughters Freda [Jackson] and Ada [Ralph] spent their later years in Three Rivers, Freda living on the North Fork and Ada living on the South Fork. Eventually, they both moved to Woodlake where they spent their last years.

Brother Albert Alfred Hengst came to the United States in 1890, arriving in San Francisco where he applied for US citizenship in what he called "this great country of opportunity and adventure."[134] He then came to Three Rivers in 1891 and worked briefly on the construction crew which was building the road from the Kaweah Colony to Giant Forest. In 1892, he was employed as construction superintendent on the flume being built for Kaweah Power House No. 1.

Alfred Hengst. *Photo courtesy of the Three Rivers Museum.*

134   History of Alfred Hengst, manuscript by Wilma Kauling.

He married Martha [Mattie] Martin in 1907.[135] Alfred had purchased a used 1905 International Autobuggy and he and Martha drove it into Visalia for their wedding ceremony. He was the first person on the North Fork to have an automobile and when it gave him troubles, he would take it to his nephew Bill Hengst for necessary repairs.

Mattie Hengst. *Photo courtesy of the Three Rivers Museum.*

Alfred Hengst and another brother Harold (Shorty) homesteaded on two pieces of land on the North Fork down river from their brother Frank's property. A fifth brother, George, who had been living in New York and Chicago also joined them with his family; however, they too eventually settled near Exeter in the Merryman area.

All the brothers raised cattle and later Alfred and Harold acquired more property farther down river on the North Fork. Then, in 1900, Alfred joined Walter Braddock in a cattle business partnership; this successful venture continued until the mid–1930s, when the death of Braddock brought it to its end. Every summer from 1905 they would take their cattle to Mineral King via the old wagon road. Their summer camp was at Cliff Creek and during those summers, Alfred built many of the original trails into the Cliff Creek country. Also, Hengst Peak in Mineral King is named for Alfred Hengst.

Alfred and his nephew Bill Hengst were the pioneers who in 1909 brought the golden trout from the Kern River drainage to the west slope of the mountains, planting them in Granite Creek, upper Granite Lake, and Eagle Scout Creek. They also planted other streams that were barren of fish such as rainbow trout in Deer Creek, Lower Granite Lake and in Spring and Cyclamen Lakes.[136] Alfred lived in Three Rivers for 53 years. During that time, he was very active in community affairs, serving as Chamber of Commerce president and on the Tulare Council Association of Chambers of Commerce that was formed for the purpose of bringing into being the Central Valley Irrigation Project. In addition, he was a leader in the development of the original Three Rivers Airport.

Alfred's wife Mattie was very active in the Three Rivers Woman's Club, serving as president for two terms. It was during her presidency that the Club inherited the home of Mrs. Anna Hays after she passed away; Mattie was in charge of filing the club incorporation papers so the organization could own property. During her 1925 term in office, the Woman's Club held an apple festival that netted the club nearly $1,000.00, a very impressive amount for that time. Mattie was always available when there was a

---

136   History of Alfred Hengst, manuscript by Wilma Kauling.

proclamation to be drawn up or legislation to be enacted; she was well known for her good business sense and was definitely an asset to the club.

FIRST MOTOR CAR
ON NORTH FORK KAWEAH RIVER
Photo taken Spring 1909

This 1907 International Car is now on display
at the Exeter Mercantile Store, Exeter, Calif.

Front Seat
    Driver - Alfred Hengst
    Standing - Dr. Forest Grunigen (age 5)
    Seated - Mattie Hengst

Rear Seat
    Seated - John Grunigen
         (Father of Forest)
    On Lap - Berrien Grunigen
         (Sister of Forest)

Photo courtesy of the Three Rivers Museum.

According to his niece, Wilma Kauling, Alfred's life ended in 1944 the way he would have wanted it to—in the hills with his horse. When he was out with his cattle, he began having chest pains; he dismounted and led his horse to a shady spot where he could sit to rest. Later the same day, he was found there, with his horse standing by. Since the majority of their range land had been previously sold, his wife Mattie sold their house and remaining land to her niece Elsa and her husband Floyd Jones. Mattie moved to a small house just south of the Kaweah Post Office until her death in 1956.

1890s

Peter Cartwright Kirkpatrick and His Family

Peter Cartwright Kirkpatrick was born in Iowa in 1859; his parents were George Washington Kirkpatrick and Sarah Hood. Peter married Martha (Mattie) Davis Stricklin and they lived in Iowa and Kansas where two of their children were born: Eva and Lora. They came west to Three Rivers and Mr. Kirkpatrick took out a homestead of 160 acres on the South Fork where the former Wells/Seaborn ranch is now. He and his wife Mattie had six more children: Nellie, Lafayette, Cedric, Amy Thirsa, Bessie and Harry while living there.

Eva Kirkpatrick (Barnard) told the late Frankie Welch one family story about her father's very skinny sow. It seems that nothing Mr. Kirkpatrick could feed her would have any benefit; she would eat and eat and eat and still remained very thin. One day he got tired of this and thought to end her misery. He added a large dose of strychnine to her food and gave her the last rites. When Mr. Kirkpatrick later told this story: "You know," he said, "that hog cleared herself out and lived! She got fat as any pig could be!" and he concluded that she must have had worms and the strychnine killed them all.[137]

---

137   Notes of Frankie Welch.

Unfortunately, the Kirkpatricks did not stay long on the South Fork; the ranch was sold to John Broder in 1898-1899. The Kirkpatrick family moved down to Ventura County where the father [Peter] found work at St. Mary's Cemetery and where he worked until retirement. He died May 26, 1943, at age 84 in Fresno, California.[138]

Photo from Ancestry.com

---

138   Ancestry.com

Abe Burdick - A Man Who Beat the Odds

Abraham ("Abe") Baldwin Burdick, an early settler, has gone down in Three Rivers history as a legendary figure. He was born August 31, 1839 in New Jersey; his father was Abraham Burdick, mother Nancy. Siblings were Nathan, Mary, Ezra and Eunice.[139] Abe became a goldsmith by trade in New York City. Burdick resigned a lieutenant's commission in the 1st New Jersey Volunteers in 1859; when the Civil War broke out, he was employed in Massachusetts in the manufacture of guns for the Union forces.

Following the war, he was superintendent of a large jewelry manufacturing plant at Springfield, Massachusetts for seven years. Migrating westward, he first went to Arizona where he was identified with mining operations there, and later, he came farther west to San Francisco; he was employed there by George Shreve until Shreve's jewelry plant was destroyed by fire. Burdick, having lost a valuable set of tools in this fire, decided to seek rest far from the crowds of the Bay metropolis and came to Three Rivers to rest and recover his health. His wife and daughter chose to stay behind in New York City.

His decision to come to Three Rivers was made when he was hired to cook for a crew that was to build what the Kaweah Colonists called the Giant Forest Railroad, a project that was doomed to failure, since the Colonists opted instead for a wagon road to access the Giant Sequoia trees.

Again out of work, Burdick was finally diagnosed with what was then called consumption—or tuberculosis as we now know it. His doctor told him he had just a few weeks to live.

By then, his wealth purportedly consisted of $1.75 and with this, he bought a sack of beans and a slab of sowbelly [bacon]. He journeyed up to Yucca Creek on the North Fork [called East Branch by the Colonists] and camped under a sloping rock, ostensibly to await his fate. However, Burdick did not succumb to his fatal illness; in fact, he lived under the rock for two years; then he moved farther up the creek and built a cabin for himself out

139   1850 U.S. Census, www.Ancestry.com.

of hand-hewn alders he had carried up from the creek. Eventually, he developed a small ranch with an apple orchard and some livestock.

Pictures of Abe Burdick's Cabin. *Photos from Author's Collection.*

Vowing that sleeping outdoors had saved his life, Burdick continued his habit of sleeping outside in a lean-to shelter for many years. During his lifetime, the Park Service tried many times to obtain his property but according to Colonel John White, then Superintendent, he refused to sell.

Mr. Burdick had a most famous [or infamous] cat that he named "Jesus." Harry Britten, who was a park ranger at the time, told the story of the day that he had ridden his horse down the Colony Mill Road on his patrol and as was his custom, stopped at Burdick's ranch to have breakfast. As Britten was riding through the apple orchard, he spotted what he called a "lynx cat" or wildcat. He pulled out his service revolver and shot the cat, thinking to protect Mr. Burdick's chickens. He carried the cat by its bob-tail up to the door and when it was opened, Britten showed his trophy to Mr. Burdick who beheld the sight with horror. Burdick promptly became infuriated and shouted that Britten had shot his cat, slammed the door, and did not speak to Harry for many years.

Years later, the families of Ernest Britten and Ora Welch held a birthday party for the then-aged Burdick; Harry was invited to attend and he presented the tanned hide of the bobcat to Burdick. Burdick graciously accepted the "peace offering" and told Britten that he would send it to his daughter who still lived in New York and had recently contacted him.

Picnic at Burdick's. *Photo from Author's Collection.*

In the 1930s, a CCC camp was established on Yucca Creek and Abe Burdick became acquainted with Camp Superintendent John Grunigen and his wife. She took food to the then-90+ year-old man and the CCCs helped him with maintenance of his ranch.

Abe Burdick lived in good health and contentment until his death in 1935; the CCC crew buried him on a knoll above his house in the shade of a large oak. Obviously, the salubrious air and climate of the Three Rivers country had allowed him to outlive his sack of beans and slab of sowbelly to reach the age of 96.[140] He was one man who truly "beat the odds!"

---

140   *Visalia Times Delta*, July 1, 1935.

The Hopping Family

The George W. Hopping family came to Three Rivers and the Kaweah district about 1893; evidently, George had read about the Kaweah Colony and was attracted to its beliefs and practices.

George W. Hopping was born about 1845 in New York State; his wife's name was Laura and in 1880, he listed his occupation as a bookkeeper.[141] At that time, their family consisted of sons Ralph, Burt, Roy, daughter Ruth and youngest son, Guy Hopping.

George W. Hopping was a veteran of the Civil War and was the chief accountant for the firm that eventually became known as Johnson & Johnson, the druggist company of fame; working there, he received the large salary of $500 per month.[142] Although he was definitely in agreement with the goals of the Colony, he was understandably somewhat reluctant to commit himself totally; instead, he sent two of his sons, Ralph and Burt, to Kaweah. They went to work at Atwell Mill for the colonists; Burt turned out to be a valuable mechanic for the group and was complimented when he was able to do the necessary repairs to the printing press for the *Commonwealth*.

Ralph and Burt were popular and well liked by the colonists and they made the Redstone Park area of Kaweah their headquarters. There they came into contact with two of the attractive Redstone daughters and it wasn't long before there were marriages between the two families. Ralph Hopping married Kate Redstone April 23, 1892, and soon after, brother Burt followed with his marriage to Dovey, Kate's sister [Tulare County records show that Burt (Bert) Hopping married a Nannie A. Redstone, January 4, 1894.][143]

In time, the other members of the Hopping family came west to Kaweah; the youngest son, Guy, and sister Jessie. Jessie Hopping married

141   1880 US Federal Census.
142   *Co-operative Dreams*, by Jay O'Connell, pg. 175.
143   Tulare County Vital Records, pg. 584.

John Grunigen in 1903, but the marriage ended in divorce. Their children were Forest J. Grunigen and Ethel Berrien Grunigen.

Jessie Hopping Grunigen. *Photo courtesy of the Three Rivers Museum.*

According to Phil Winser, a member of the Colony, when the father, George W. Hopping, finally arrived in 1911 with much fanfare, "By paying off Kaweah's mortgage, he [Hopping] acquired title to that 240 acres and thus insured greater permanency for the Redstone-Hopping section of Redstone Park and a choice of home sites for himself, Mrs. Hopping and two maiden sisters when they finally came west."[144] George W. Hopping and family continued to live in the Redstone area for many years. In 1923,

144   *Co-Operative Dreams*, by Jay O'Connell, pg176.

George went to Pasadena to live with his daughter, Jessie; he passed away there January 22, 1924.[145]

The Hoppings of Kaweah made Three Rivers their home; Guy Hopping went on to work for the Park Service at Sequoia, eventually being appointed superintendent of General Grant National Park in 1933. When this Park was absorbed by the creation of Kings Canyon National Park, he became the assistant superintendent. He retired from the park service in 1942. Guy married Daisy DeMasters, a native of Visalia and daughter of Newton DeMasters in 1907 and they made their home on his Salt Creek Ranch. They had no children.

Guy was considered an expert forest and brush firefighter and directed the crews which battled several major fires, including one which came from Eshom Valley in the 1930s and for a time threatened Giant Forest. In addition to his service in the parks, Guy was also a cattleman and an authority on early park history, remembering distinctly the days when the park was controlled by the US Army and its cavalry troops every summer. Guy passed away June 22, 1961 at the age of 84.

Guy Hopping, Ranger. *Photo courtesy of the Three Rivers Museum.*

145   *The Fresno Bee,* January 23, 1924.

Guy's brother Ralph was also enterprising and his endeavors left their mark on early-day Three Rivers and Giant Forest. Ralph went into partnership with John Broder and they operated the first stock packing outfit to the high country. Broder & Hopping became known for its trips into the back country, enabling the tourists in those days to see the beauties of the mountains for themselves. They established their way station at Redstone Park with a hotel and "Queen Anne" cottages for guests. They also opened a tent-style hotel in Giant Forest; the stage line at that time came all the way up from Visalia.

Like his brother Guy, Ralph also served as a park ranger; in addition, he had an interest in studying entomology and, in fact, discovered a species of insect unknown at the time, bringing him great notice and success and launching his career as an entomologist. Ralph died October 29, 1941 in Vernon, BC, Canada, at the age of 73.

The Doctor Downing D. Nice Family

In 1918, Dr. Downing D. (Or Dr. D. D. Nice as he was locally known) and his son Bert [Hubert C.] moved to the small orange and apple ranch on the old highway into Three Rivers (eventually Highway 198) that had previously been known as the Joe Carter place. It later became the Spotts Cider Mill and eventually, the Sequoia Cider Mill. The Nice family moved here from Los Angeles, where Dr. Nice had practiced medicine since 1890.[146] Evidently, his wife Jessy E. Nice had passed away sometime before his move to Three Rivers.[147]

Joe Carter Home, Later Sequoia Cider Mill. *Photo courtesy of the Three Rivers Museum.*

Doctor Nice was the only doctor in Three Rivers for the next ten years and his home became known as the "house beside the road." It became a stopping place for the local people as well as many nationally known individuals and prominent doctors who stopped over for a few hours or

146   Ancestry.com
147   1920 US Federal Census shows "widowed."

a day or two. This was the period of development of Sequoia Park, and Doctor Nice took an active interest in the work.

Dr. Nice's son Hubert was born in Bowen, Illinois, February 2, 1896. The family moved to Los Angeles where the doctor established his practice and Bert received his education. According to Bert's obituary, the Nice family were California pioneers, the first of whom established themselves in the 1850s. They had interests in land in the Yosemite area, Yuma, Arizona and owned acreage and mineral rights in the San Gabriel Canyon.

Quite a bit of Bert's growing up years were spent exploring the San Gabriel Canyon, ranching with his grandfather in the Yuma area and at the ranch near Yosemite. They vacationed in Yosemite by traveling on horseback and wagon.

In addition to maintaining the small ranch at Three Rivers, Bert spent his summers working as a packer and guide for Earl McKee, Sr. during the mid-1920s.

Bert's father, Dr. Downing Nice, passed away December 17, 1927 from influenza and pneumonia.[148] Bert eventually married Violet Vinding, and in 1931, they sold the Three Rivers ranch and moved to Lemon Cove, where Bert became associated with the Sequoia Citrus Association. He was the manager of the Association and assisted in the management of the Henry Howison ranches.

With the closing of the Citrus Association in 1950, Bert moved to Elderwood, where he managed the Elderwood Association for about eight years. Bert and Violet's sons Hubert and Don spent their high school days at Woodlake High.

In 1958, the family moved south to Glendora and became semi-retired. Interest in the San Gabriel property took up much of Bert's time. The oldest son Hubert died in 1969 and then Bert's wife Violet in 1970. Bert Nice then passed away suddenly after heart surgery January 20, 1973.[149]

---

148   *Directory of Deceased American Physicians,* 1804-1929.
149   *Three Rivers Sentinel,* January 26, 1973.

Fred Savage and His Family

The patriarch of the Savage family and the first to settle in Three Rivers was Fred Samuel Savage. He was born March 19, 1868 in West Derby, Liverpool, England.[150] He came to this country in 1890 at the urging of his friend Philip Winser to join the Kaweah Colony. Fred Savage was the son of a cabinet maker from Liverpool who took a great interest in social experiments and cooperative ventures. Early in 1891, he had sent money to Kaweah toward a membership, and also to help with the Colony's Defense Fund. Sometime later, he had a financially disastrous business venture in Sinola, Mexico on behalf of another cooperative colony there; this one was similar to the concept of the Kaweah Colony. Savage boarded another ship for passage to San Diego and from there, he literally walked all the way to Kaweah.[151] And walk he did; through the Mojave Desert where the temperature reached 120 degrees in the shade, as the leather on his shoes continued to crack and curl around his feet.[152]

When he had walked as far as Lemon Cove, he noticed Phil Winser's sign advertising lemonade there. Jay O'Connell shares a portion of Phil Winser's memoirs as follows:

> It was this sign [Winser wrote in his memoirs] which lured in Fred Savage one hot day. A little conversation convinced Blanche [Winser] that here was a man I must meet, so she induced him to stop that night and we talked.
>
> Then we sent him on up to Bert and when he returned, it was to get a job in Lemon Cove and we planned to pool our resources and extend our orchard enterprise together. And so it went, throughout the summer and autumn, Fred would come over some Sundays and we talked everything over; he sent to England for some savings and with my pay we were able to negotiate a

---

150   www.ancestry.com.
151   *Co-operative Dreams*, Jay O'Connell, pg. 178.
152   *Sequoia Sentinal*, "I Remember When" by Mary Anne Savage, July 22, 1992.

further purchase of [some of Halstead's] land on which there was a clearing to be done by Bert.

As soon as we returned to Kaweah, we arranged a form of partnership to fit conditions; Blanche and I by virtue of holdings already established took two-fifths interest and Fred and Bert divided the remaining three-fifths equally; all outside earnings were to be pooled and the common fund to supply housekeeping and ranch outlays.[153]

So a partnership was born—a very small scale cooperative, but it continued to thrive and become a viable business venture for all concerned.

Fred Savage then sent for his childhood sweetheart, Annie Harrison, who was living in England. She joined him and when Fred went to meet her in Visalia, they stopped in Exeter on their way to Kaweah and were married in the old Montgomery house on what is now Highway 65. Fred and Annie had three children: Allan, Kenneth and Enid. Allan was born in the house Phil Winser had built and named "Merrington" for his old farm in far-off England. The late Ord Loverin remembered when Allan was born; his mother, Mary Lovern, had left home for a few days to take care of Mrs. Savage who was "ill." Then Ord was very surprised to find out that Allan had "magically appeared" and everyone was fine![154]

The boys, Allan and Kenneth, went to grade school at the Sulphur Springs School. They often walked or rode horseback. Sister Enid was later sent to be educated in England.

Their mother, Annie Harrison Savage, died in 1913 and she was buried above the orchard in the private family cemetery. According to a column written by Annie's granddaughter, Mary Anne Savage [daughter of Allan]:

I always felt that I had missed a lot by never knowing her since I was named for her and heard such nice things about her as I grew up. But I do remember Grandad (Fred S.) and was always a little awed by him.

---

153   *Co-operative Dreams*, pg. 178.
154   Memories of the author.

Whenever I would visit him, he would take my hand and gravely shake it rather than a hug; he was a very reserved man.

Fred Samuel Savage married again; this time to Jessie Ann; they married in 1937. At the time of their marriage, Jessie was 53 and she had been born in England also. Again, according to Mary Anne Savage,

> Jessie was the only grandmother I knew. She had come from England and was a delightful person, well known in Three Rivers. There were Christmas parties held in the big arched living-room with a log fire burning in the fireplace and all my cousins, Milton, Merritt and Stoney, and of course Uncle Ken and Aunt Myrtle and my own family gathered together. Granddad would tell stories of Christmas in England and Grandma Jessie would play the piano and we all sang. I loved every minute of it. I was six years old when Grandad died in 1942. It was the end of quite a saga and of a different life and time. It took much courage and foresight by him and his fellowmen [sic] to come so far and build so much.[155]

Fred S. Savage. *Photo from www.ancestry.com public photos.*

---

155   *I Remember When*, by Mary Anne Savage, Sequoia Sentinel, July 22, 1992.

Colonel Charles Young, Citizen, Soldier

[NOTE: while it is true that Colonel Young was not a "pioneer" settler of the Three Rivers district, his presence and those of his troops by completing the road into Giant Forest made an impact on this community; it opened up tourist travel to and from the Park. His story is one of inspiration and dedication; to omit it would be to ignore an important part of Three Rivers history.]

* * * * *

In Arlington National Cemetery in Washington, DC lies the grave of Colonel Charles Young, a man of distinction and dignity, whose entire life was devoted to serving his country and his race.

His career has a particular interest to the residents of Three Rivers, because in 1903, he was acting superintendent of Sequoia National Park. He was the only Black to ever serve in that capacity, and in that year, he was responsible for completion of the first road into Giant Forest.

He was a cavalry officer of the 9th Cavalry troop and a graduate of West Point with an enviable record of military service in the Philippines with the Rough Riders in Cuba and with General John J. Pershing in Mexico.

He was born in Mayslick, Kentucky in 1864 and was distinguished from his youth. At age sixteen, he was the first Black person graduated from a white high school in Ripley, Ohio. Following graduation, he taught in the Black person's high school in Ripley and also prepared to enter a Jesuit College. However, he had an opportunity to take the competitive examination for appointment to West Point through Representative Alonzo Hart and he won, entering the academy in 1884.

While he was the third Black person graduated from West Point, he was the first to achieve distinction. He received a medal for his outstanding contribution while serving as a military attaché in Africa, and he was promoted to captain for conspicuous bravery while riding in the famous charge up San Juan Hill in Cuba.

Colonel Young was a scholar, as well as a soldier and gentleman. He was a professor of military science and tactics at Wilberforce University, Xenia, Ohio. He spoke six foreign languages and had a magnificent collection of books in those languages; he wrote poetry, and was an accomplished musician and composer for piano and violin.

Completion of the road to Giant Forest under his direction was a milestone in the development of Sequoia National Park for it opened up that area to tourists. Although the park was formed in 1890, there were no administrative funds available and each summer, troops were sent to prevent trespassing on the government lands previously used for lumbering and also as summer range for cattle and sheep.

Young and his all-Black troops of the 9th Cavalry rode from the Presidio in San Francisco to Three Rivers, taking sixteen days to make the trip. In the next three months, in addition to directing work on trails and fighting fires, he obtained options on patented lands and pushed and completed the road.

Captain Young, front row left, with road crew. Celebrating completion of first road to Giant Forest. 1903.

Road Crew, Capt. Young, front row left, George Welch, Engineer & Surveyor, second row, middle. *Photo from Author's Collection.*

Captain L. W. Cornish, who relieved him of duty in September, wrote in his report to Washington, "An examination of the work done on the roads and trails under the direction of Captain Charles Young, shows that it has been well done, and the quantity is largely in excess of that done in previous years with the same amount of money."

The job was not an easy one. There was bitterness and resentment against the government, particularly from Kaweah Commonwealth Colonists who had built the road up the North Fork of the Kaweah River as far as Colony Mill for their lumbering activities. They lost their holdings there when their timber claims were declared invalid, thus including them in the new park. Previous cavalry officers had administered construction of the extension of the road each summer, but Young got it completed in record time under the direction of George Welch, a civil engineer from Lima, Ohio.

Mounted troop of the 9th Cavalry "Buffalo" Soldiers, led by Captain Young on Old Three Rivers Drive. *Photo from Author's Collection.*

Young encouraged the workmen by promising them a sumptuous dinner at its completion. He kept his word and that dinner was the talk of the whole county for a long time. Everyone who had been connected with the road building, including notables from the valley, were invited and none declined. The food was set out on a huge log and Young and his troops served the guests from blasting powder boxes attached to shovels. Pleased at his guest's enjoyment of the food, Young remarked that the traditional regard of black people for fried chicken was well matched by those of the whites present.

While the archives at Sequoia National Park, West Point and Ripley High School supply many details, Young was vividly recalled by old-timers in Three Rivers as being a splendid officer and a fine man. He was a dynamic man, described as handsome and powerful with a pleasant expression and direct eyes that reflected intelligence and kindness. This author can remember her late husband, John Britten, Sr., telling the story of his father, Ernest Britten, when he was the first park ranger; Ernest spent much time with Colonel Young and his 9th Cavalry unit. In the evenings, they would play poker and one of the prizes that was won and passed around to the winner every night was a money belt sewn with many silver dollars. At the end of the summer season, the cavalry troop gave it to Ranger Britten for his kindnesses to them. Unfortunately, this money belt was lost in a fire at the home of Ernest's sister Eureka Williams in La Cañada, where he had left it for safekeeping.

Young was philosophical about his color, but he admitted to friends that he "went through hell" to get his commission, and "so I have no fear for the future life." He also said that the worst he could wish for any enemy would be to make him a Negro and send him to West Point.

Colonel Young also purchased the house at Pierce Corner from Montgomery Barton and lived there for a while, making it his headquarters. Among the stories that are told about him in Three Rivers is one that reveals the incongruity of his life. While on his way to address the students and faculty at Stanford University by special invitation, he stopped at a restaurant in Visalia, but was refused service.

There is a story about the Grunigens who had accommodations at Lake Canyon on the Mineral King Road. Young and a crew of troopers had been fighting fire at Oriole Lake above Lake Canyon and it had taken them longer than expected. It was late; they were tired and out of rations. Young asked Mrs. Grunigen if she would feed his men and she agreed until he added that the men would come in and pick up their plates and eat outside. Highly indignant, she declared they would either come inside and eat at the table or they would not eat at all. They came inside and ate the hearty supper she prepared, but Young insisted his men clean up the kitchen in return. They did, and when they were through, the kitchen shone from ceiling to floor.

Another incident related about him could possibly be the origin of a well-known legend. Young was at the Presidio when two young officers walked by and failed to salute; he called them back and questioned them about the breach of discipline. They replied that they would refuse to salute a Black person. Without a word, Captain Young hung his coat and cap on a post. "Now! You will stand at attention and salute the uniform of the United States Army! No matter what is inside that uniform, and officers, you should know you are saluting your government." They saluted to the amusement of others passing by.

Young married Ada Mills in San Francisco in February 1904 and shortly thereafter received assignment for duty as a military attaché in Haiti. A Washington newspaper article carrying a dateline from the Legation of the United States, Port au Prince, Haiti, June 21, 1904 states, "A military attaché will be sent to Haiti and San Domingo and for this duty Captain Charles Young of the 9th Cavalry has been selected. He is a colored man, a graduate of the military academy and has a fine record. His ability and fitness for the place led to his destination."

He also served as a military attaché in Monrovia, Liberia. His accomplishments in this field earned for him the Springarm Medal for African Work.

Young had been promoted to the rank of colonel by 1916 when he was with General Pershing on the expedition against Francisco [Pancho]

Villa in Mexico, and his indomitable spirit is exemplified by an episode in World War I. He was in Ohio and retired, but he applied for a command overseas. When doctors claimed his health was too poor for active duty, Young mounted his favorite horse and rode the 500 miles to Washington to prove he was physically fit.

The determined colonel was recalled to active duty and assigned to train Black troops at Fort Grant, Illinois. He returned to Liberia later as a military attaché, but soon after his arrival, he died in Lagos Nigeria in 1922. His body was brought back to the United States in 1923 and buried in Arlington Cemetery with full honors.

He and his wife had two children; Charles, who became a professor at Wilberforce University, and his daughter, Mrs. Marie Ware, became a teacher there. At the time this manuscript was written [1967], they were compiling a biography of their father.[156] Since that time, several other biographies have been written about this heroic, compelling American.

Colonel Charles Young. *Photo courtesy the Three Rivers Museum.*

---

156   *The Fresno Bee*, November 5, 1967. A manuscript by Virginia Williams.

Walter Fry

Walter Fry was born in 1859 in Watseka, Iroquois County, Illinois. His father was Samuel Fry, a native of Ohio, who died in 1897; his mother was Mary Catherine McCullough; she passed away when Walter was young. When he was nine, Walter was taken from Illinois to Kansas and he lived there as well as in Oklahoma. As he got older, he made a living by being a cowboy, a miner, a rancher and deputy US Marshal. He married Sarah A. Higgins July 21, 1879 in Fredonia, Kansas; she accompanied him to California when they came to Tulare in 1887.

In Tulare, he was given employment with the railroad company and was made a peace officer; he served in that capacity until 1894 or 1895. At that time, he moved to Three Rivers and settled on the South Fork in the Cinnamon Creek district where their children Clarence and Bessie attended the Cinnamon Creek School.

In 1899, the family moved closer to Three Rivers and purchased a home and acreage from Daniel Clotfelter (near the location of the current Three Rivers Historical Museum). Clotfelter was a pioneer stockman who had received a patent for his homestead on the Middle Fork in 1870. The parcel he sold to the Frys included a very distinctive two-story house built about 1880.

Civilian Walter Fry was appointed to the job of Road Foreman for Sequoia Park in 1901; in 1905 he became a Park Ranger. By 1910, Fry was Chief Ranger, managing the parks for the military superintendents that were appointed to supervise each summer. When the Army gave up caretaking the parks in 1914, the choice for a civilian superintendent was a clear one. Fry went on to lead the parks through challenging times that included a world war and the creation of the National Park Service.[157] From 1914–1920, he served as the Superintendent of Sequoia.

When Colonel White became superintendent in 1920, Fry again shifted jobs, becoming U.S. Commissioner, or Federal "Judge" in the Parks. Colonel White recognized Fry's worth immediately: "[I]t would be almost

157   www.ancestry.com

impossible to overstate the affection and esteem in which Judge Fry is held by both the Park employees and visitors. He has been able to enforce park regulations with such sympathetic insight into the needs of visitors and residents that the enforcement has won friends for the Park Service."

The Fry house became a famous landmark and was subsequently listed on an early map as just "Frys." According to the late Jessie Bequette, Judge Fry's granddaughter, the large frame house had lots of bedrooms; the second floor was just one large open room, well suited for parties and dances. Jessie fondly remembered many affairs as part of the "good life" at Frys.

As she recalled, "The families would come at nightfall in their buggies or buckboards. With them they brought their babies and young children all bundled up, as well as bringing with them food, music, and candles. The second floor [of the house] was ablaze with the candles securely fastened in plate racks around the room. Everybody would dance to the music of banjo, fiddle and guitars. Around midnight, the aroma of fried chicken, baked ham, chocolate cake and apple pies would entice the party to their potluck feast. Then it would be back to dancing until daylight."

First Home of Walter Fry & Family. *Photo courtesy the Three Rivers Museum.*

Square and round dancing were occasions for plenty of foot stomping. As a precaution, the Frys would place 1 x 12s in the dining room and kitchen to support the upstairs floor and also save the downstairs ceilings.[158]

The Fry home was also used for visiting dignitaries and Park guests. In addition, there were three telephones strategically placed there that served the entire community.[159]

Tragedy struck this lovely home in August 1917; a grass fire had started near the home of Walter's son Clarence; the fire consumed Clarence's house, then continued burning up the canyon until it had ravaged several structures, including the large and lovely home of Judge and Mrs. Fry. It was reported that this was the most serious fire of that season; it also destroyed the home of Dan Southward and swept up the canyon toward Hammond and Kaweah No. 1, burning the power lines as it went. All three power houses were closed until the repairs were made.[160]

Both Fry families soon re-built; Walter's second home was purchased in 1930 by Ben Packard, who was an employee of Sequoia Park at the time. Clarence's home was enlarged and eventually sold as well.

Unfortunately, their homes, previously known locally as "Frys," this Three Rivers place name is now consigned to history. The enduring memory of Judge Walter Fry is not; the nature center at Lodgepole Campground was re-dedicated as the "Walter Fry Nature Center" in the summer of 1994. Children come to this building each summer for hands-on involvement with the things of these parks: huge trees, awesome geology and fascinating wildlife. Each child takes home a sense of the Sierra, and in so doing, carries on a bit of Judge Walter Fry's distinctive legacy.[161]

---

158   John F. Elliott, *Sequoia Sentinel*, December 8, 1993.
159   Ibid.
160   *Bakersfield Morning Echo*, August 12, 1917.
161   www.ancestry.com

Judge and Mrs. Walter Fry. *Photo from Author's Collection.*

Walter Fry's Second Home. *Photo courtesy of the Three Rivers Museum.*

1900s

Byron Allen

Byron Allen was a native son of California, Tulare County and Visalia; he was born October 10, 1868 and was a pioneer cattleman in Visalia and Three Rivers. He was the son of William Byron Allen and Margaret Houston, a niece of Sam Houston of Texas. His father died shortly after Byron was born; his mother remarried and he was brought up by his stepfather, James W. Oakes. When he finished school, he was associated with Oakes in the cattle business. The family brand, the Square Top Three, was registered in Tulare County in 1858.

Byron went to Arizona, New Mexico and Old Mexico on a prospecting tour before returning to Visalia, where he again engaged in the breeding of cattle and horses. With all his experiences and travels, he had found ranching to be more promising than mining. Following the death of Mr. Oakes, he had the management of the interests left by his stepfather and made a success of the ranching business. With 280 acres of valley land, he made a specialty of raising fine-blooded horses and ranging his large herd of cattle in the mountains on two thousand acres there. His herd numbered 250 head of beef cattle, 150 hogs and forty turkeys.

Byron Allen married Miss Della Carter in 1904; she was the daughter of a pioneer Lemon Cove family where her father was the postmaster for many years.

Byron passed away at his family home in Visalia, December 12, 1954; he was 87.

Byron Allen. *Photo from Visalia Times-Delta.*

The Blick Family

The Blick Family came to Three Rivers in 1908. The family consisted of the father, James Shannon Blickensderfer (later changed to Blick) and his wife Phoebe Elenor Dunning. They came to Three Rivers from their home in Eldorado, Kansas and settled on the South Fork of the Kaweah. Along with Frederick Burnham, husband of their daughter Blanche, they bought the property from John Broder. Originally, this consisted of 800 acres; however, in succeeding years, the ranch was enlarged to encompass over 4,000 acres. They built three adobe houses for all the families with labor and supplies imported from Mexico.

The Blick family consisted of eight children: Madge, who married a John Ford; Blanche, who married the famous Frederick Russell Burnham; Homer Ephraim, who married Linnie Nye; Joseph James, who married Daisy Russell; Grace (spouse unknown); Judd, who married Edith Lovering; John C., who remained a bachelor; and Kate F. (no record of marriage).[162]

The ranch, or La Cuesta as it was named, was located about five miles up the South Fork; it was a combination of homesteads and open land, bought up by the Blick brothers, Judd and John, and Fred Burnham between 1905 and 1910.

However, in the mid-1890s, John and Judd Blick, along with Fred Burnham, all U. S. citizens, nevertheless became members of the British Army in South Africa during the Boer Wars, where their many adventures have been told. Burnham wrote two books himself, *Scouting on Two Continents*, and *Taking Chances*; several other books have been written by different authors.[163]

When gold was discovered in the Yukon Territory in 1898, Major Burnham and the Blick brothers made their way across the globe to the gold fields there. Burnham told a tale of ice and snow, 40-degree-below temperatures that they endured on the 300-mile trek to the Klondike,

---

162   Family names and info from www.ancestry.com
163   *American Family on the African Frontier*, Mary & Richard Bradford; *King of Scouts*, Peter van Wyk.

returning to Skagway, Alaska one year later with one-hundred pounds of gold.

Coming back to California, Homer Blick worked in Pasadena for about twenty years, finally returning to Three Rivers where he took over the operation of the Mount Whitney Power Company hydro plant at Hammond.

Judd Blick returned to Three Rivers, where he managed the large ranch; he married Edith Lovering from Three Rivers; they had no children. After members of the large family drifted away, only Judd and his wife remained; the range was leased to Gill Brothers for 10 or 15 years before finally being sold. The loss of the Hockett Meadows range, when it became part of Sequoia Park, further discouraged Judd from cattle raising.

Although John C. Blick was a mining engineer in Africa, the Alaskan Klondike and Mexico, he spent many years at the ranch, living there until it was sold in 1926.

At that time, he became associated with the Museum of Natural History in New York City as a paleontologist. Eventually, he moved to Visalia in 1954 and made his home with his niece, Mrs. Helen Gardiner. He died July 11, 1960 at the age of 84.

James Arthur Mehrten

James (Jim) Mehrten was born September 7, 1879, at his family home on the Mehrten "Swamp Ranch" near the site of the old Cottage Post Office, west of Woodlake. His father was Louis Mehrten, who had been born in Germany, and his mother was Mae Elizabeth Poppe Mehrten. Jim had a twin sister, Matilda Mae, who married Tom Homer. He had three brothers, Bernard, Charles and William, and one other sister, Louisa. By the time Jim had reached the age of thirteen, both of his parents had died and he went to live with his older brother William in Dinuba for a while. At the age of sixteen, he went with his brother Charles and Charles' wife Dora to Mexico to go into the hog business on the 200 acres of land that Charles had already purchased there. After a trip of several weeks from home, they arrived at the American Colony at Metlaltoyuca in the state of Veracruz. This venture did not work out for them due to the inhospitable climate for animal raising, so they switched to growing corn, bananas, pineapples and other crops instead. At time passed, they were threatened by neighboring Mexican landholders, forcing them to sell out and they left for Mexico City, eventually returning home.

On December 7, 1902, James married Amy Myrtle Odenbaugh in Tulare at the home of her parents Mr. And Mrs. G. W. Odenbaugh. This family had migrated to California from Severy, Kansas when Amy was seven.

Jim and Amy's first home was in the Exeter District for a few years and their first daughter Norma May was born there in 1904. The family then came to Three Rivers in 1906, buying the Purdy place on the North Fork near the Kaweah Post Office; two years later, their home there was completed.

That summer was spent at Atwell Mill, where Jim made redwood posts and shakes to sell during the fall in the valley. Amy told the story of traveling up the old Mineral King Road with their balky horse in their team. She said she had to walk practically all the way up the River Hill

Grade, carrying their small daughter, blocking the wagon wheels to keep them from rolling back when the horse balked. This happened every time the grade of the road became too steep, causing him to rear back.

After that summer, Jim Mehrten went into the freighting business; he carried the mail up the old Colony Mill Road on the North Fork to the earliest post office at Giant Forest, first with a horse and cart, and later by stagecoach. Three two-day trips a week with the mail were made, up one day and back the next. Starting about 1908, he carried both passengers and mail while driving the stage for Broder and Hopping, the first park tourist company. In 1910, he took over the Broder and Hopping stage line; again hauling mail and passengers. This type of operation required a four-horse team with three relay stations to change teams. Starting at Lemon Cove, he drove to Three Rivers for a change of horses, then on to the relay stations at Minnehaha Gulch and Colony Mill; then on to Giant Forest. One day, he was carrying the mail by cart when his horse smelled a bear and started backing up, trying to turn around. However, the more Jim whacked and shouted at the mare, the more she snorted, finally backing the cart, horse, mail and driver right over the bank. They all survived, but for a time things were in a real mess.

Giant Forest Stage, Jim Mehrten, Driver, Abe Burdick passenger. *Photo from Author's Collection.*

When Jim first started carrying parcel post, the weight limit was three pounds. Then it went up to eleven pounds, then to 25 and up to 50 pounds the last two months of his contract. He was so disgusted by this practice that he would not renew his contract, and he quit the business. However, Jim continued to haul freight and to team for many years, including hauling for the Mt. Whitney Power Company when they were constructing Power House No.3 on the Middle Fork above Three Rivers.

Jim and Amy's second daughter, Myrtle Evelyn, was born February 26, 1907. Both girls attended the Sulphur Springs School, and for several years their teacher was Eula Graham, who soon after married Will Mehrten of Lind Cove.

During the early years in the winter months, Jim did carpentry work and construction in Three Rivers; in the spring and fall, he worked in their apple orchard; then he, Amy and the family would spend their summers in the mountains, which they continued doing for over thirty years. Jim was connected with part of the early building in Giant Forest, and he made the shakes for roofing some of the earliest buildings there. For several years, he also worked as a checker at the Park at Cedar Creek Checking Station, and he admitted the first automobile ever to enter the Sequoia National Park.

Jim continued to operate and work in his apple orchard that had originally been on the property when he purchased it from the Purdys. His apples became well known, and in later years, many people from the valley would make the drive up to the Mehrten Ranch and purchase most of his entire crop. He was also known for the cider he and Amy produced each fall. Among the varieties he grew were Ben Davis, Winesaps, Stamens, and Black Twigs. Careful handling and occasional replacement of the old trees kept the orchard in top production. The biggest problem was keeping the bears from breaking down the trees and the deer out of the orchard.

For thirteen years, Jim had a fruit and vegetable stand at Giant Forest, which was an outlet for his apples and the large vegetable garden that Amy had; he would haul the produce up when he was teaming, and later on he used his 1917 Dodge truck to do the freighting. For two summers, he hired his nephew, Edward Homer, to work for him and it was there in Giant Forest that Edward met his future wife, Esther Prestage.

In the 1930s, Jim built and operated the mountain resort of Silver City, located on the Mineral King Road. He ran the store, restaurant, gasoline station and cabins, as well as organizing most of the social activities and dances there. In addition, he built many other summer homes for people who purchased lots in Silver City. Frank Blain had obtained 320 acres of land there and the north half was leased to Jim.

During several summers there, daughter Myrtle and her husband Merritt would join her parents, Jim and Amy, and they would enjoy the back country as a family outing. One time, one of the pack horses fell into Forester Lake with his hobbles still on. Jim managed to coax the animal to the bank, removed the hobbles and the horse proceeded to swim out of the lake.

Jim Mehrten continued constructing homes and buildings in Three Rivers, including the old Community Hall and the home of Anna Hays, which eventually became the Three Rivers Woman's Club House. In addition, he built the Tom Homer home on Dry Creek, as well as the John and Louise Mehrten Taylor home just a mile or so below Jim and Amy on the North Fork Road.

The Mehrtens always took an active part in the community and the social life of Three Rivers, especially the old-time square dances. Assisted by their daughters, the Mehrtens entertained a large group of friends and relatives at the Three Rivers Woman's Club House for their 25th wedding anniversary in 1927. They hosted over 150 well wishers at their Golden wedding anniversary party that was held at their home in Kaweah in 1952.

Old age did not seem to bother either Jim or Amy; Jim continued to care for his orchard by himself; it was one of the few remaining commercial orchards left in the Three Rivers area. However, while working at his place, Jim died suddenly with a heart attack at his home at the age of 81. He was the last living child of the Louis Mehrten family. He was buried in the Three Rivers Cemetery. Amy stayed on for a few years in the old home with the aid of her two daughters. She also suffered from heart trouble and she died November 7, 1965 at the age of 80. She is buried beside her husband.

The growth of Three Rivers over the years is much of an open book, part of which was authored by Jim Mehrten. At his death, he was eulogized as a "pioneer in development"; he had spent a long span of years working and doing things with his hands almost until to the time of his death. His efforts to bring civilization to the mountain area would fill volumes. His career was varied to fit the pioneer times from hauling mail, passengers and freight by horse and buggy to being a first-class carpenter and lumber man, to building and operating successfully a mountain resort and at the same time being an expert in agriculture, especially in the planting and the growing of apples. The resort at Silver City still stands, as do numerous buildings in Three Rivers, Lemon Cove and Giant Forest that he either constructed or hauled the lumber so they could be built. Jim Mehrten lived to see the transition from the horse to the stagecoach, to the automobile and truck as the principle means of transportation. All that he did required a rugged constitution and a special way of getting along with his neighbors to survive the history-laden years that composed his life span.[164]

Jim Mehrten in his orchard. *Photo from Los Angeles Times.*

---

164   Mehrtens of the San Joaquin Family Newsletter, pg. 614. September 1969, editor Rodney Homer.

The Finch Family

Frank Finch was the pioneer member of the Finch family to settle in Three Rivers. Frank was the son of Jesse Finch and Grace Simmons Finch. Frank was born in Iowa in 1867 into a family that included five boys and one girl. Frank lived in Hale, Jones County, Iowa, where he attended school. He met Rhoda Mary Rice, born September 13, 1867, daughter of James N. Rice and Mary A. Williams Rice; they were married in Aurelia, Iowa August 20, 1889. Rhoda was the sister of William Rice who had settled on what is now Kaweah Lake bottom in 1887. Frank and Rhoda's children were Jesse Frank, born 1890; Edna Blanche (who married Earl McKee, Sr.), born 1893; Loren James, born 1895; and Zola Evelyn, born 1901. They were all born in Cherokee County, Iowa, except for the youngest daughter, Marjorie, who was born after they moved to California.

Will Rice (Frank's brother-in-law) told Frank about a property east of Lemon Cove that was for sale, so Frank and his family came to Tulare County to settle about 1902. He purchased 80 acres on the south side of what is now Highway 198 at the intersection of the road to Woodlake. Frank and his family traveled to California by train, and Frank actually carried $2,500 in gold coin with him.

Frank and Rhoda Finch. *Photo courtesy of Earl McKee.*

They lived at this location for about two years, then Frank purchased 160 acres on Old Three Rivers Drive in Three Rivers, beginning near where the McKee house is now, then leading north, taking in part of the area now known as the Three Rivers Golf Course. Frank planted orange and apple orchards there as well as raising cattle. He kept his acreage in the Lemon Cove area, too; he commuted back and forth between the two properties by horseback or buggy until automobiles came into use.

Unfortunately, the orange and apple orchards that Frank planted in Three Rivers did not thrive like they should have, mainly due to the lack of irrigation water. They depended on water from the Britten Ditch and during dry years, the ditch was dry for the last part of the growing season. Frank also opened a small store on Old Three Rivers Drive at the intersection of South Fork Drive. The store was also the location of the post office, where Rhoda Finch served as postmistress from 1903 to 1907.

Frank and his family continued in the cattle and citrus business, although Frank had other interests outside of Three Rivers; he was known throughout the state of California for his work in the citrus industry. For 15 years, he was manager of the Lemon Cove packing plant for the Sequoia Citrus Association; he served on the Three Rivers Union school board for a number of years and he was instrumental in the building of an addition to the school.

Frank was a member of the Kiwanis Club at Woodlake where he served as president; in addition, he was president of the Three Rivers Chamber of Commerce for several years. Frank and Rhoda Finch were faithful supporters of the Visalia Cubs, the local baseball team, and they very seldom missed going to home games until ill health prevented him from traveling to Visalia.

Frank Finch died April 10, 1955 after a lengthy illness. His wife Rhoda passed away December 2, 1955. They are both buried in the Three Rivers Cemetery. Frank and his family played a very major role in the development of Three Rivers during the 53 years he called Three Rivers his home.

Rhoda & Frank, 2nd Row: Zola, Jess, Marjorie, Lauren, Edna Finch. *Photo courtesy of Earl McKee.*

The Lovering Family

Roy Ingersoll Lovering (better known as Bob) came to the Three Rivers district in 1908 with his wife Nellie Evelyn [Weaver] Lovering and their small daughter Norma. Roy's sister Edith had married Judd Blick of the Blick/Burnham family and when Judd told him of a property available further up the canyon from their ranch, acting upon his suggestion, Roy took his advice and brought his family north.

Roy Lovering had been born in Lucas County, Iowa in 1882, the son of Martin Van Buren Lovering and Mary Ann Molly Baker. Roy's father Martin had moved from Iowa to Fullerton, California about 1888 and remained in that area until his death in 1912. There were nine children in Martin's family, six girls and three boys.

Roy, the sixth child, grew up in Fullerton, went to school there and in 1904, he married Nellie, who was born in 1881 in Kansas; she was the daughter of Willis Wesley Weaver and Flora Evelyn Birtch. Their first daughter was Norma, who was born in Fullerton in 1906. The family lived there until they came to Three Rivers and settled on the South Fork.

Roy and Nell Lovering. *Photo courtesy of Gaynor McKee.*

Roy had shipped much of the family furnishings by train and they left Fullerton with two different wagons, four horses, two mules and one milk cow. The trip took three weeks, going through Bouquet Canyon and Lancaster to reach the San Joaquin Valley. In her book, Norma Lovering Hardison recounts a little of the trip:

> In the evening, one of the camps we made was by a cottonwood spring and my papa and uncle came into camp with a sack full of wild doves for dinner. They fried just the breasts in the frying pan over hot coals. We stayed the night and had pancakes for breakfast a long time before the sun came up. They hitched up the mules, tethered the cow and we started off again.[165]

She continued:

> My papa bought 560 acres of hills and pasture for cattle and horses. There was a house there with a lean-to kitchen, two bedrooms and a small living room. I remember my first Christmas there, the Christmas tree in the corner of the living room, bright with candles and popcorn strings, tinsel, packages beneath the tree, and Santa Claus. The house was full of people I didn't know making over me as I was the only child there. One of them asked me how old I was, and as I sat rocking in my Christmas chair I told them, holding up my fingers that I would be three years old in June; I remember that![166]

In 1911, Roy was hired to go to Mexico to be a foreman of a large wheat ranch that belonged to his brother-in-law, Homer Clever, husband of Roy's sister Stella. They had been on the Mexico ranch for the year before and were building the house for Roy's family.

Norma describes the conditions they found there:

---

165   *Memories,* by Norma Lovering Hardison, June 1988.
166   Ibid.

Our adobe house was not finished yet. It was set out in a field with no trees anywhere except in the Mexican workmen camp on the other side of the fence near the barns, and they were just mesquite trees. The fields and sheds for the work animals were some distance from our house. The Mexican workmen built the walls all of adobe and the house had a sheet iron roof. There was one bedroom and kitchen on one side of the "sijuan" and two unfinished rooms on the other side. A sijuan is a large room open on both ends between the kitchen and bedroom on one side and the other rooms on the other side. Both ends were secured with a screen door. The floors were dirt, packed hard and kept swept clean. The kitchen had a wood stove and a work table, a wooden drain board and a sink. There was a barrel of water packed up from the canal for washing. Our drinking water was packed in to us on donkeys.

We had no plumbing at all. The sheets and larger things went into the large iron kettle that sat on a bed of coals, and she would stomp them out with a clothes stomper, dunk them into a cold tub and Papa would help wring them out and hang them on the wire fence that enclosed the yard.

One day a thunder and lightning storm came up, and Mama ran out to grab her clothes off the fence, when Papa chased after her and caught her by the legs and threw her to the ground just as a bolt of lightning struck the fence. I watched the little blue flames run along the fence and drop off in the dirt.[167]

As time went on, the political turmoil in Mexico became very dangerous for any Americans living there. The Yaqui Indians went on the "war path" and were killing the settlers. Roy and Nell packed all the belongings they could in boxes and barrels and prepared to leave. Norma tells this story:

---

167   Ibid.

At 2 a.m. on the set time, Mama made me a bed in the spring wagon, drawn by the mule team of Pete and Jenny and we set out on the sandy one-wagon track to Cajemie where our belongings were waiting to board the train. From my bed in the wagon, I could see the bright stars, and Saguaro cactus lifting their ghostly arms all around us. Papa wasn't quite sure of the road and he kept looking at a certain star in the sky to guide us. We were taking a short cut over the desert road, my Mam was so scared, then I was too cause she was. It was almost 4 p.m. when we came to Cajemie and boarded the train . . . . We went home to Three Rivers, where Papa's brother-in-law [Judd Blick] and Aunt Deedee, [Edith] Papa's sister were living.[168]

Roy Lovering and Nell remained in Three Rivers and soon the second daughter, Jessie, was born in 1911. Roy decided to build his family a new house and he used the talents of Nell's three brothers from Fullerton, who were all carpenters. This house today is the home of Paul and Nancy Smith.

Roy and his family continued living in their home, and in her book, Norma gives many insights into what life was like in those early days:

Mama could make the best bread I ever ate. Bake day was Wednesday. Papa always wanted pie, cobbler, cake or custard for desert so most of Wednesday was devoted to the baking for the week. When evening came, Mama wiped all the glass chimney tops for our coal oil lamps. Two for the kitchen, one that sat in a little brass bracket above the stove and the other one on the kitchen table. We usually had two on the mantle of the fireplace and one was a hanging lamp over the dining room table in the living room.

Papa always had a haunch of venison hanging in the screen porch, with a canvas around it, most anytime of the year except summers. We usually ate ducks, chicken, wild pigeons and

168   *Memories.*

whatever meat was around, maybe beef. We ate a lot of beans. Papa loved them, cooked with garlic, onions and bacon rind.

We went to buy food at least every two weeks. On the days we went to the store, Mama bought a sack of flour, a sack of sugar and packages of ground coffee. The sacks weighed from 20 to 50 pounds each. Papa always gave me a nickel to buy a sack of candy. The store [Britten Brothers Store] was full of everything; they sold shoes, underwear, overalls and lots of different materials for dresses, etc., and harness and pickles in big kegs. There was an old pot belly wood stove in the middle of the store with five or six chairs around it, and spittoons by the chairs. On a cold winter day, the men folks used to come and sit around by stove, chewing tobacco and exchanging stories while the women did the shopping.

The stagecoach from Visalia to Mineral King used to stop at the store, sometimes the big wagon teams that hauled lumber from the redwood mills at Colony Creek would stop there and the horses with the bell yokes on their shoulders would make beautiful sounds, stomping the ground and shaking their heads.[169]

In the spring of 1916, Roy's father Martin died and his property was divided among the nine children. Roy's share was the large family house in Fullerton and five acres of Valencia orange trees. So Roy moved his family to Fullerton and his brothers and sisters hired him to take care of their groves as well. Roy bought another eight acres of oranges and walnuts from his brother Guy. Roy sold their property in Three Rivers to Earl Davis and his wife Freddie Maxon Davis. Not many years after, Mr. Davis died and Roy had to take back the property. The Loverings then spent all their summers and school vacations at the Three Rivers ranch and in the high mountains.

Eventually, Roy sold the Fullerton property and he and Nell spent most of their time on their ranch. Although she was not in good health,

---

169   Ibid.

Nell Lovering started writing poetry in 1948. She wrote about life in Three Rivers, her family and the wonders of nature that she saw every day. Her health grew worse, and in 1951 she passed away from cancer. Roy married Amy Ray, a widow who had been a family friend; she passed away in 1962 from complications of a stroke. Then in 1963, Roy passed away from burns suffered in an accident at his home. This man lived a very colorful, rewarding life—in the outdoors working his cattle, in the southland working in the orange groves and in Mexico where he and his family made their harrowing escape.

Martin Lovering and Family, Roy Lovering on far right. *Photo from* Memories, *by Norma Hardison.*

[The author wishes to thank Gaynor McKee, daughter of Norma Lovering Hardison, for the loan of her mother's wonderful book full of memories and stories of the times in which she and her family lived.]

1910s

Onis Brown

Onis Imus Brown was born in 1885 near Santa Maria, and his life was filled with experiences and adventures that even in his generation were very unique. His parents were Marcellus and Elisa Jane Pogue Brown, early settlers of Tulare County. His mother was a daughter of J. W. C. Pogue, well-known early citrus grower and rancher of Lemon Cove. Onis married Mabel Annie Lewis in 1909.

At the age of fourteen, when California Grizzlies still roamed the country, he carried mail twice a week on a 42-mile route from Matilija near Ojai to Sheideck in the Cuyama Valley. In 1904, he was a cowboy for Jim Wagy, who later became a State Senator. Onis and Wagy's brother Cliff once drove a herd of horses from Bakersfield to Oakland.

After driving a team for his uncle, J. W. C. [John Lee] Pogue, and harvesting grain where the city of Woodlake is now, he bought the Henry Schneider homestead on the North Fork of the Kaweah about two miles above the Kaweah Post Office; there he went into the cattle and horse business. In taking horses to summer meadows in the Tamarack Lake country (northwest of Mt. Stewart) and later on to the Lost Canyon area (east of Mineral King over Sawtooth Pass), he built many cutoff trails that saved time and distance for future travelers.

In 1913, he hauled freight into Wolverton with an eight-horse team for the Wolverton Dam that was a Mt. Whitney Power Company project; he also drove a freight wagon into Mineral King over the first, infamous Mineral King Road. The following year, he hauled grain into the Tulare Lake bottom with a "long team line"—14 horses pulling three wagons and controlled with a jerk line.

During this time, he and his brother Marcellus had a ranch near Parkfield; it was there in 1916 that he got word that his wife, Mabel, was ill in Visalia. He made an outstanding ride from Parkfield to Visalia in about twelve hours without injuring his horse.

After working on the famous Peach Tree Ranch owned by Miller and Lux, Onis moved to Lemon Cove and there he became a packer, guide, hunter and trapper in the high mountains.

In 1920, he and Earl McKee, Sr. were packers for the McDuffy-Hutchinson party and climbed with them on the first ascent of the 13,752-foot Black Kaweah Peak. They were also the first legalized pack train over Colby Pass from west to east.

Onis took the first pack train of large stock over Glenn and Mather Pass in 1921, well before there were any trails. He was also probably the first man to catch fish in Hamilton Lake. About 1910, Jim Hamilton told of planting fish in the lake back in 1900 and since the lake was almost unknown and inaccessible at the time, it was thought no one had tried fishing there. Onis made the trip and caught a fine lot of fish.

Three Packers - Onis Brown, Jim Kindred & Allan Savage. *Photo from the Three Rivers Museum.*

During his years in the high mountains, he took pack stock over the high passes long before there were any trails, climbed most of the mountain peaks, and fished every lake and stream. Onis was completely at home in the Sierra—from Bakersfield to Sonora Pass—and in living so close to nature, he accumulated a priceless knowledge of wildlife. The automobile never quite replaced the horse in his life. He started breaking horses when he was just ten years old and often stated that he had broken all of his bones except the ones in his back.

He was highly respected for his ability to break and train horses as well as outstanding hunting dogs. The late John Britten often commented to this writer that Onis would first train the horse to "ground drive" and never even tried mounting his steed until this task was completed. John always said that Onis had an uncanny way with animals—even though the term "horse whisperer" was unknown at the time, he most certainly would have qualified for the title!

Onis was a popular storyteller, filled with an unending variety of tales. He continued to train and ride horses, pack into the mountains, and hunt until illness began to slow him down.

A highlight of his later years and his last big pack trip was when he was hired by Walt Disney to assist in making the film *High Sierra Trail*, which told the story of the John Muir Trail. Since Onis had known John Muir personally and had become almost a legend himself, he was asked to take part in the picture. The film company made an unforgettable three-week trip from Mineral King to Yosemite that included climbing Mt. Whitney.

Onis was a member of the Three Rivers Community Presbyterian Church and an honorary member of the Three Rivers Lions Club. He was once written up in the *Saturday Evening Post* as a mountain packer when the magazine was at the height of its popularity.[170] He died November 7, 1959 at the age of 74. Onis was definitely a living legend who added to the colorful history of Three Rivers.[171]

---

170   *Exeter Sun*, August 21, 1991, pg. A2.
171   *Woodlake Echo*, November 12, 1959.

Marcellus Brown home in Cuyama, California, about 1897
L. to R.
Standing, back row: Onis Imus Brown, Laura Josephine Brown Fraser, Luce
        Celesta Brown, Sarah Elisabeth Brown Marx

Seated: Eliza Jane Pogue Brown, Baby Lawrence Talmadge Brown, Marcellus
        Brown, Joseph Carl Brown, Meda Virginia Brown Keener

Brown Family. *Photo from the Three Rivers Museum.*

The Ogilvie Family

Albert Gallatin Ogilvie was the first of this family to settle in Three Rivers. He was the son of Johnson and Margaret [Norman] Ogilvie. Albert was born March 25, 1856 in Delaware County, Ohio. Johnson and Margaret also had the following children: Elbert, Myrl, Dora, Laura, William, Fred, Howard, Benjamin, Oscar, Raymond [Kelly] and John Ogilvie.[172]

US Census records show that A. G. Ogilvie was in the Los Angeles area as early as 1880 with his brother James. His occupation was listed as a "sewing machine agent" and he was single at the time. By 1900, he was married, living in Visalia with a daughter Anna, three years old and a son William, one year. By 1910, the family had increased in size and was living in the Three Rivers area on the Middle Fork. Their house burned and A.G. moved his family to a ranch that was later to be known as the "Buckman place" on the north side of the Middle Fork of the Kaweah.

Along with his brothers and sisters, Fred Ogilvie went to school at Sulphur Springs School. When the original building burned, A. G. Ogilvie donated the land for the second schoolhouse where it sits today as a private home at the beginning of Kaweah River Drive.

In an interview that he gave in 1964, Fred Ogilvie told of going to school there with his brothers and sisters. He said that the only difference in school kids in those days was that they walked instead of riding in a car or school bus. He said, "Might as well of walked as rode a horse cause you usually had to walk as far to find the horse!"[173]

Fred's family moved to Orange Cove soon after he graduated from grammar school. He worked in the oilfields until he was seventeen. This was during the first World War, so he signed up, took his exams, and was waiting for placement when the Armistice was signed.

Soon after, he moved to Lemon Cove and went into business with his brother Bill and his half-brother Al Askins. They formed the Sequoia National Park Trucking Company and were engaged in hauling freight

---

172   1910 US Federal Census.
173   *Woodlake Echo*, October 1, 1964.

and passengers to the park. At this time, there were seventeen children in Three Rivers who were of high school age, so the Woodlake Union School District hired Fred as its first bus driver to transport these children to high school.

Woodlake High School had just completed a mechanical arts building and had hired an electrical engineer to teach mechanics, so Fred decided to go to school and drive the bus at the same time. Driving a bus in those days was not easy; few of the roads were paved and every winter there were flooded areas to go through just east of Woodlake. One of the passengers who rode with Fred during that time was Rena Alles, daughter of Phil and Grace Alles. Cupid shot his arrows and Fred and Rena were married in 1926.

Fred drove the high school bus until 1922 and then spent his senior year just being a student. After he graduated, he continued in the trucking business; he and his brothers hauled hay and supplies to the Park up the Colony Mill Road in the summer and oranges and logs to Atwell Mill in the off-season. Fred also worked at the service station at Giant Forest in the summers.

In 1930, a GMC candy wagon that had been confiscated from a bootlegger was acquired by the Park and donated to the Three Rivers school. Up until this time, the school children had been taken to school by private means. The school board, whose members at the time were Bob Barton, Violet Nice, Ken Savage, Legrand Ellis and Ed Riggs, decided that Three Rivers needed a permanent bus driver and custodian. Because of his experience, they approached Fred, and he accepted their offer.

By 1932 the candy wagon was getting quite crowded. "Sorta like sardines," Fred said, so the school board bought a second-hand International bus from the Beardsley school district for $1,300; the rear end went out the first week of operation. Due to a school bus accident outside of Modesto, the state set requirements for all bus drivers to pass a physical and written examination. Fred said the school had a hard time getting the bus to pass the safety requirements, because the brakes "could hardly make the bus hesitate, let alone stop." This bus was used until 1936 when the school bought a new Studebaker "Boss," and it hauled the school children until 1951.

Photo courtesy of the Three Rivers Museum.

The bus route in those days went from Ash Mountain, down to Slick Rock then back up the North Fork to the Elliot Ranch. Children on the South Fork either rode horses or were transported by automobile. In 1939 the school acquired a new International bus to make the South Fork run, where 17 school age boys were located in the CCC Camp there.

After their daughter Alice was born, Fred's wife Rena went to work at the school also, helping with the custodial duties. They enjoyed working together and shared a love for Indian lore, spending a great deal of time exploring old Indian camping grounds. Rena kept track of the historical data and Fred seemed to have a knack for finding artifacts. In 1992 Rena told this author about the time she and Fred assisted at the archeological explorations below the present site of Terminus Dam that was sponsored by College of the Sequoias. They uncovered eleven skeletons and many, many artifacts. She and Fred also found a skeleton of an Indian at Cherokee

Flat; they notified the professor at College of the Sequoias but when he didn't respond, Rena covered the Indian with one of her mother's quilts and they closed his grave.[174] Several homes are built on this site today.

Fred and Rena Ogilvie. *Photo courtesy of the Three Rivers Museum.*

Fred passed away February 25, 1988 and is buried in the Three Rivers Cemetery. This mild-mannered, warm-hearted man, who gave so much of himself to the school and the children was honored by the Chamber of Commerce and the PTA, but his greatest tribute is still in the hearts of those who "went to school with Fred."[175] His wife Rena passed away in 2001 and is buried in the Three Rivers Cemetery as well.

One of Fred's younger brothers was J. Raymond Ogilvie, otherwise known as "Kelly." He was also a kind-hearted soul, liking everyone. He had a problem that set him apart from others in his family, however; he was very, very fond of alcoholic beverages. Even with this handicap, he was

---

174   [NOTE: could this have been "Cherokee Nels" who rescued the Work family at the time of the 1867 flood? More research is needed.]
175   Ibid.

able to keep a job for many years. He worked for Dick Britten at Britten Construction and was capable and adept on the bull-dozer and other heavy equipment. John Britten, Sr. always told the story of how Dick could never find where Kelly kept his bottle of whiskey hidden while on the job; however, one day he was seen to lift something out of the diesel fuel tank of the bulldozer he was driving; it was his whiskey bottle, warm from the diesel fuel but still containing his whiskey! He was dedicated to his work and to his drink.

Kelly married Dora Magly, the daughter of George Magly who was Mrs. Walter Braddock's nephew. Dora was a few years older than Kelly but they had a very compatible relationship. Although she did not share his liking for strong drink, she did make the best pies for miles around! Her name for Kelly was "Presh" which this author thinks meant Precious. Their home was on the little knoll just above the Lion's Roping Arena. Kelly and Dora had a wonderful cattle dog by the name of "Sparky"; he was a coal black McNab shepherd; this author and her step-dad Ord would borrow Sparky to help herd their cattle. Sparky was wonderful help, especially when it came to flushing the cattle out of the brush. He had one fault though; he barked constantly in the back of the pick-up but we suffered this drawback for the good help he gave. When our day with Sparky was over, we would just let him out at the junction of North Fork Drive and Kaweah River Drive and tell him to "go home," which he did immediately to find Dora waiting with his meal.

Kelly Ogilvie survived several bad auto accidents, probably due to his habit; he passed away July 15, 1969; Dora preceded Kelly in death November 23, 1966. She and her "Presh" are buried in the Three Rivers Cemetery.

The Pierce Family

The Pierce family came to Three Rivers on a camping trip in 1910. They had traveled from Coalinga, where they were living at the time, to Lemon Cove by train and to the North Fork by stage coach. The stage stopped at the Montgomery Barton ranch for lunch, and evidently the Pierces fell in love with the place and the area. The Bartons were willing to sell the property and the offer was accepted. As a consequence, the family then moved to Three Rivers to the property that was to become known as the Pierce place.

James H. Pierce was born in Pen Yan, New York in 1871. He was an only child and left home at an early age. He began his working years as a roustabout in the Pennsylvania oilfields. According to his granddaughter, Juanita Tolle, James Pierce was a gifted artist; self-educated, spontaneous and impulsive, quick to act from loyalty. He was in the process of going to the Yukon to search for gold; however, the Spanish-American War drew his attention and he enlisted to fight.

James met his future wife, Julia Van Arsdale, while he was a patient at the Pacific Hospital in San Francisco in 1899; she had been visiting her father who was also a patient there. Julia had been born in Canton, China, the first of four children of Presbyterian missionary parents. She received her early education in China and spoke Chinese before she spoke English. She came to the United States in 1890 to attend college in Pennsylvania and after graduation and several years of teaching, she came to California due to her mother's illness.

James and Julia were married the next year and spent their early years of marriage in Coalinga, where James worked for both Peerless Pump and Standard Oil Company. Their first daughter Frances was born in Bakersfield in 1902 and second daughter Elizabeth in Coalinga in 1907; her birth coincided with her older sister's first day of school.

Julia adapted to ranch life in Three Rivers that had little in the way of amenities; there was no electricity or other conveniences of that day.

Kerosene lamps were used for light; the ranch house was heated by a large wood stove in the kitchen and a fireplace in the living room. The kitchen was a gathering place for the family; the hot water was supplied not by a water heater but instead by the water tank on the side of the cookstove where it was heated by pipes going through the firebox.

After dinner, the family's entertainment time was spent listening to favorite music on a wind-up Victrola. The bedrooms were not heated and hot rocks or flat irons were wrapped in newspaper and put into the beds at bedtime. During World War I, Julia made soap in a large copper kettle inherited from the Bartons. In the summertime, she boiled clothes in this same kettle outdoors over an open fire.

An account by Julia's daughter Elizabeth tells some interesting stories about life on "Pierce's Corner":

The North Fork road went directly in front of the house and it was very dusty since the road was never oiled. The U. S. Cavalry troop came each summer to supervise the Park and the troops rode by on that road. We used to hose down the dust before they galloped by, but there was still plenty of dust. In addition, the Hengst cattle were driven past each year on their way to summer forage higher in the mountains. They returned in the fall, too. Can you imagine the experience of dust, bellowing cattle and cowboy Hengst shouts!

There were many picket fences outlining our 160-acre ranch and its fields. My father said there were miles of picket fencing with the exception of some real log fences. Redwood was easily available then—so much had been washed down by the flood of 1867.

As always in the country, many mice came into the house from outdoors; wood rats built nests in the attic, skunks raided the chicken coops—even coming into the house. One evening we were all sitting in the living room and a skunk ran around the room, hiding in a bedroom. My mother had heard of enticing skunks out of the house with dabs of tuna on newspapers to an open door, so we tried this and watched. Sure enough, the skunk came out of the bedroom and began to eat his way to the open back door. But coming in the back door was another skunk eating his way in! All we could do was shut the door behind the inside skunk and hope for the best![176]

James Pierce planted groves of orange and grapefruit trees, several varieties of apples, as well as plum, peach, apricot and nectarine trees. The oranges and grapefruit were income crops transported to the Lemon Cove packing house. Apples and apple cider were sold to customers in the fall as well. The Pierce family livestock consisted of horses, cows, pigs and chickens. A root cellar under the house held many quarts of home-canned fresh fruits and vegetables as well as thick cream from the milk cows that was skimmed off for cereal or homemade ice cream.

By the 1920s, electricity made its appearance in the house and the family enjoyed electric lights, a radio and an electric refrigerator instead of the ice box. The large porches around the house were screened so the family could eat on the porch during the summer months, while the upstairs porch was used for a year-round bedroom.

James and Julia Pierce developed very large, beautiful gardens around the house that included roses, iris, bridal wreath, jasmine and many others, as well as a Concord grape arbor. An almond tree stood by the driveway; also, a large English Walnut tree grew on the south side of the house, providing needed shade as well as quantities of nuts each year. Julia planted 75 different varieties of iris and her garden was a source of joy to her family and friends who came to see its beauty. James enjoyed teaching his children the botanical names for the wild flowers they would see during their hikes in the foothills and nearby mountains.

Julia Pierce became an active member of the Three Rivers community; she served as chairman of the local Red Cross chapter and was successful in promoting community support for various charitable projects. She

---

176   *The Pierce Family and Ranch*, Elizabeth Pierce Roy, September 25, 1977.

was also an active member of the Three Rivers Woman's Club, American Association of University Women, and others.

Jim Pierce's health began failing him after years of trying to make a living from the ranch, as well personal tragedy caused by the death of his son from an earlier marriage, and the death of two children at birth during his marriage to Julia. He developed severe health problems, forcing him to move to the Mojave Desert for his health. He eventually settled in Banning, California and established a vegetable and flower/cactus garden that provided food and nurtured his love of flowers. The family visited him as often as possible and maintained a stream of correspondence with him until his death in 1952.

Julia applied to the State Department of Education for a teaching credential in 1934. After studying at home and taking the exam, she passed and began teaching elementary education to young men in the CCC camps at Buckeye, Potwisha, Salt Creek, Yucca Creek, Marble Fork and Kings Canyon. She was treated with great respect by her students because of her sincere efforts to help them receive a basic education, and although she did not drive, they often provided transportation for her to the various CCC facilities. Julia also served as a substitute teacher at the Three Rivers Union School and from 1942 to 1948, she taught at Hanby School, a small two-room schoolhouse south of Tipton, commuting to the ranch on weekends by Greyhound bus to Visalia, then riding with family or friends to Three Rivers. Julia later formed a close relationship with the mother of her son-in-law William H. Roy, who had married her daughter Elizabeth. Bill Roy's mother was a contemporary of Julia's and they enjoyed memorable visits with each other, maintaining contact until Julia's death in May 1948.[177]

---

[177] *Julia Van Arsdale Henry Pierce, 1874–1948*, by Juanita E. Tolle and Elizabeth M. Roy, April 1992.

Pierce House. *Photo from Author's Collection.*

Asa Peck and His Family

Asa Peck was born in Tipton, California on October 23, 1888. His father had died just before Asa's birth and he was raised by his mother and stepfather Lon Elster, who was a freighter in the Randsburg and Johannesburg mining area of Kern County. Asa attended school in Randsburg as well as Pixley.

In 1911, he went to Mexico with some friends who had mining interests there; included in the party were two mining engineers. While searching for water to drink, they were fired upon by a roving band of Yaqui Indians. Finally reduced to one mule on which the two engineers perched with young Asa holding on to the beast's tail, they made a run for it only to find themselves in the midst of revolutionaries under the command of General Blanco. The two engineers bought their release but young Peck found himself a captive and only after some heavy skirmishes and severe injuries was he able to escape and get back to the U. S. A.

In 1914, he got a job with the Forest Service stationed at Mineral King, supervising the building of trails and patrolling the area. After about two years, he joined the Army, fighting in World War I. His army service was in Siberia where as a sergeant with three enlisted men, he captured a Bolshevik supply boat and had some shooting scrapes which left his hand severely wounded.

When he received his discharge, he spent time at his homestead on Blue Ridge until his hand healed. In 1924, he went into the Park Service as a Ranger, stationed at Ash Mountain and then at Redwood Meadow. At that time, Colonel White was superintendent and Guy Hopping was the Chief Ranger. Asa remained stationed at Redwood Meadow for about four seasons, and when the Kern River District was added to the Park, he was stationed at Lewis Camp, spending winters at Ash Mountain. He remained there until 1931, when he moved over to Grant Grove National Park.

While still stationed at Lewis Camp, Asa married Ester Mires of Three Rivers, and in 1933, they were sent to Hawaii with the Park Service where they lived from 1933-1939. There they had one daughter, Maile. Their last move was back to Three Rivers and Asa again worked for the Park Service until his retirement in 1955. They continued to live in their home on La Cienega Drive in Alta Acres. Asa Peck died in January 1981 and is buried in the Three Rivers Cemetery.

His wife Ester was born June 19, 1909 in Cashion, Oklahoma, the daughter of Wilber and Susie McCollum Mires. Ester was six years old when her family moved to Atwell Mill. Several years after her husband Asa passed away, Ester added another career—from wife and mother to wife, mother and librarian. She worked in the Exeter Library from 1957 to 1960. After the county library branches merged to form the Three Rivers Branch Library, she became the official librarian here. The library at that time was housed in the building where the *Kaweah Commonwealth* is now located; at that time, the library took up the entire building. Ester was the librarian there from 1960–1974 when she retired from that library and went to work for another: the Sequoia Natural History Association at their library at Ash Mountain. Ester died suddenly of a stroke in a local bank in December 1995.

While Ester was filing, shelving and checking out books at the Three Rivers Library, she hired her daughter Maile as an assistant. Maile had been born in Hawaii while her parents were stationed there with the Park Service in 1936. Her name was taken from the fragrant flowering vine that grows in the Haleakala forests on Maui.

As a toddler, Maile spent her summers with Asa and Ester at Giant Forest, Atwell Mill, Colony Mill, Hockett Meadows, Kern Canyon and other places in the Sierra. She learned to love the mountains and was very proud of her early life spent there. In an interview she gave to Sarah Elliot for the *Kaweah Commonwealth*, she said her goal was to live to be 95; to have lived longer than either her mother or father.[178] However, her wish wasn't granted; at age 70 she passed away, having spent the last two years of her life in a nursing home due to injuries caused in a fall. On August 5, 2006, Maile suffered a fatal heart attack at a residential care facility in

178   *The Kaweah Commonwealth*, August 11, 2006.

Woodlake. Maile, her mother Ester, and her father Asa Peck are all buried in the Three Rivers Cemetery.

Asa Peck. *Photo from Sequoia Sentinel.*

Jessie Bequette

Jessie Agatha [MacKinnon] Bequette was born in Fresno, California, September 11, 1906. Her parents were John MacKinnon and Bessie Fry, daughter of Walter Fry, Superintendent of Sequoia Park at the time. Jessie's father, John MacKinnon, was from Saskatchewan, Canada where he had been a wheat farmer, cattleman, and drover; he emigrated to the United States just after 1900. MacKinnon was also a telegraph operator and was working in Fresno's Old Polaski Depot. He and his wife Bessie had an apartment on the second floor of the depot and that is where Jessie was born. The family moved back to Canada in 1907 and they lived for a while on a wheat farm that included a sod barn. Jessie later recalled that the winters were so cold the milk would freeze as it was rushed from the barn to the house. Her mother Bessie supplemented the family larder by shooting prairie chickens from the front porch.

After two years of crop failures and hard times, the family moved back to California and settled on the Walter Fry property where MacKinnon built their first home, located about a mile from the Frys'. Jessie's sister Edith was born in Visalia in 1910 and Thelma in 1914. A terrible tragedy struck the family August 14, 1914, when fire completely destroyed the MacKinnon home. Jessie's father John lost his life in the blaze, evidently trying to save Bessie's grand piano. Bessie then took her three daughters and moved to Visalia for a short time, but returned to Three Rivers to work in the Park, eventually becoming her father's secretary. In 1916, she married Kenneth Weckert and in 1920, Jessie's half-brother Russell was born.

Jessie went to Sulphur Springs Grammar School from 1912 to 1920. It was the largest school district in Tulare County stretching from Three Rivers to Mt. Whitney. The school was north of the main river; it was reached by crossing a foot bridge located just about where the "dome" houses stood. There were between 10 and 25 pupils, and the teachers boarded with local families; the 8th grade boys would make life miserable for the young teachers just out of Normal School. Jessie attended high school in Woodlake and rode the bus every day. She recalled that the bus was so cold and drafty that in the winter, everyone carried a hot brick wrapped in newspaper to keep their feet warm. At one time, there was an epidemic of hoof and mouth disease in the county, and a large pit was dug on the road to Woodlake, filled with sheep dip and not only the bus's wheels but the children's feet had to go through it every trip.

Jessie remembered her high school days with much fondness. "Sneak Day" was especially memorable for her; that was when the senior class played hooky and spent the day swimming, picnicking and partying at Terminus Beach. While there in 1924, she attracted the attention of a young man playing golf nearby who was an alumnus of the Woodlake class of 1919. That was Bruce Bequette, and according to Jessie, the "vibrations were never to cease." They were married six months later. Bruce had been born in Lemon Cove; he was the first child Dr. Montgomery of that town had delivered and Bruce always had a special place in the heart of the Montgomery family, since he was given the doctor's first name of Bruce. When Bruce and Jessie Bequette were married, Dr. Montgomery arranged for them to have the small apartment on the second floor of what is now the Lemon Cove Woman's Clubhouse.

Jessie and Bruce Bequette. *Photo from the Three Rivers Museum.*

Bruce worked up in Dry Creek for his uncle Lynn Bequette that first year, but like his father-in-law, John MacKinnon, he was happiest working with trees, flowers and things of nature. He was delighted to go into the Park Service in 1926; he bought Jessie a 1925 Ford roadster, and he built their own home into which they soon moved; here they lived for many happy years. The little white house still stands on the knoll just to the west of the Three Rivers Museum.

Bruce and Jessie Bequette. *Photo from the Three Rivers Museum.*

Bruce and Jessie spent every summer up in the Parks, sometimes in a cabin, more frequently, however, in a tent. One snowy year they were stationed on the Marble Fork, going in at Easter and not coming out until Thanksgiving.

With the start of World War II, the Park activities slowed down and Bruce was offered positions in other areas. He was beyond active military service but still concerned with the war effort; so he chose to go to work in the San Diego shipyards. His brother-in-law Russ Weckert was already there working in a defense plant and the three of them—Bruce, Jessie and Russ—joined forces. They found a big old estate, a three-story house on a city block of walled grounds and while the men went off to work every day, Jessie kept the house and the estate in good running order. After three years, they bought a house in Pacific Beach expecting to stay in the area permanently, but after the war, they decided to return to Three Rivers and came home in 1948.

For a time, Jessie was a telephone operator in the Three Rivers Telephone Company office with Rena and Dora Ogilvie, as well as Ester Peck. When the dial system was introduced, she worked 1½ years for Pacific Telephone and Telegraph Company at the Lemon Cove office.

During this time, Bruce leased the old Noisy Water service station (the current location of the Brewery) and Jessie helped out as needed, pumping gas but refusing her husband Bruce's pals who were always teasing her to wash their cars. In 1953, Bruce and Jessie built their own shop with two Richfield gas pumps along with a plant nursery where Bruce grew and sold trees, ferns, azaleas, and camellias; Jessie had a gift shop as well in the same building [the site of the current Three Rivers Museum]. Another career opened for Jessie in 1958 when Mary McDowell, principal of the Three Rivers Union School, asked her to lend a hand in the school cafeteria. Jessie began helping out wherever she was needed and soon became a full-fledged faculty member that included yard duty. She supervised the lower grades after school until the bus or their parents came to meet them. In 1962, she became cafeteria manager where she served for five years.

Her husband Bruce was struck down by a massive heart attack and died in March 1967; they had been married for 43 years. Jessie finished out the school year, then resigned and with her sister Edith's support, they took care of their bedridden mother Bessie for the next five years until her death.

Later, Jessie traveled extensively around the world in the 1970s and 1980s, visiting the Bible lands, Greece and the Mediterranean, Hawaii, Spain, Morocco and other interesting places, traveling with Three Rivers' own High Sierra Jazz Band.

Throughout the years, she was an active participant in the life of the community. The MacKinnons, as well as the Frys, were members of the Lemon Cove Presbyterian Church until the Three Rivers church was built in 1938. She was a charter member of the Lady Lions and was a loyal and hard worker. Jessie was very proud of a bracelet presented to her by the Lady Lions Club for thirteen years of perfect attendance. For fifteen years, she served on the Board of Directors of the American Cancer Society of Tulare County and she was an inspirational counselor to recovering patients.

Her longtime membership in the Three Rivers Woman's Club began in 1924 when her mother Bessie gave the 18-year-old bride this advice: "Jessie, now that you are a married woman, you'll have to join the Woman's Club."

Jessie lived to see the age of 103. She passed away April 9, 2010 in Visalia. Her bright smile and happy disposition still light up her memory in the minds of the people who knew, loved and still remember this kind and wonderful lady.[179]

---

179   Information from manuscript by Louise Bosshard from her presentation to the Three Rivers Woman's Club March 4, 1992.

1920s

The Balch Family

Herbert C. Balch came to Three Rivers with his son, Arthur, a short time before May 1925. He was an old wood-turner from the mills of Michigan; while in Michigan, he had patented a citrus picker in 1904 called the "Balch's Hand Fruit Picker." When he settled in Three Rivers, he established a curio shop on the South Fork Road in 1925 and proceeded to make souvenirs for tourists visiting Sequoia National Park. His first shop was located across the road from the Britten Brothers Store and just north of the Three Rivers Lodge. While there, he produced candlesticks, nut bowls, baseball bats, sock darners, trinket boxes and many other novelties. He used as his wood source the many large logs of redwood that had been washed down the South Fork in the flood of December 1867.

Later, his business was sold to a Mr. Morris Macy, who had obtained a contract from the State of California in 1933 to sharpen the drill bits used in the jackhammers during the construction of Highway 198. The late John Britten, Sr. recalled that he and Mr. Macy's nephew, Joe Pillsbury, were paid 5 cents per drill bit for this work; often they worked until after midnight so the bits would be ready for use the next day. Mr. Macy later moved the shop to a location on Highway 198—across the street from where the office of the *Kaweah Commonwealth* building now stands.

H. C. Balch. *Photo from Author's Collection.*

Herbert Balch's son Arthur worked for a packing house in Lemon Cove for many years. He and his wife owned property on Pierce Drive; they had no children. After Arthur's wife was seriously injured in an automobile accident which left her paralyzed, she required nursing home care for a long time. Arthur was forced to deed his property over to the County of Tulare for her continued care. This property is where the County Maintenance Yard is now located.

The McKees - Four Generations

The first members of the McKee family to come to Tulare County were John C. McKee and his wife Martha. Accompanying him was his son William Alfred McKee and William's wife Mary (or Molly). John and his son William both served in the Civil War where William was wounded.

William A. and Molly McKee. *Photo courtesy of Earl McKee.*

John C. McKee was born in Greene County, Tennessee about 1822. He married Babe Nancy Pogue, who had also been born in the same county.

She was born in 1823 and they married on 1842. Nancy Pogue McKee was the aunt of Lemon Cove's J. W. C. (Or Jim) Pogue. John and Nancy had five children; she passed away in 1856 and John McKee then married Martha Simms, another resident of Greene County. Three more children were born to this marriage. Since the McKees and the Pogues were cousins, John and William settled on Pogue land up Dry Creek on what was later to become the Ward Ranch. William's father John died there in 1882. William and his wife Molly had four children: Lena, Maud, Stella and Earl A. [father of Earl McKee].

William went to work for J. W. C. Pogue and his son, Earl Alford McKee, was born there on Dry Creek January 13, 1891. In 1904, Fred Ward bought the Pogue ranch on Dry Creek, so William and his family moved to Naranjo where he continued to work for the Pogue holdings. By 1910, the family had moved to Lemon Cove and William bought several acres of oranges from Jim Pogue.[180]

William's family then moved to Ivanhoe on October 12, 1911. While he was working in the wheat fields there, he had a heart attack and passed away at the age of 66. He is buried in the Antelope Cemetery.[181]

William's son Earl Alford McKee was born January 13, 1891 on Dry Creek where his father had been employed by the Pogue family. He attended school in Lemon Cove, and since there was no high school for students in those days, he went to work at the Lemon Cove packing house where he met his future wife, Edna Finch; they were married August 11, 1912. Edna was the daughter of Frank and Rhoda Finch of Lemon Cove and Three Rivers.

In 1918, Earl and Edna filed on a homestead of 320 acres on the west side of Highway 198 across from the old Buckaroo Restaurant. They built their house there and after three years when they had "proved up," Earl purchased property on Old Three Rivers Drive from a Mr. Underwood. They built their home there where his son and wife live today.

---

180   Oral Interview with Earl McKee, September 13, 2012.
181   *Tulare County Cemetery Index.*

Earl and Edna McKee on their wedding day. *Photos courtesy of Earl McKee.*

Then Earl purchased the Lewis Place on the South Fork in 1921, and in 1936, during the Depression, he purchased the Greasy Cove property [northeast of Lake Kaweah] and the Canfield property above Britten Cove. With his wife Edna, they had three children: Blanche, who married Lee Maloy; Earleen, who married Dan Monaghan; and Earl, who married Gaynor Hardison.

From an early age, Earl had an interest in packing with mules and horses. He had his first string of five mules when he was 13.[182] It was natural for him to develop this talent, and with his wife Edna, Earl began his stock packing business in earnest, providing them with a very active life at their pack station and riding stables in Giant Forest.

They spent thirty summers at the pack station, going at first by horse and buggy up the old Colony Mill road but later by Model T Ford. Edna acted as a guide and she and Earl met many famous and interesting persons who made long trips into the high country of the Sierra; many of the trips lasted thirty days from start to finish.

---

182   *Mule Men*, by Louise Jackson, pg. 148.

Earl McKee, Sr. *Photo courtesy of Earl McKee.*

Although Earl began his venture of commercial packing in 1901 with only about ten animals, he eventually was able to buy out other packers until his stock had increased to at least 80 pack animals.

In 1935, the *Oakland Tribune* had the following article:

> To keep inviolate the Sierra backwoods country and to preserve the charm of the mountains' natural resources that thousands of nature lovers hold dear, a group of Sierra sportsmen have organized the "High Sierra Packers Association," dedicated to halt the construction of more roads into the "back country."

Elected president of the organization was Art Griswald, Springville. Other officers were Earl McKee, Three Rivers, vice-president, and N. Livermore, Mineral King, secretary and treasurer. Membership in the sportsmen's club has reached 35. A co-club has also been organized on the eastern side of the Sierra.

"Thousands of nature lovers who love to pack in the mountains of California during vacation periods are with us in our movement to halt the destroying of the backwoods country," said Griswald. "The building of mountain roads and the movement of autos into wilderness territory has gradually isolated many of our natural beauties.

"There are still many persons who want to pack back in the mountains, sleep in sleeping bags, hunt and fish in wild territory, and to enjoy the pleasures of nature. They don't want that destroyed by automobile roads. We are circulating petitions to that effect." Persons interested in joining this movement to preserve the backwoods country, may write Hugh Traweck, Dunlap, California.[183]

Earl McKee did very well with his packing business. Here is another article, "Deluxe Pack Trip," that tells the story:

Thomas Lamont, a New York financier, and a party of seven friends left here today for a two-week pack trip through the wilderness of the Kern and Kings River Canyons.

Earl McKee, park commissioner of packing, said the party was equipped with the most elaborate outfit ever packed through the Sierra. It included table service and hot and cold running water in the tents, he said.

McKee, who led the party, said it would traverse one of the most rugged areas of the Sierra Nevada Mountains.[184]

In 1946, Earl McKee was bucked off a "bronc" horse and hit his head on a rock; two weeks later, he was in the Cartridge Creek Basin with the

---

183   *Oakland Tribune*, August 18, 1935.
184   *Berkeley Daily Gazette*, July 7, 1938.

Fuller party when he was attempting to repair a picket line for the stock. Unfortunately, the line broke, causing him to fall and hit his head again. One week later, he was in Sixty Lakes Basin where he died suddenly. Although many people thought he'd had a heart attack, his son, Earl, still thinks to this day that his death was caused by a embolism that burst in his brain.[185] Earl McKee was greatly missed in Three Rivers; the author can remember her stepdad Ord Loverin telling about his death even years afterward.

After Earl's death, his wife Edna remained in Three Rivers and stayed active in community affairs for a long time. She was a charter member of the Three Rivers Woman's Club and also served on the Session as an Elder in the Presbyterian Church, as well as many other social events in the community. In 1961, she attended the 50th wedding anniversary reception and dinner for Mr. and Mrs. W. P. Fuller of the Fuller Paint Company at the Burlingame Country Club. The Fuller family had been guided through the high Sierra by Edna's husband Earl and his son, starting in 1938 for 25 years, usually on month-long trips with a large party of friends and relatives.[186]

Edna enjoyed the company of her family members and her many friends in the community and beyond. At her death at age 93, she had ten grandchildren, seventeen great-grandchildren and six great-great-grandchildren. She passed away August 8, 1986 and is buried in the Three Rivers Cemetery beside her husband Earl.

---

185   Oral Interview with Earl McKee.
186   *Visalia Times-Delta*, March 3, 1961.

The Whitney Family

Dow Calloway Whitney was born March 6, 1900, the son of Cassius Henry Whitney and Hattie [Records] Whitney. Dow's father Cassius was a lawyer who came from Iowa, through Nebraska, eventually settling in Ontario, California in 1908. He was very successful in the course of his career, one that provided him with the ability to purchase a number of pieces of land across the state, including the acreage in the Horse Creek drainage known as Little Oak Flat from a Johnny Mayben. Mayben was from Visalia where he owned several businesses, including two saloons.

Dow Whitney had two sisters, Agnes and Ruth. When he was eighteen, Dow worked as a teamster near Blythe, California and also in the rice fields at Woodland, California. He married Clara Koch April 5, 1921. Dow went to the University of California at Davis to study agriculture, but he always wanted to be a rancher, so he left his studies and gained his practical experiences from ranching and all that it entails.

Whitney cattle on the old Ewing homestead on Big Oak Flat. *Photo courtesy of Gene Whitney.*

Dow and Clara built their home in Little Oak Flat [near Big Oak Flat]; Dow started his herd with 180 cows and became very successful in the ranching business. Dow and Clara had three boys, Gene, born 1925, Kenneth, born 1929, and Leroy, born 1931. The boys grew up in the Little Oak Flat country; they loved the outdoors and the life of being cowboys and cattlemen. Because the dividing line for the school districts was Horse Creek, the Whitneys went to grammar school in Lemon Cove and not Three Rivers; Gene and his brothers went to high school in Woodlake.

Whitney Home in Little Oak Flat. *Photo courtesy of the Gene Whitney Family.*

Gene went to college at Cal Poly, receiving his degree in animal husbandry. After he graduated, his dad assured him he had plenty of help on the ranch, so he took his saddle and boarded a bus and went north to seek his fortune—in Fortuna, California, where he remained for the major portion of his life. He was employed by the county there working in the agriculture industry, specifically with pesticides and quarantines. During this time, Gene returned to work for a while at the Rocky Hill Cattle

Company from 1950 to 1957. Gene married Mary Christiansen; her family had come from Denmark and was living in Arcata, California.

In a recent interview, Gene told the author about the time he was very young and helped during a big cattle drive out of Big Oak Flat and down through Yokohl in the 1930s. There were 1,000 head of Mexican steers that the Gill Cattle Company had fed on pastureland for the Green Cattle Company of Arizona. Gene and his father Dow helped drive them down to the pens and loaded them on the Visalia Electric Railroad stock cars where they were eventually shipped to the stockyards at Los Angeles. He said that the sight of all those steers lined up to drink out of the canal before loading them was a sight to see.

Gene remembered the flood of 1937 and how their lives were impacted by it. He said that because of the high waters, they missed six weeks of school and the family had to live at the Cobble Lodges and also at the Tharp place, since there was no way to get back up to the homestead.

Dow and Clara's son Kenneth went to college at Cal Poly and after he graduated, he taught Ag classes in Bakersfield; he has since retired and he and his wife Donna still live there in Bakersfield.

Leroy, the youngest son, remained on the ranch after Dow died in 1976. He was very successful with the cattle ranch; he was well liked and respected by the other cattlemen in Three Rivers as well as Tulare County and beyond. He and his wife Catherine reared a family of two boys and two girls. The family continued in the cattle ranching business until Leroy's death in 2002.

Gene Whitney's wife Mary passed away August 10, 2010. He returned to the Horse Creek Ranch where he recently married Leroy's widow Catherine. It was a joy for this author to have had the opportunity to interview them and record their collective memories of early days on Little Oak Flat, Big Oak Flat and the Horse Creek country. They are living examples of a story having a happy ending![187]

---

187   Oral Interview, Gene and Catherine Whitney, September 4, 2012.

Big Oak Flat, Looking Southeast. *Photo courtesy of Mike Whitney.*

Old apple tree planted by early settlers on Big Oak Flat. *Photo courtesy of Mike Whitney.*

Special Section

The Life of Major Frederick Russell Burnham - From an Interview with Frankie Luella Welch

[NOTE: The following is a lengthy account of the life of Major Frederick Russell Burnham. During his later years, he gave an interview to the late Frankie Welch as well as giving her his two books, autographing them both for her. Frankie wrote the following account of his life and tried unsuccessfully to convince the newspapers for which she wrote to carry the Major's story; she was refused by both publications. The author found this manuscript among Frankie's papers and has decided that Frankie at last will get her story into print through this book. Only light editing has been done, since it was the author's goal to present the story as Frankie's alone. Please enjoy the exciting exploits of one of Three River's true heroes.]

As the last rays of a setting sun throw deep shadows on the mountains west of the Kaweah River and reach across to the little Three Rivers Cemetery, they linger briefly on a tall shaft of rugged granite which marks the grave of one of the world's great scouts.

Major Frederick Russell Burnham was endowed with courage, exceptional endurance and the ability to make instant and accurate decisions in time of peril—attributes which saved his life in many a confrontation with death and contributed to his success in daring reconnoiters into enemy territory for information which would determine the movements of troops, safeguard life and save towns from destruction.

American-born, wanderlust led Burnham afar. In the 1890s he cast his lot with the British in South Africa and became so valuable to them in two Matabele Wars and the Boer War that he was made chief of scouts under Lord Roberts and invested with the Distinguished Service Order by the King of England, highest honor bestowed by the empire.

Once he entered a cave in the Matoppo mountains and killed the M'Limo, a high priest who was inciting the blacks to uprisings and diabolical torture killings of the whites. This ended the second Matabele War. When on a mission to blow up a railroad used by the Boers in their last stand at Pretoria, he was desperately injured but finished the mission, which helped win the war. He got back to the British lines by compelling his crumpling body, through sheer force of will, to stagger and crawl for two days between periods of unconsciousness and hiding from the enemy.

Sir Rider Haggard, an English writer of the period, said of this American scout: "Burnham in real life is more interesting than any of my heroes of romance." Richard Harding Davis featured him in his book, *Real Soldiers of Fortune*. He was offered a large sum by Lord Northcliff for an account of his exploits but impelled by the modesty characteristic of him, he turned down the offer.

In appearance, Burnham was short of stature and unassuming. He was not particularly arresting—not until one caught the glint of his brilliant blue eyes —"Eyes so expressive of alertness, force and self-control, that see everything from his feet to the horizon without seeming to see," is the description given of him by Mary Nixon Everett, who elicited and arranged his two books, *Scouting on Two Continents* and *Taking Chances*. Mrs. Everett pictured him as having abounding vigor of mind and body, "with a step as elastic and noiseless as a prowling lion," erect broad-chested body, regular features and the fair skin of his English ancestors.

Major Frederick Russell Burnham. *Photo from Author's Collection.*

Burnham was born March 11, 1861, on an Indian reservation at Tivols, Minnesota. His parents were Edwin O. Burnham, a Congregational minister and Rebecca Russel Burnham. Both were of English lineage. When he was not yet two years old, they took him to a homestead near the ill-fated New Elm settlement which was set ablaze by Indians. Three hundred men, women and children were scalped, burned alive or otherwise tortured and killed.

The child early developed an acute sense of the requirements for self-preservation. Once when Indians were raiding, the father left to get powder and bullets to protect his family. Standing in the cabin door at evening, the mother was horrified to see Indians emerging from the thicket along the creek. Knowing that she could not escape with the child, she made an instant decision, a characteristic of her son in adult life. She swiftly carried him to a nearby corn patch and secreted him in the hollow cleft of a corn shock too green to burn.

Over and over in a low tense voice, she cautioned him, "Don't move, or make the slightest sound until I return."

Just as the Indians were surrounding the cabin, she slipped across an opening to some hazel bushes. They took up her trail but with the swiftness desperation lent [to] her feet and the screening of the cottonwoods, she was able to elude them in the waning light. Spent of breath, clothes torn by the grasping hands of brush and vine, she reached a barricaded cabin six miles distant, but not until she had seen the flames of her own home licking skyward.

At daybreak the next morning, she hurried back with armed neighbors. As she parted the corn stalks with anxious hands and peered in, her little son blinked up at her—just as she had left him.

As Frederick was growing up on the Minnesota frontier, he played with Indian boys and learned through feats of endurance and cunning much that was to serve him later; he also attended the little pioneer school there.

When tales of Stanley and Livingston came to his attention, he read everything available and there grew a dream of becoming a great scout and going to Africa. The dream never left him.

The family of four (Frederick now had a little brother named Howard) left for California in the winter of 1870 in search of a better climate for the father, whose chest had been crushed when he slipped on an icy spot and a log he had swung on his shoulder in the exuberance of his great strength fell on him. It took two weeks from the Mississippi to the California border on the new railroad through areas where buffalo roamed.

The care-free life of early California   hospitable haciendas, vast herds of cattle and thousands of horses, the exciting rodeos, fiestas, fandangoes—fascinated the youthful Frederick.

But his life took on a more serious aspect when his father died in 1873. His mother's health had broken, Howard was only three years old and Fred not yet thirteen. Since there was no visible means of support, relatives in the East offered a home to them all, but young Fred decided to stay in California and make his own way. A friend lent his mother money for the fare back and he set himself the task of repaying this, to him a vast sum of $125.00.

At thirteen years of age, he became a mounted messenger for the old Western Union Telegraph Company. The company wire ended at the old pueblo in Los Angeles and messages were carried by means of swift horses to all the surrounding towns and haciendas within thirty miles. Burnham tells in one of his books that he provided his own horses and received $20.00 per month for regular runs—when he had to go farther, often in the dead of night, he received more. There were times when the clattering hoof-beats of his speeding mount under the stars would rouse the barking dogs at far off Lucky Baldwin's ranch or, bridle reins over his arm, he would pound a street door in the little coast town of Santa Monica at 2:00 a.m.

The boy had remarkable endurance and was able to stay in the saddle all day and far into the night, changing mounts and tiring out four horses in a long, hard ride.

His mother's last debt repaid, young Frederick gave rein to his passion for roaming and exploring, an urge which in adult life led to discovery of ancient treasures in Africa of immense archeological value. Intrigued by the great wagon trains of bullion coming in [to Los Angeles] over the desert from old Cerro Gordo [Inyo County], he wandered and hunted over their route, often alone for weeks at a time. He once met the famous General Crook, who fired his imagination with tales of the little-known frontiers of Arizona and old Mexico.

When on a hunting trip in the Tejunga Canyon, his horse was stolen. He had left camp at daylight to watch for deer at a water hole and when he returned, he found that his staked-out mount had been taken minutes before, since warm horse sign showed. Small boot heel tracks indicated that the thief was a Spaniard or Mexican.

The trail out of the canyon made a big horse-shoe bend. Spurred by anger at his loss, the boy scrambled frantically up a steep ridge and ran desperately for two hard miles down the other side through brush and boulders, hoping to intercept the thief. But when he reached the trail, the thief had already passed. Mexicans at a wood chopper's camp said yes, they had seen the black horse and the rider was Tiburcio Vasquez, the famous bandit.

This was perhaps the last horse Vasquez ever stole. One hot day soon after, Frederick and another boy were walking up Figueroa Street with the intention of taking a swim in a nearby xanca [community fountain]. Their attention was attracted by a wagon jolting along with an armed man riding on either side. On some hay in the wagon bed lay a man with bloody clothes and beside him knelt a fellow plying a fan.

"I'll bet they've caught Vasquez," shouted one of the boys. The armed men would tell them nothing so they trailed along in the deep dust to the old Spring Street jail where the jailer, kindly disposed to the boys, confirmed their suspicions.

Later the jailer let a few boys in to see the bandit. Young Fred mentioned his sorely-missed black horse and told of his attempt to cut the thief off back on the trail. Vasquez assured him that he would not have taken the horse if he had known that it belonged to a boy like him, then laughingly added, "Now ride a better one; take mine." Vasquez predicted that some day Frederick would be a great robber, "like me." The sheriff let Frederick ride the bandit's pinto around Los Angeles and he felt very important when people stared at him.

Some six weeks later in San Jose, the scene of his first killing, Tiburcio Vasquez paid by way of the hangman's noose for the many lives he had snuffed out during his long career of banditry from the San Joaquin Valley to Southern California.

The pendulum of young Frederick Burnham's life swung from assuming the responsibilities of a man to playing with other boys. At the age of fourteen, he realized that he needed more education and accepted the invitation of an uncle to a small midwestern town on the Mississippi where he received a year's schooling.

But the restraints of this type of community and the mold into which he was being forced increasingly irked the freedom-loving spirit of the lad. One dark night, a canoe in the big river released Fred from the prospects of becoming a small-town merchant, and instead led to the exciting life of an adventurer who finally landed in *Who's Who* and who numbered sovereigns and dignitaries of the world among his friends.

There followed years of glorious wanderings over the Southwest—years in which he knew hardships, danger and hunger but never lost his zest for new experiences and fresh horizons.

He worked as needed to supply the necessities of life. Once he drove a band of wild Texas ponies up to Missouri and sold them for a neat sum. He then reveled in spurs, sombrero and other trappings of a cowboy. After losing his horse one time, he continued alone on foot the 500 miles from Santa Fe, New Mexico to Prescott, Arizona, traveling by night and sleeping in the daytime, as the Indians were on the war path. The savages had driven off all settlers and "stock and food was scarce. There were swollen creeks to swim, Indians and the snow and cold of the Mogollon Mountains almost got me," he tells in one of his accounts.

During his earlier wanderings, he was joined for a time by the brother of his boyhood sweetheart back in the little town on the Mississippi. Homer Blick [the Blick who in later years was associated with the operation of electric plants in Three Rivers] invited him to their new home where the Blicks had moved even further west.

The boy and girl friendship was renewed and Frederick rode away with disturbing dreams in his heart of a life very different from that which he had planned for himself.

He was 18 before he realized his long-cherished dream of exploring the frontiers of civilization on the Mexican border. During this period, he received his first definite lessons in scouting from an old man named Holmes who had served under Fremont, Kit Carson and other great scouts. Holmes had lost all his family in the Indian wars and he wished to pass on to Frederick the scouting skills acquired during a lifetime on the frontiers. For six months he led the slight, keen-eyed youth with the receptive mind, over the mountains of Arizona, New Mexico and Sonora, Mexico, and taught him with infinite pains the details of trailing and hunting that make up a scout's work.

"He showed me how to ascend and descend precipices," Burnham recounted; "how to protect one's self from snakes, forest fires, falling trees or floods, how to double back and cover a trail, time one's self at night, travel in the direction intended, find water in the desert and endless other details, much of it given around the campfire at night. The old scout's remembered words often proved the deciding factor between destruction and survival."

Another old scout named Lee told him that it was almost as important to know the habits, social customs, religions and superstitions of a people as the topography and climate of the country. Lee had been successful in ferreting Indians out of the deep, torturous canyons of the rough Santa Maria country through knowing their use of mescal, a desert aloe which is stripped of its thorns and roasted in a bed of hot boulders. Made into patties and dried it was a nourishing food; fermented, it became an intoxicating drink.

The Indians found ways of controlling tell-tale smoke clouds but they could not prevent the odor of burning mescal from drifting for miles up and down the canyons. By tracing these odors, Lee could mark the most secret hiding places of the savages.

A frugal diet adapted by Burnham when making a long, hard ride in dangerous country without fire was equal parts of ground venison and flour, baked. Ten pounds of this ration would keep a man in strength ten days, he tells, though lean and hungry. He took infinite care of his horse, so important to the work of a scout. Sometimes he slaked the saddle blanket in water found at the bottom of an almost impenetrable canyon and by turning it over and over as he climbed back out, he was able to squeeze a drink for his grateful mount into his hat or a depression in some rock. Scouting brought extreme hardships but he emulated the Indian and hardened his mind and body to stoical endurance.

Trying to help a family which had befriended him and now was being forced to join a faction in order to save their cattle, young Burnham was drawn into the Tonto Basin feud. He practiced pistol shooting incessantly with both right and left hands and from a galloping horse. Gradually he found himself actively participating in the turbulent life of Arizona at that time when the cattle men were trying to run the sheep men out. Powerful politicians furthered their sordid ends by secretly inciting factions to kill each other off, with the Apache Indians' raids adding further danger.

A man was out to get Fred because he knew too much about his machinations with cattle brands. So he changed names often and worked under various disguises; a prospector with burros [he had worked in the mines and knew the lingo], a game hunter on the Black Mesa—or his best role because of his youth and slight stature—just a harmless, tenderfoot kid from the East.

He became the liaison for certain men in Prescott, Globe and the Basin. Taking care never to ride a horse, which was always noted in those days as to brand and characteristics from one district to another, he kept a cache with a friend in each place. He found that he could travel long distances swiftly on foot. A complete outfit of clothes was kept with loyal friends in Prescott, where he could disarm and rest. The editor of the *Silver Belt* in Globe was interested in the young chap and was instrumental in changing his associates from those who broke the law to those who enforced it; he got Fred a job with the deputy sheriff. He guarded Wells Fargo's valuable shipments by secreting himself in the big leather boot in the back of the coach and discouraged would-be robbers with unexpected shots from the rear instead of from the driver's seat.

Despite the rough life, Burnham did not smoke or drink—never did. He explains that he did not require a stimulant or a sedative and "as a scout, I needed all five senses and every faculty of mind at highest pitch."

The fever of mining ran strongly in Burnham's blood. He roamed the mountains and deserts at every opportunity to prospect and learned the use of horn spoon, gold pan and every kind of explosive. When one venture did not bring wealth, he would work and earn money for outfitting and try it again. Over a period of years, his mining efforts earned him little and cost him much until one happy day near Casa Granda; he and his partner shot out over a thousand dollars with the first stick of dynamite.

Burnham promptly went East and married his boyhood sweetheart, Blanche Blick in Clinton, Iowa, in March 1882, and brought her to a home in an orange grove at Pasadena, California.

Fred Burnham, 1884. *Photo from Author's Collection.*
Blanche Blick Burnham, 1884. *Photo from Author's Collection.*

He was able to send for his mother and young brother in the east and contribute a small allowance to his grandparents in their old age.

A compulsive wanderer, the twenty-three-year-old Burnham decided that he was not fitted for operating an orange grove successfully and there followed various mining expeditions into Canada, Colorado, and Mexico as well as in California. The bottom dropped out of one promising mine and another burned just as the first bar of gold bullion was melted out and much money was lost.

There was an adventurous homesteading incident: Burnham, his wife and their little son, Roderick, now old enough to walk and therefore old enough to ride, decided to join all of Mrs. Burnham's family from the East in a migration out onto the desert to take up claims of various kinds. The eight eligible to file on government land controlled several thousand acres. They built cabins for themselves and tried to keep their unenclosed horses from being enticed away by a beautiful and wild stallion with silver mane and tail which would dash to within a quarter of a mile and call and cavort for an hour at a time.

The call to Africa came when Burnham's imagination was fired by the personality of Cecil Rhodes, a man he believed to be not only a colossal empire builder but a man of just dealings. Then thirty-one years old, Burnham considered himself to be in the prime of his strength and usefulness and believed that his knowledge of scouting and fighting Indians on the American frontiers could be made of value to Rhodes. On January 1, 1893, he and his wife and son, Roderick, now aged six, embarked from San Francisco and followed along a route to the English colonial town of Durban on the coast of South Africa.

Burnham's dream of Africa was coming true. But the dream did not foretell that the wonder and the glory of the great continent would be so tinctured with the desperate dangers, hardships and the horrors he was to know during the next few years.

Outfitting in Durban for the long trek north to Mashonaland was a problem. The gold rush to Johannesburg had drawn heavily on the African means of travel and created boom prices. The ponderous ox wagon, the lightest requiring ten or more oxen, a fore-loper to lead them and a driver with a thirty-foot whip was out. Undaunted, Burnham made a thorough search of the town and found the running gear of an American Studebaker buckboard stored in the attic of a warehouse and forgotten because it was considered too light for African travel. He was able to buy it for $100; then had a bed and spring seat put on it. Mrs. Burnham quilted a covering for the floor boards and sewed a canvas cover. Four burros had been purchased at $15 apiece but there was no suitable harness to be found for them. The resourceful Westerner bought a good hide, some tools and rivets and made the harnesses.

The burros had never been harnessed or driven and it took some laughable efforts to break them in—one could not learn at all and kept turning around to face the wagon. When the proprietress of the inn saw this uncertain little outfit with which the family of three Americans proposed to travel for months over deserts, rivers and mountains in a land where they could not speak a word of the native language, she begged Mrs. Burnham to let her foolhardy husband go on ahead and she and the boy could wait until there was an opportunity to travel with more safety and comfort in some wagon train. But Mrs. Burnham politely rejected the suggestion.

Out on the desert, the little donkeys gradually broke in under the stern guidance of their master (the dumb one was traded off for a more intelligent one) and could make fifteen to seventeen miles a day—better than an ox team. On the uphill grades, the family walked to spare them.

Roderick Burnham, now living in Idylwild, California [at the time of this manuscript], vividly remembers his boyhood participation in this trek. He has commemorated it on one of the bronze plaques he had placed around the base of the obelisk which marks his parents' crypt.

"I had fun," he recalls, "riding and naming the burros: Dock, Ah Sin, Ta-Ra, Ty Wink and the last two acquired, Babe and Chub. It was my job to herd them on the grass during rest stops and I trained them to come to my call and they would almost nose me over for a handful of shelled mealies."

The order of the day was up at dawn, breakfast of bacon, corn cakes and coffee, inspan [hitch up the donkeys] at sunrise, trek about four hours and outspan [un-hitch the donkeys] for three. The afternoon trek was usually about three hours. Enough water was carried to make a dry camp if necessary, also wood when not in a brush country or where the buffalo chips were not plentiful. Burnham supplemented the rations by shooting game or buying from occasional farms. Sundays were usually spent with washing clothes, doing some extra cooking, greasing the buckboard, oiling the harness and grazing the stock.

The trek was going well, the days were pleasant and there was an inclination to disregard any suggestions of danger in this mode of travel. On the Transvaal, a gray-bearded Boer urged the party to lay over at his farm for a couple of weeks until he and his sons were ready to start north in their great wagons. The Boer took Burnham aside and told him that he should not risk the lives of his wife and child going through the wilderness in such an outfit. "Some of my people were eaten by lion," he said; "yours might be also."

But the trusting travelers pushed on. The next day, the Boer overtook them on a horse and again urged them to wait over. He offered a Scotch cart and six oxen if the little family would stay and join his wagon train. "But with more determination than judgement," Burnham tells, "we continued on."

Johannesburg was reached—a fabulous mining center and then Pretoria, the Boer capitol. Here the American scout saw the great Boer leader Paul Kruger, "that forceful character of African soil" against whom he was to fight some years later when in the service of Cecil Rhodes, the masterminded head of the British forces.

In Pretoria, supplies were laid in for continuing the trek. A sawed-off shotgun and ammunition for keeping the lion from eating Roderick or the stock was bought and two more burros purchased.

Roderick Burnham, telling his recollections of this remarkable journey, says, "As we trekked further and further north, the country became wilder and the natives less accustomed to seeing white people, let alone a woman and child in a spidery buckboard drawn by burros instead of oxen." He has a mental picture of the little outfit which seemed to "bend and twist and crawl like a crab through streams, over boulders and up rough canyons of the mountainous country we traversed."

A little hand powered sewing machine which Roderick's mother carried on the trek was magic to the natives, he recounts. "They called her 'Tagetti,' meaning bewitched, because of the machine she ran. I would set it up for her on a box of dynamite, with another box of the explosives for her seat. When the savages saw two pieces of cloth going together, they would crowd excitedly around, like a football huddle," he recalls. "Too close for comfort. Then my Dad made them sit in rows on the ground out in front of Mama."

"I can see her now," he fondly pictures, "sitting on the box of dynamite with Dad's old .44 Remington six-shooter on her lap and cranking the little machine as the goggle-eyed savages watched."

"Dynamite occasioned no fear in our family," Roderick Burnham tells. "It was always around because of the Dad's incurable mining fever. The bed on which my mother and father slept, I remember, were poles lashed together with rawhide and slung under the buckboard when traveling; it was set up at night on four forty-pound boxes of dynamite for legs."

When the little outfit reached the lion country, Roderick was not allowed off the buckboard. Besides lions, there were leopards and hyenas to cope with. Fires were built at night and replenished often to keep the animals away from the burros. As the country grew wilder and more dangerous, treks were made at night as well as day, the quicker to get through it. Mrs. Burnham drove and Burnham walked with cocked gun beside the team. Stealthy movements, sometimes ahead of the outfit and sometimes behind, informed them [they] were being stalked by wild beasts. Burnham had occasion often on these night marches to think of the old Boer's warning words.

Happily the little family fell in with some trek wagons and felt much safer. Burnham, always sensitive to beauty, whether in nature or human relations, gives this enthusiastic picture: "The nights were wonderful. Laager (fortified camp) was formed by drawing the great wagons into a circle protecting man and beast. The blazing fires, the steaming coffee and the roasting biltong banished all fatigue. Outside the circle wild animals sent up their cries and overhead the stars, so brilliant in the clear African atmosphere, shone down on us."

Two young Americans, trekking north with the big wagons, visited the Burnham camp. They were Bain and Ingram, both destined to play important parts with Burnham in savage warfare and Ingram to become Burnham's brother-in-law.

Crossing the Crocodile River was looked forward to with considerable apprehension by all concerned and there were dire predictions that the little Yankee outfit would never make it. Burnham put his family and possessions, including a little fox terrier which the crocodiles would surely have eaten, into one of the big wagons. Shooting into the water to scare away the long-jawed lizards of the river, he, Bain and Ingram brought the swimming burros and the floating buckboard across without mishap, to the amazement of the other trekkers.

Camp was established just across the river at Ingonsloop while the men did some hunting. Bringing into play his Western training in snap shooting at running game, the American was able to far out-bag a Boer and his son who made their living hunting on the veldt. In ten days, Burnham got more game than the two Boers combined.

The country was too dangerous to let Roderick herd the burros and one night his father failed to bring them in to laager before dark; two came in of their own accord. About 7 o'clock Chub and Dock, with a great braying and crashing through the brush, charged into camp. Burnham seized a rifle and rushed into the bush in an attempt to save the other two burros. Looking back, he realized his wife was following him with a lantern and sawed-off shotgun. One of the trekkers, an Australian, confided to him later, "I've been looking for a woman like that for many years."

The next morning Ah Sin and Ta-ra were found in a thicket of thorn-bush. They were so delighted to be reunited with the family that they almost knocked Roderick and his mother down with their joyous, braying rush. Ah-sin showed some claw marks but evidently had escaped the lion by plunging into the deadly thorn-bush.

As the wagon train proceeded, rumors of impending war with the blacks sifted down from the north. Lobengola, the Matabele king, was preparing his imipis (regiments) for battle. Suddenly word came from the British administration at Salsbury to press on at all speed.

The old rule, "Let not the sun shine on yoked oxen," had to be disregarded and day treks as well as night ones were made. Burnham recounts that the oxen became hollow-eyed and their great frames seemed to shrivel from the long hot hours. Grass of this dry season had little nourishment and the animals grew weak. Instead of the loud pops of the whips now was heard the dull thud of the great lashes flaying the struggling, staggering brutes. On the sandy spots, it became necessary to resort to the severe punishment of the sjomboks, six-foot heavy hippo hide whips. The voices of the cape boys grew hoarse or ceased from exhaustion. In crossing rivers, it was necessary to put thirty-six oxen to one wagon to make the opposite bank.

The loose cattle began to die off. Hyenas and jackals flanked the train and overhead the great vultures wheeled and dipped. Their food supply increased daily as the trekker's decreased.

Burnham was able to maintain the strength of his burro team with mealies he carried to supplement the grass. His outfit could out-distance the wagon train and as the oxen grew weaker and the treks shorter, he decided to leave the train and push on alone, despite the sinister rumors. A woman in an outfit fleeing from Victoria told Mrs. Burnham that the town was about to be attacked by the savages, that all the women would be killed in a horrible manner and that her little boy's tongue might be cut out.

As it was not advisable to build fires to protect their camp at night because of the danger of attracting hostiles, the family decided to travel at night and hide in the tall grass during the day. The hyenas, unusually large in this area, persistently padded alongside as the outfit moved along in the dark. Burnham knew with what suddenness they could attack, he relates, because he saw one pull down a saddle horse at Ingonsloop. He always carried the sawed-off shotgun at full cock as he walked beside the burros.

One night a wheel bearing absorbed too much sand and as Burnham was struggling with the hot wheel, measured footsteps were heard approaching. His wife handed him the gun which he had put in her hands as he worked. As he stood tensely waiting, the footsteps ceased, a great head lifted out of the tall grass and an ox looked at them; Burnham says that he never knew before that an ox could have so sweet a face.

One happy night they sighted the lights of Victoria, then a far-flung outpost of the British Empire. Here Burnham immediately joined the feverish preparations for war and they did not go on to Salisbury as planned.

This ended the saga of a four month's trek by a little American family over 1400 miles of some of the wildest and most dangerous country in Africa with a light Yankee buckboard drawn by six small burros.

Fortunately, the blacks were slow to get into action. Burnham found them not as keen as the American Indian—their minds were slower [Disclaimer: these are Burnham's words, not the author's!]. "Their tongues must wag and wag before an idea is brought forth," he said. The British had time to bring horses and ammunition up from the south, drill men, gather cattle and fortify Victoria. But there were increasingly disturbing rumors of the vast army that was being formed by the Matabele.

With seven hundred men recruited from Victoria and Salisbury, as against a hundred thousand blacks, the British decided to take the offensive and push two hundred miles through totally unknown wilderness territory to Bulawayo, capitol of the powerful African king Lobengula.

The time had come for parting, dreaded by men in all wars, when the warrior looks into the eyes of loved ones knowing that it may be the last time. And there was the anxiety of leaving the women and children guarded only by a few old men and youths. Every woman, girl and boy was assigned to a task in case the savages should attack. The Burnhams' young son was equipped with a bandolier for carrying ammunition to the men at the loop holes.

Twenty-odd trek wagons, protected by mounted men on either side, moved off into unknown wilderness of enemy country. Constant scouting was necessary; Burnham used to good advantage the scouting skill he had acquired on the American frontiers. He had the cunning to outwit the savages and the endurance for long, hard rides and severe hardships. He was able to locate the column from Salisbury and bring the two outfits together.

Accompanied by another scout, he located Bulawayo, the objective of the expedition.

Many men were lost in the constant encounters with natives, and there was desperate hardship. After twenty-three days of continuous patrolling and fighting on five days' rations, Burnham and his companions were forced to eat one of their starving horses, in which there was little nourishment. Burnham chose the brain, knowing that this is the last portion of a failing body to lose nourishment.

Burnham faced death daily; out of the forest there once leaped a savage, leopard skin over his shoulder, shouting to his followers, "quasi" (come and stab), as he fired at the white man. He missed and paused to reload. Burnham, holding his rifle at his side, rode straight at the black warrior. This confused him and he tried to tug a cartridge out of his bandolier instead of lifting it with the tip of his finger.

Frustrated, the black threw down his gun and quick as a flash, drew a stabbing spear from under his shield and rushed. As his arm was raised for the deadly thrust, Burnham, whose strong wrists enabled him to handle a rifle in one hand as one would a pistol, crumpled the savage. Seeing their leader fall, the other spearsmen jumped back into the bush.

Lobengula fled his capitol after burning his stores of ivory, skins and other treasures. He died later in the wilderness; after a few more skirmishes with the blacks, the war was over.

Land was thrown open for entry after the war and the whites rapidly moved in, creating boom prices. Building material was scarce, but Burnham put up the first brick house in Bulawayo, flooring it with small boards salvaged from whiskey crates at fifty cents per foot. He says that he felt his wife, who had lived under the stars, or at best thatch or buck sail for over a year, deserved a real roof and board floor.

Burnham often paid tribute to his wife's courage and devotion in unfalteringly accompanying him over desert, river and forbidding jungle. He dedicated one of his books to her: "my dear companion of many a mile."

Three young Blick brothers-in-law joined Burnham and his family to pioneer in South Africa, the bright new land of high hopes. Eventually his 65-year-old father-in-law came and also a sister-in-law, who married Ingram, Burnham's companion in many dangerous missions during the black war.

Between wars, Burnham did some exploring and hunting as well as gold mining. He and Ingram discovered the ruins of Dhlo-Dhlo, where gold ornaments and inlay work were found and a great treasure of gold— six hundred and forty-one ounces. In the Zimbabwe ruins, dating back to before the Christian era, gold beads in quantity were washed out of the sand.

On a safari across the desert, the blacks grew tired of carrying water and trusting with childlike faith that there would be another water hole ahead, they quietly poured the water from the calabashes onto the sands. Several of the natives died from thirst and heat and Burnham himself almost perished. On an expedition through cannibal country, two of the porters, leaving the trail against orders, were eaten by cannibals.

Burnham headed a large expedition with twenty white officers and over five hundred black askaris and porters which was financed by the British East Africa Company. Cecil Rhodes was desirous of gaining information as to the feasibility of a railroad from Cape Town to Cari— the company wanted reports on mineral and agriculture resources. The most important discovery was of the lost M'Gardi, a vast lake of almost pure carbonate of soda, to which a railroad was later built. Burnham, seeing it first under moonlight, poetically described it as a great white jewel held in Africa's black palm.

When hunting elephants in East Africa, well-placed bullets failed to stop a huge "rogue" elephant and Burnham escaped being trampled by the enraged, charging animal only by dodging between his fore legs. The elephant finally dropped and the hunter was rewarded with a pair of ivory tusks over six feet in length. Another elephant he shot had tusks over seven feet long but not so large an animal. The size of the elephant did not determine the lengths of the tusks, Burnham found.

One night the dozing askari did not keep the fire blazing brightly in the center of the encampment and Burnham was awakened by a frightful yelling and shouts of "Simba, Basa" ("Lion, Master"). He aimed a shot at the faint blur of a tawny mane in the brush but the animal made off. Searching in the brush with firebrands was to no avail. When Burnham returned, he discovered that it was his tent the lion had entered and carried off his mule boy, sleeping on the ground, as a cat would carry a mouse. The next morning, the lion was trailed. Not far from there, the partially eaten body was found; there was a sudden mighty roar, which sent the askari scurrying. As the lion came into sight, Burnham killed it with one lucky shot.

In 1896, the blacks rose again and were murdering settlers and the whites who had befriended them. The second Matabele War was on. Burnham took active part in this war under Sir Frederick Carington. One of the most desperate situations he had to meet was when the native uprising was complicated by drought and cessation of supplies to the wilderness settlement of Bulawayo. The only means of bringing anything to the frontier town from the end of the railroad at Mafeking, five hundred miles distant, was by ox team and wagon. It required about five hundred such outfits to keep the community of several thousand supplied. The dread rinderpest disease settled down on the land like a black pall and whole spans of oxen (eighteen head) dropped in their tracks and the precious necessities of life in the great wagons had to be abandoned to hostiles. Thousands of huge, swollen carcasses choked the route which led through wilderness areas, across flooding rivers and over long, rugged passes in the Matoppa Mountains.

There were four thousand whites to feed and about two thousand friendly blacks. Desperation led to slaughtering the cattle stricken with rinderpest and frying the diseased meat in the sun or salting it down to eke out the food supply.

Bulawayo was surrounded by bloated, rotting bodies so numerous that the scavenger hyena and great vultures made no impression. Stench pervaded the town unremittingly. There was no wood to burn the carcasses and the manpower it would have required to bury them had to be devoted to warding off attacks of the blacks. At night their campfires could be seen for six miles around the town.

Wagons were drawn up on laager, completely surrounding the brick marketplace in the center of town, the wheels chained together and the spaces between yokes barricaded with sand bags. All empty bottles in town were broken and scattered inch deep about twenty feet in front of the wagons. Barbed wire was skillfully used; improvised bombs were placed on the roofs of outlaying huts to be touched off in case of night attack to illuminate the enemy and give riflemen more accurate aim.

It was learned that friendly natives were selling the town's precious ammunition to the enemy; the situation grew increasingly acute. Burnham tells in his account that each night "certain ones of us were grimly ordered that in case a rush was made and the laager broken, to kill our own women and children and not let them fall into the hands of the blacks."

The Burnham's little daughter, Nada, not yet three years old, had died from the deprivations of the siege.

It was learned by the underground that a satanic plan to slay all the whites in Rhodesia, killing the women in a frightful manner, was being promoted by the M'Limo, a witch doctor, or high priest, who had great influence with the blacks and exacted a high tax from them. All servants were to turn upon their masters. A black woman coming into Bulawayo with a large bundle of faggots [a bundle of sticks or twigs, with which to use for a fire] was found to be carrying concealed assagais, or stabbing spears.

Burnham was then ordered to take the M'Limo, dead or alive. He and young Armstrong, who had learned the whereabouts of the high priest, went into the Matoppos and located his cave. A regiment of warriors encamped nearby and numerous savages, moving about preparing for a ceremonial dance, made it necessary for the men to use the greatest care in approaching the cave. Camouflaging themselves with bunches of grass or brush, they were able to slip into the cave unobserved and secret themselves there.

When the M'Limo came to the opening, a shot from Burnham's rifle ended the black reign of terror. Their high priest was killed by the white man's bullet, which he had boasted he could turn to water; the savages subsided and the war was over.

The American family did not regard all blacks as treacherous and cruel. One servant in Bulawayo, Longwan, a former warrior of gigantic frame who was still very strong, always camped on the doorstep with assagai and knobkerrie to protect Mrs. Burnham when her husband was away on night patrol. The time Burnham was about to ride away on his mission to the M'Limo's cave, Longwon, sensing something unusual and that he might never come back, said, "Master, if the Matabele come to this house there will be many dead with me around the door."

In 1897, Burnham was lured to Alaska by the call of gold, along with his brothers-in-law, John and Judd Blick and Ingram, all of whom had been associated with him in campaigning or exploring in Africa. They dog-sledded, packed over treacherous passes and shot rapids. Building fires on the age-old ice to reach pay gravel, they probed down to the skeletons of pre-historic animals, ivory tusks still white.

Burnham took the first gold from the Klondike to England—one hundred pounds in large nuggets which were displayed at Rothschild's in London. This started plans for a great development in Alaska, not then consummated but in later years carried out.

After arduous excursions of the frozen North, Burnham built a house in Skagway and brought the family there. But the Alaskan interlude was soon to end.

In 1899, Burnham was called back to Africa and made Chief of Scouts under Lord Roberts to serve in the Boer War. He was captured in this war when he valiantly stepped in the enemy's view and frantically waved a red kerchief in a desperate effort to warn the advancing British columns of an ambush they were heading into. He later escaped to continue service until the war was almost over, when he was injured as his horse was shot from under him and he was invalided to England.

Much was made of the American scout. He carried a personal letter of appreciation from Lord Roberts which opened wide the doors of England to him and his wife. He received a command invitation to dine with Queen Victoria and spent the night at Osborne House. In appreciation for his services, he was commissioned a major in the British Army with the privilege of retaining his American citizenship.

The Prince of Wales, later King Edward VII, made him a member of the Distinguished Service Order and presented to him the South African Medal with five bars and the cross of the D. S. O.

L to R: Winston Churchill, Judd Blick, John Blick, Frederick Burnham and the Earl of Kent. *Photo from Author's Collection.*

The actual investiture took place later in St. James's Palace at an impressive ceremony witnessed by many distinguished figures of the British Empire. The intrepid scout and warrior confessed that this momentous event was more nerve shattering than any of his confrontations with death. "The steps seemed very high that led up to the throne where King Edward pinned the cross over my heart. I received congratulations from my fellow officers in a daze." Major Burnham was previously given a large tract of land and a sum of money for his services in Africa.

The Burnhams frequently visited England—they had a house in London and put their son, Roderick, in a military school. One of their sojourns there was saddened by the tragic loss of their six-year-old son Bruce, who was drowned in the Thames.

Major Burnham's personality won him many friends. Lord Baden Powell, with whom he scouted in Africa, wrote of him in a letter to his mother in 1896; "Burnham is a most delightful companion, amusing, interesting and most instructive. He was associated with Cecil Rhodes as friend as well as scout during the wars in Africa. Lord Gray, one time administrator of Rhodesia and later Governor General of Canada, was among his devoted admirers, as well as many other prominent Englishmen." Among noted Americans who enjoyed his company were Thomas Nelson Page, Hopkins Smith (who regarded him as the best storyteller he knew) and President Theodore Roosevelt. The President invited Burnham to a luncheon and listened enthralled to his tales of his African adventures. John Hays Hammond, world-famous mining engineer, in speaking of Major Burnham's part in winning South Africa from barbarism, said of him in 1925: "His extraordinary accomplishments, unblemished character and winning personality fully earned the high praise bestowed on him by the people of South Africa and the patriotic pride of his fellow countrymen there."

Major Burnham was associated with Hammond after the African wars in diverting the Yacqui River in Mexico through a system of canals to a delta of 700 square miles.

In 1908, Major Burnham and a group of Mrs. Burnham's family, including John and Judd Blick, acquired 5000 acres of patented land on the South Fork of the Kaweah River below Sequoia National Park; leased about 20,000 acres more from the government and stocked the range with cattle. In the summers, the stock was driven to summer range at Hockett Meadows in the park.

Three adobe houses were built with labor brought from Mexico. A large upstairs room in one of the dwellings was devoted to a magnificent collection of trophies of the men's hunts in Africa and elsewhere. An extensive area was fenced and small, white-tailed deer brought up from Mexico. Many other rare animals and birds were added; La Cuesta became a show place.

Burnham's Home at La Cuesta. *Photo from Author's Collection.*

Passers-by would sometimes shoot one of the little deer. Burnham fastened the skull of an Indian that had been killed in Mexico to a board marked with cross bones and the words: "Tame deer - please do not shoot." Whether it was the polite request or the ominous skull and cross-bones, Major Burnham did not know, but no more deer were shot.

Major and Mrs. Burnham with their Mexican deer. *Photo from Author's Collection.*

The big, close-knit family became a valued part of the community life during the twenty-odd years the members lived in Three Rivers. But Burnham never stayed very long at one time on the ranch. His chronic wanderlust would tingle his toes and he would be off on another adventure—hunting for a buried city in Yucatan or directing a new project for the Dominguez Oil Company of California, of which he was vice-president. However, he was so sure that of all the places he had seen in his wanderings over the earth, Three Rivers was where he wanted to take his long rest, that he had a crypt and monument placed in the cemetery here.

Major and Mrs. Burnham, 1934. *Photo from Author's Collection.*

Some four years after Mrs. Burnham's death, Major Burnham was married in 1943 to Ilo Willits, secretary of an oil firm with which he was associated. She nursed him into the sunset of his life at their home near Santa Barbara.

When this remarkable scout, explorer and adventurer died September 1, 1947, at the age of 87 years, his ashes were brought to the little Three Rivers Cemetery and placed beside those of his wife, Blanche Blick Burnham, who followed him over the world to share the dangers, the hardships and the joys of his eventful life.

Bibliography

Newspapers and Periodicals:

Bakersfield Morning Echo; August 12, 1917.

Berkeley Daily Gazette, July 7, 1938.

Daily Morning Delta, February 17, 1893.

Directory of Deceased American Physicians, 1804–1929.

Heritage, Exeter Sun, February 22, 1961; Joe Doctor; May 21, 1986. September 14, 1988; August 21,1991; January 25, 1995.

Fresno Bee, October 18, 1924; December 16, 1924; January 23, 1924; January,1924; January 8, 1925; October 3, 1954; February 15, 1955; April 18, 1961; November 5,1967; May 27, 1970.

Fresno Morning Republican, February 7, 1926.

Heritage, Three Rivers Historical Society, Vol. I, No. 1, February 1992.

Heritage, Three Rivers Historical Society, Vol. IV, No. 3, September 1955. Sophie Britten.

Kaweah Commonwealth, April 9, 1999–August 6, 1999; May 29, 1999; August 11, 2006.

Los Tulares, March 1955; June 1972; September 1986.

Mehrtens of the San Joaquin Family Newsletter; September 1969.

Oakland Tribune, August 4, 1916; August 18, 1935.

Sequoia Sentinel, February 15, 1974; July 22, 1992; *Remember When* Column by Pauline Grunigen, no date; Elliott, John F. December 8, 1993.

SNP Nature News Bulletin; Fry, Walter; First Ascent of Moro Rock.

Three Rivers Current, March 3, 1950.

Three Rivers Sentinal, January 26, 1973; February 2, 1973.

The Valley Voice, November 1987.

Visalia Daily Morning Delta, January 21, 1894.

Visalia Morning Times, August 5, 1926.

Visalia Times-Delta, March 18, 1924; July 21, 1925; July 8, 1926; October 2, 1926; October 30, 1926; December. 6, 1926; July 1, 1935; March 24, 1951; February 27, 1955; March 3, 1961; January 26, 1966.

The Weekly Delta, Visalia, CA; July 8, 1886; September16, 1887; October13,1887; October 27, 1887.

Woodlake Echo, November 12, 1959; November 17, 1960; October 1, 1964; December 7, 1977; May 28, 1986; February 6, 1988; April 8, 1992; February 9, 1994; *Heritage*, Doctor, Joe; *The Kaweah's Springtime Toll*; no date.

Books:

Bradford, Mary & Richard, *American Family on the African Frontier,* Colorado: Roberts Rinehart, 1993.

Ingles, Lloyd Glenn, *Mammals of California,* California: Stanford University Press, 1948.

Jackson, Louise, *Beulah,* Arizona: Westernlore Press, 1988.

Jackson, Louise, *Mule Men,* Montana: Mountain Press, 2004.

Keesey, Gladieux & Merrill, *Silver City History,* California: Silver City Service Club, 2009.

O'Connell, Jay, *Co-operative Dreams,* California: *Raven River, 1999.*

Small, Kathleen Edwards, *History of Tulare County,* Chicago: S. J. Clarke, 1926.

van Wyck, Peter, *King of Scouts,* British Columbia, CAN: Trafford, 2003.

Electronic Research Materials:

Menefee, Eugene, and Fred A. Dodge, *History of Tulare and Kings Counties, California,* Los Angeles: Historic Record Co., 1913, CD.

Tulare County Vital Records, 1859-1899, CD.

Government Documents:

California Voter Registration, 1867.

Tulare County Cemetery Index.

Tulare County Marriage Records.

Tulare County Record of Wills

United States Federal Census - 1850

United States Federal Census - 1880.

United States Federal Census - 1910

United States Federal Census - 1920.

Unpublished Materials:

Frankie Luella Welch's miscellaneous notes, no date.

Hardison, Norma Lovering, *Memories*; unpublished manuscript, 1988.

Junep, Herbert, *Junep's History of Sequoia National Park*; (unpublished), 1937.

Kauling, Wilma, *History of Alfred Hengst*; unpublished manuscript, no date.

Manuscript by Dan Alles, no date.

Manuscript by Bob Barton, no date.

Manuscript by Louise Bosshard; March 4, 1992

Manuscript of Carrie Swanson, no date.

Roy, Elizabeth Pierce, *The Pierce Family and Ranch,* unpublished manuscript, Sept. 25, 1977.

Tolle, Juanita and Elizabeth M. Roy, *Julia Van Arsdale Henry Pierce, 1874-1948,* unpublished manuscript, April, 1992.

Welch, Frankie Luella, *No Apples for the Teacher,* unpublished manuscript, no date.

Web Pages:

www.ancestry.com

www.familysearch.com

www.findagrave.com

Oral Interviews:

Oral Interview with Ord Loverin by Barry Bartlett, August, 1973.

Oral Interview, Ellen Hill by Louise Jackson, July 16, 1994.

Oral Interview, Gene & Catherine Whitney, September 4, 2012.

Oral Interview with Earl and Gaynor McKee, September 13, 2012

Index

(Photos are indicated by italics)

About the Author

Stewart M. Green, living in Colorado Springs, Colorado, is a freelance writer and photographer for FalconGuides and Globe Pequot, imprints of The Rowman & Littlefield Publishing Group, Inc. He's written over forty adventure travel, hiking, and climbing books, including *Best Climbs Moab, Best Climbs Denver and Boulder, Best Climbs Phoenix, Arizona, KNACK Rock Climbing, Rock Climbing Colorado, Rock Climbing Europe, Rock Climbing Utah, Rock Climbing Arizona,* and *Rock Climbing New England*. Stewart, a lifelong climber, began his climbing career in Colorado at age twelve in 1965 and has since climbed all over the world. He's also a professional climbing guide with Front Range Climbing Company in Colorado Springs. Visit him at http://green1109.wixsite.com/stewartmgreenphoto.